SACRED SPACE

SACRED SPACE

The Prayer Book 2016

from the website www.sacredspace.ie

Prayer from the Irish Jesuits

LOYOLA PRESS.
A JESUIT MINISTRY
Chicago

LOYOLA PRESS.
A JESUIT MINISTRY

3441 N. Ashland Avenue
Chicago, Illinois 60657
(800) 621-1008
www.loyolapress.com

Scripture quotations are from the *New Revised Standard Version Bible: Catholic Edition*, copyright © 1989, 1993 National Council of the Churches of Christ in the United States of America. Used by permission. All rights reserved.

Cover art credit: © iStock/Qweek

ISBN-13: 978-0-8294-4366-0
ISBN-10: 0-8294-4366-5
Library of Congress Control Number: 2015946929

15 16 17 18 19 20 Versa 10 9 8 7 6 5 4 3 2 1

Contents

Sacred Space Prayer

Bless all who worship you, almighty God,
from the rising of the sun to its setting:
from your goodness enrich us,
by your love inspire us,
by your Spirit guide us,
by your power protect us,
in your mercy receive us,
now and always.

Preface

In 1999 an Irish Jesuit named Alan McGuckian had the simple—but at the time, radical—idea of bringing daily prayer to the Internet. No one imagined that his experimental project would grow into a global community with volunteers translating the prayer experience into seventeen different languages.

Millions of people, from numerous Christian traditions, visit www.sacredspace.ie each year, and what they find is an invitation to step away from their busy routine for a few minutes each day to concentrate on what is really important in their lives. Sacred Space offers its visitors the opportunity to grow in prayerful awareness of their friendship with God.

Besides the daily prayer experience, Sacred Space also offers Living Space, with commentaries on the Scripture readings for each day's Catholic Mass. The Chapel of Intentions allows people to add their own prayers, while Pray with the Pope joins the community to the international Apostleship of Prayer. In addition, Sacred Space provides Lenten and Advent retreats, often in partnership with Pray as You Go, an audio prayer service from the British Jesuits.

The contents of this printed edition, first produced in 2004, are taken directly from our Internet site. Despite the increased use of Sacred Space on mobile devices, many people want a book they can hold and carry, and this book has proven especially helpful for prayer groups.

In 2014, the Irish Jesuits entered into an apostolic agreement with the Chicago-Detroit Jesuits, and Sacred Space now operates in partnership with Loyola Press.

I am delighted to bring you the *Sacred Space* book, and I pray that your prayer life will flourish with its help.

Yours in Christ,

Paul Brian Campbell, SJ

Introduction to *Sacred Space*, 2016

Saint Ignatius of Loyola, founder of the Society of Jesus, is famously known for wanting to find God in all things. *Is that even possible?* you might ask. He believed it was, but only as a gift from God and only as the fruit of our paying attention to our experience. Ignatius developed an optimistic spiritual practice that assumed the presence of God at every moment of our existence. While we tend to think of God's presence as a "sometime thing," Ignatius came to believe that our perception of God's presence as a sometime occurrence is a major spiritual hindrance. Ignatius believed that God is always creating this universe, always keeping it in existence, always working to bring about God's purpose in creation, and always trying to move us to join God in the great adventure of bringing about what Jesus called the Kingdom of God.

In order to experience this ever-present God, we need to develop a regular spiritual practice, a practice Ignatius had learned from his experience as a relatively untutored layman. Ignatius began to teach people and to write down the spiritual practices that helped him move toward uniting himself with God's purposes and thus toward finding God in all things. *Spiritual Exercises* is Ignatius's manual for those who want to follow his example of helping others get in touch with our ever-present God. God wants a close personal relationship with each of us, and he wants each of us to join him in the great work of bringing about a world where peace and justice prevail. Over the almost five centuries since the time of Ignatius, Jesuits and many others have found through these spiritual practices the answer to their own deepest desires.

Over the centuries, the Spiritual Exercises have been adapted in many ways. Jesuits originally followed Ignatius's own practice of giving the Exercises to individuals for thirty days. But they also used the methods of prayer suggested in the Exercises in their preaching, missions, and talks to larger groups. Eventually, houses were set aside for the giving of the Exercises to individuals and large groups. One of the adaptations suggested by Ignatius himself was to make the Exercises in daily life under the direction of someone trained in giving them. In this format, an individual maintained his or her regular daily life and work but promised to devote time every day to the spiritual practices suggested by Ignatius and to see the spiritual director once a week. In the past fifty years, this adaptation has seen a worldwide resurgence and has touched many lives. It has also been used with groups to great advantage. In modern times, the giving of the Spiritual Exercises has become something of a cottage industry in many countries.

Enter the age of the Internet. Could this new tool be used to help large numbers of people move toward finding God in all things? The answer is a resounding *yes*! Many websites, in multiple languages, try to help people become more aware of God's presence in their lives, using practices stemming from the *Spiritual Exercises*. One example is the book you have in your hands. In 1999 the Irish Jesuits started to offer daily prompts for prayer based on Ignatius's Exercises on the website Sacred Space (www.sacredspace.ie). The English edition was soon translated into other languages, and the site now features twenty-one languages that span the globe.

In my work as a spiritual director and in my travels, I have come across many, many people of various walks of life who use the daily prompts for prayer provided through Sacred Space. People find the site and the daily suggestions to be user-friendly, inviting, and, in keeping with Ignatian spirituality, optimistic. The suggestions help them pay attention to their experience, notice intimations of God's presence in that experience, and engage in an honest conversation with God.

For each week, there is an overarching suggested theme and a method for spending time with God each day. One of the methods is to turn to the Scripture and reflections suggested for each day of the week. Each day's text is taken from the Gospel reading for Mass that day. Thus, someone who follows Sacred Space every day will, in the course of a year, work prayerfully through all four of the Gospels. No wonder that so many have been enthralled by this site.

In spite of the digital age, many of us still like the feel of a book in our hands. The book *Sacred Space*, which you now hold in your hands, was designed for the likes of us. I am very happy to introduce the book and even happier that Loyola Press, a Jesuit institution, is now the publisher. Ignatian spiritual practice has brought me closer to God, for which I am immensely grateful. Through Ignatius's spiritual practices I have experienced God's desire for my friendship, and I figure, if God wants *my* friendship, he wants *everyone's* friendship. If you take this book seriously and engage in the relationship with God that it suggests, you will, I'm sure, find as much joy in God's friendship as I have. Try it—you'll like it.

William A. Barry, SJ

How to Use This Book

During each week of the Liturgical year, begin by reading the "Something to think and pray about each day this week." Then proceed through "The Presence of God," "Freedom," and "Consciousness" steps to prepare yourself to hear the Word of God in your heart. In the next step, "The Word," turn to the Scripture reading for each day of the week. Inspiration points are provided if you need them. Then return to the "Conversation" and "Conclusion" steps. Use this process every day of the year.

November 29—December 5, 2015

Something to think and pray about each day this week:

Imagination and Hope

We used to imagine that, despite the diversity within societies and across the world, we could somehow all achieve safe middle-class ambitions like basic financial security, a wholesome family life, an education for excellence, a fulfilling job with a handsome wage, good health and white teeth, a house in the suburbs, freedom to worship, protection from terrorism, and an environment ready to do our bidding. Now we know that life is not so straightforward. We are not here only to make money, though we need that too. We are not here just to enjoy good health, though we all know what an incredible difference that makes. We are not here solely to live morally good lives, admirable though moral living is. We are here for a project so audacious that something within us finds it hard to believe: we are here to transform ourselves and our world. If we cannot believe this, it is because we have downsized our beliefs. It is our greatness rather than our littleness that intimidates us. But hope can heal us, for hope unsettles us with the passionate unrest that propels us toward great things, and it is imagination that gives us the entrance ticket into the hope-filled world of possibility. We can hope in God, for God is the true fulfillment of everything for which we long and desire. God promises us that the best is yet to come.

The Presence of God

"Come to me all you who are burdened, and I will give you rest."
Here I am, Lord. I come to seek your presence.
I long for your healing power.

Freedom

Lord, grant me the grace to be free from the excesses of this life.
Let me not get caught up with the desire for wealth.
Keep my heart and mind free to love and serve you.

Consciousness

At this moment, Lord, I turn my thoughts to you.
I will leave aside my chores and preoccupations.
I will take rest and refreshment in your presence, Lord.

The Word

The Word of God comes down to us through the Scriptures. May the
Holy Spirit enlighten my mind and my heart to respond to the gospel teachings. (Please turn to the Scripture on the following pages.
Inspiration points are provided should you need them. When you are
ready, return here to continue.)

Conversation

Jesus, you speak to me through the words of the Gospels.
May I respond to your call today.
Teach me to recognize your hand at work in my daily living.

Conclusion

Glory be to the Father, and to the Son, and to the Holy Spirit,
As it was in the beginning, is now and ever shall be,
world without end. Amen.

Sunday 29th November
First Sunday of Advent
Luke 21:25–28, 34–36

Jesus said, "There will be signs in the sun, the moon, and the stars, and on the earth distress among nations confused by the roaring of the sea and the waves. People will faint from fear and foreboding of what is coming upon the world, for the powers of the heavens will be shaken. Then they will see 'the Son of Man coming in a cloud' with power and great glory. Now when these things begin to take place, stand up and raise your heads because your redemption is drawing near. Be on guard so that your hearts are not weighed down with dissipation and drunkenness and the worries of this life, and that day does not catch you unexpectedly, like a trap. For it will come upon all who live on the face of the whole earth. Be alert at all times, praying that you may have the strength to escape all these things that will take place, and to stand before the Son of Man."

• Jesus is using traditional Jewish symbolism to describe what will happen when God's final judgment occurs. He says that people will see "the Son of Man coming in a cloud." The cloud is a symbol for God's presence. Jesus' message bursts with hope and confidence because, unlike those who have reason to fear his coming, Jesus' followers will be able to hold their heads high because their liberation is at hand.

• Jesus urges me to be on guard so that my heart is not weighed down by the worries of life. What are the worries and cares of life that weigh me down today? As I prepare for a conversation with Jesus, can I bring my worries and cares to him in prayer?

Monday 30th November
Matthew 4:18–22

As Jesus walked by the Sea of Galilee, he saw two brothers, Simon, who is called Peter, and Andrew his brother, casting a net into the lake—for they were fishermen. And he said to them, "Follow me, and I will make you fish for people." Immediately they left their nets and followed him. As he went from there, he saw two other brothers, James son of Zebedee and his brother John, in the boat with their father Zebedee, mending their nets, and he called them. Immediately they left the boat and their father, and followed him.

- The call of the disciples is rooted in the call of Jesus, and this call is to change their lives forever. The disciples are not only to hear the Word of God; they act on it. So the first disciples leave everything and follow him. Jesus will go on to teach the disciples a new way of life, for they cannot be open to the work of God unless they have their ears opened by his word.

- I pray: "Jesus, show me what I need to leave behind in order to be a good disciple. Do not let me fall far behind you and lose sight of you. Keep me close. Thank you for these times of prayer, and for inviting me to share a meal with you in the Eucharist."

Tuesday 1st December
Luke 10:21–24

Jesus rejoiced in the Holy Spirit and said, "I thank you, Father, Lord of heaven and earth, because you have hidden these things from the wise and the intelligent and have revealed them to infants; yes, Father, for such was your gracious will. All things have been handed over to me by my Father; and no one knows who the Son is except the Father, or who the Father is except the Son and anyone to whom the Son chooses to reveal him." Then turning to the disciples, Jesus said to them privately, "Blessed are the eyes that see what you see! For I tell you that many prophets and kings desired to see what you see, but did not see it, and to hear what you hear, but did not hear it."

- To rejoice in the Holy Spirit is to be aware of the Father's infinite and unconditional love poured out on me. Are there moments in my life when I have felt such love? What may be preventing me from experiencing such love today?

- How blessed are we to see Jesus and to hear his words! And Jesus has chosen to reveal his Father to us! I consider how this message might make me glad and grateful.

Wednesday 2nd December

Matthew 15:29–37

Jesus passed along the Sea of Galilee, and he went up the mountain, where he sat down. Great crowds came to him, bringing with them the lame, the maimed, the blind, the mute, and many others. They put them at his feet, and he cured them, so that the crowd was amazed when they saw the mute speaking, the maimed whole, the lame walking, and the blind seeing. And they praised the God of Israel. Then Jesus called his disciples to him and said, "I have compassion for the crowd, because they have been with me now for three days and have nothing to eat; and I do not want to send them away hungry, for they might faint on the way." Jesus asked them, "How many loaves have you?" They said, "Seven, and a few small fish." Then ordering the crowd to sit down on the ground, he took the seven loaves and the fish; and after giving thanks he broke them and gave them to the disciples, and the disciples gave them to the crowds. And all of them ate and were filled; and they took up the broken pieces left over, seven baskets full.

- I imagine the crowd, with everyone bringing their problems to Jesus. The people who approach him have an illness or are accompanying a person with an illness. What problem might I bring, and how does Jesus deal with it? Is this how I deal with the problems others bring to me?

- Jesus takes in the bigger picture: He is in touch with our basic human need for nourishment. What joy he must have had in providing this party in the wilderness! Everything is for sharing; how might I be glad to share what I can? What do my bread and fish look like?

Thursday 3rd December

Matthew 7:21, 24–27

Jesus said to the people, "Not everyone who says to me, 'Lord, Lord,' will enter the kingdom of heaven, but only one who does the will of my Father in heaven. Everyone then who hears these words of mine and acts on them will be like a wise man who built his house on rock. The rain fell, the floods came, and the winds blew and beat on that house, but it did not fall, because it had been founded on rock. And everyone who hears these words of mine and does not act on them will be like a foolish man who built his house on sand. The rain fell, and the floods came, and the winds blew and beat against that house, and it fell—and great was its fall!"

- There are many ways to "hear" words. They can be just sound, external meaning, like giving information or directions. The Word of God is more like the word of a friend, spoken to the mind and to the heart. Or it is like the words of a caring parent, giving advice or directions out of love. The Word of God gives meaning to life and is spoken always in love. Prayer is giving time to hearing this word on the deepest levels of our heart.

- Lord, you never let me forget that love is shown in deeds, not words or feelings. I could fill notebooks with resolutions and in the end be further from you. As the psychologist William James put it, "A resolution that is a fine flame of feeling allowed to burn itself out without appropriate action, is not merely a lost opportunity, but a bar to future action."

Friday 4th December
Matthew 9:27–31

As Jesus went on his way, two blind men followed him, crying loudly, "Have mercy on us, Son of David!" When he entered the house, the blind men came to him; and Jesus said to them, "Do you believe that I am able to do this?" They said to him, "Yes, Lord." Then he touched their eyes and said, "According to your faith let it be done to you." And their eyes were opened. Then Jesus sternly ordered them, "See that no one knows of this." But they went away and spread the news about him throughout that district.

- The start of this encounter is in public. There are crowds around Jesus, and the blind men are caught up in the general emotion. They shout at Jesus using a formal title, Son of David, as though he were a powerful messianic figure dispensing health to crowds. Jesus waits until he is inside the house, where he can meet the blind men in person and question their faith.

- I hope I have the faith to call out to Jesus, whom I cannot see, and to follow him into a darkened house. I hope I can answer, "Yes, Lord" to the question, "Do you believe that I am able to do this?" and mean it.

Saturday 5th December
Matthew 9:35—10:1, 5a, 6–8

Jesus went about all the cities and villages, teaching in their synagogues, and proclaiming the good news of the kingdom, and curing every disease and every sickness. When he saw the crowds, he had compassion for them, because they were harassed and helpless, like sheep without a shepherd. Then he said to his disciples, "The harvest is plentiful, but the laborers are few; therefore ask the Lord of the harvest to send out laborers into his harvest." Then Jesus summoned his twelve disciples and gave them authority over unclean spirits, to cast them out, and to cure every disease and every sickness. These twelve Jesus sent out with the following instructions: "Go to the lost sheep of the house of Israel. As you go, proclaim the good news, 'The kingdom of heaven has come near.' Cure the sick, raise the dead, cleanse the lepers, cast out demons. You received without payment; give without payment."

- Do I know any people who are harassed and helpless like sheep without a shepherd? Let me hold them before my mind's eye for a moment. Can I now imagine Jesus looking at them? How does he see them?

- There is so much good that is not noticed, so many blessings that are unacknowledged. I pray for a deeper appreciation of the rich harvest that is around me.

December 6—December 12

Something to think and pray about each day this week:

Endings and Beginnings

There's something at this time of the year about endings and beginnings. An old year is coming to an end with its memories, and a new year will soon begin with its hope. The endings and the beginnings— past and future—are always in the present tense of love. Isn't that where prayer comes in? There are moments in the day—or in the night—in which we immerse ourselves in this mystery of the divine love for us. This love brings healing of the past and trust for the future. All religion worth its name surrounds the past with a wide healing and the possibility of forgiveness and enlightens the future with the same breadth of hope and trust. No matter what our prayer and its content, its context is of healing and trust in the space of a love so large that it is the name given to God. What I live in the ordinariness of the day also forms a context for prayer, and what I experience or think of in prayer forms a context for my life. Neither is separate from the other. Everything that this annual transition of the years evokes in me, I bring to the One who is love beyond all telling.

The Presence of God
The more we call on God, the more we can feel God's presence.
Day by day we are drawn closer to the loving heart of God.

Freedom
God is not foreign to my freedom.
Instead, the Spirit breathes life into my most intimate desires, gently nudging me toward all that is good.
I ask for the grace to let myself be enfolded by the Spirit.

Consciousness
How do I find myself today?
Where am I with God? With others?
Do I have something to be grateful for? Then I give thanks.
Is there something I am sorry for? Then I ask forgiveness.

The Word
I take my time to read the Word of God, slowly, a few times, allowing myself to dwell on anything that strikes me. (Please turn to the Scripture on the following pages. Inspiration points are provided should you need them. When you are ready, return here to continue.)

Conversation
How has God's Word moved me? Has it left me cold?
Has it consoled me or moved me to act in a new way?
I imagine Jesus standing or sitting beside me.
I turn and share my feelings with him.

Conclusion
I thank God for these few moments we have spent alone together and for any insights I may have been given concerning the text.

Sunday 6th December
Second Sunday of Advent
Luke 3:1–6

In the fifteenth year of the reign of Emperor Tiberius, when Pontius Pilate was governor of Judea, and Herod was ruler of Galilee, and his brother Philip ruler of the region of Ituraea and Trachonitis, and Lysanias ruler of Abilene, during the high priesthood of Annas and Caiaphas, the word of God came to John son of Zechariah in the wilderness. He went into all the region around the Jordan, proclaiming a baptism of repentance for the forgiveness of sins, as it is written in the book of the words of the prophet Isaiah, "The voice of one crying out in the wilderness: 'Prepare the way of the Lord, make his paths straight. Every valley shall be filled, and every mountain and hill shall be made low, and the crooked shall be made straight, and the rough ways made smooth; and all flesh shall see the salvation of God.'"

- The Gospel positions John the Baptist in the history of his time, signposting the date of God's intervention in human history. It was not a one-off intervention; it continues through everyone who works to prepare the way of the Lord.

- The paths I follow are often crooked, diverting me from my eternal goal. What can I do to make my path to God straight?

Monday 7th December
Luke 5:17–26

One day, while Jesus was teaching, Pharisees and teachers of the law were sitting nearby (they had come from every village of Galilee and Judea and from Jerusalem); and the power of the Lord was with him to heal. Just then some men came, carrying a paralyzed man on a bed. They were trying to bring him in and lay him before Jesus; but finding no way to bring him in because of the crowd, they went up on the roof and let him down with his bed through the tiles into the middle of the crowd in front of Jesus. When he saw their faith, he said, "Friend, your sins are forgiven you." Then the scribes and the Pharisees began to ask themselves, "Who is this who is speaking blasphemies? Who can forgive sins but God alone?" When Jesus perceived their questionings, he answered them, "Why do you raise such questions in your hearts? Which is easier, to say, 'Your sins are forgiven you,' or to say, 'Stand up and walk'? But so that you may know that the Son of Man has authority on earth to forgive sins"—he said to the one who was paralyzed—"I say to you, stand up and take your bed and go to your home." Immediately he stood up before them, picked up what he had been lying on, and went home, glorifying God. Amazement seized all of them, and they glorified God and were filled with awe, saying, "We have seen strange things today."

- Without the help of his determined friends, the paralyzed man could never have made his way to Jesus to be healed. How might I help a friend find healing in Christ?

- Jesus speaks forgiveness to me. I receive the healing that he offers and ask to understand the new life he has in mind for me.

Tuesday 8th December
The Immaculate Conception of the Blessed Virgin Mary
Luke 1:26–38

In the sixth month the angel Gabriel was sent by God to a town in Galilee called Nazareth, to a virgin engaged to a man whose name was Joseph, of the house of David. The virgin's name was Mary. And he came to her and said, "Greetings, favored one! The Lord is with you." But she was much perplexed by his words and pondered what sort of greeting this might be. The angel said to her, "Do not be afraid, Mary, for you have found favor with God. And now, you will conceive in your womb and bear a son, and you will name him Jesus. He will be great, and will be called the Son of the Most High, and the Lord God will give to him the throne of his ancestor David. He will reign over the house of Jacob forever, and of his kingdom there will be no end." Mary said to the angel, "How can this be, since I am a virgin?" The angel said to her, "The Holy Spirit will come upon you, and the power of the

Most High will overshadow you; therefore the child to be born will be holy; he will be called Son of God. And now, your relative Elizabeth in her old age has also conceived a son; and this is the sixth month for her who was said to be barren. For nothing will be impossible with God." Then Mary said, "Here am I, the servant of the Lord; let it be with me according to your word." Then the angel departed from her.

- Mary was prepared to say "Yes" to the direction God had in mind for her. How might I be as perceptive and as humble as she was, ready to notice and respond?

- Repeating a phrase in prayer may make it go deep within us. It's like a favorite piece of music that we can hum over and over again. It is part of us. "I am the servant of the Lord" was such a phrase for Mary, spoken first at one of the biggest moments in her life. In dry times of prayer, a sentence like that can occupy mind and heart and raise us close to God.

Wednesday 9th December
Matthew 11:28–30

Jesus said, "Come to me, all you that are weary and are carrying heavy burdens, and I will give you rest. Take my yoke upon you, and learn from me; for I am gentle and humble in heart, and you will find rest for your souls. For my yoke is easy, and my burden is light."

- A yoke is a wooden or iron frame that joins two oxen for the purpose of pulling a plow or cart. Here, Jesus invites us to share the burden of our worries and fears with him because he is only too willing to help us cope with and manage them. It is an open invitation spoken to us by Jesus, who is forever "gentle and humble in heart."

- Lord, let me share your work. Open my eyes to the burdens borne by others. Open my heart to the pain that cannot be shared, to the fear that cannot be spoken, to those who face darkness alone.

Thursday 10th December

Matthew 11:11–15

Jesus said, "Truly I tell you, among those born of women no one has arisen greater than John the Baptist; yet the least in the kingdom of heaven is greater than he. From the days of John the Baptist until now the kingdom of heaven has suffered violence, and the violent take it by force. For all the prophets and the law prophesied until John came; and if you are willing to accept it, he is Elijah who is to come. Let anyone with ears listen!"

- I ponder what Jesus said about the greatness of John. I think of what Jesus had seen and heard so that I might profit from understanding what he valued. John proclaimed the gospel, allowing his disciples to leave him to follow Jesus. I think of what it might mean to be less so that Jesus might be more.

- Lord, make me a better listener. Empty me of noise and clutter, to hear what needs to be heard. Let me not be afraid of silence because then you can speak to me. "Let anyone with ears listen!" What is Jesus saying to me in this time of meditation?

Friday 11th December

Matthew 11:16–19

Jesus spoke to the crowds, "But to what will I compare this generation? It is like children sitting in the market-places and calling to one another, 'We played the flute for you, and you did not dance; we wailed, and you did not mourn.' For John came neither eating nor drinking, and they say, 'He has a demon'; the Son of Man came eating and drinking, and they say, 'Look, a glutton and a drunkard, a friend of tax collectors and sinners!' Yet wisdom is vindicated by her deeds."

- Jesus notices those who sit back and do nothing except judge others. John is too strange while Jesus is too normal for such people. Am I occasionally cynical and critical? Do I disparage the humble efforts of others when they do their best?

- Do I bear faithful witness to Jesus by good deeds? Such deeds may be costly, but the ultimate course of events will reveal that they were wise decisions.

Saturday 12th December

Luke 1:26–38

In the sixth month the angel Gabriel was sent by God to a town in Galilee called Nazareth, to a virgin engaged to a man whose name was Joseph, of the house of David. The virgin's name was Mary. And he came to her and said, "Greetings, favored one! The Lord is with you." But she was much perplexed by his words and pondered what sort of greeting this might be. The angel said to her, "Do not be afraid, Mary, for you have found favor with God. And now, you will conceive in your womb and bear a son, and you will name him Jesus. He will be great, and will be called the Son of the Most High, and the Lord God will give to him the throne of his ancestor David. He will reign over the house of Jacob forever, and of his kingdom there will be no end." Mary said to the angel, "How can this be, since I am a virgin?" The angel said to her, "The Holy Spirit will come upon you, and the power of the Most High will overshadow you; therefore the child to be born will be holy; he will be called Son of God. And now, your relative Elizabeth in her old age has also conceived a son; and this is the sixth month for her who was said to be barren. For nothing will be impossible with God." Then Mary said, "Here am I, the servant of the Lord; let it be with me according to your word." Then the angel departed from her.

- How does Mary react in a crisis? She hears God's messenger but wonders, Can it be true? And how does it square with my virginity? She knows that she is free to say "Yes" or "No," and her response is from a full heart.

- Lord, this is not an easy prayer to make. You prayed it yourself in Gethsemane in a sweat of blood: "Not my will but yours be done." Help me make it the pattern of my life. What issues of surrender and trust does it raise for me?

December 13—December 19

Something to think and pray about each day this week:

Touching the Flesh of Christ

The ecclesial community is a place to grow our faith. Pope Francis often urges Christians not to lose confidence in the Church, despite its obvious failings. It makes mistakes and clearly needs institutional reform, and this is a major task for the Holy Spirit. But the Church will be chiefly reformed by dedicating itself to its central mission. This means that it must move "to the periphery" and proclaim the Good News to all people from the standpoint of solidarity with the poor. In an address to families, Pope Benedict XVI stressed that Christian charity is best understood in terms of "self-gift." Only in self-giving, he said, do we find ourselves. We must open ourselves to the ecclesial community and to the world. We cannot turn our backs on our struggling sisters and brothers. In the words of Pope Francis, we are to "touch the flesh of Christ" by caring for the needy. The Church is meant to be a servant of all in need. This is a humble role. According to the Second Vatican Council, whatever promotes human dignity among the people of the world becomes the agenda of the Church. Injustice anywhere must stir the Christian heart to an appropriate response.

The Presence of God

Dear Jesus, as I call on you today, I realize that I often come asking for favors.

Today I'd like just to be in your presence.

Let my heart respond to your love.

Freedom

If God were trying to tell me something, would I know?

If God were reassuring me or challenging me, would I notice?

I ask for the grace to be free of my own preoccupations and open to what God may be saying to me.

Consciousness

Help me, Lord, to be more conscious of your presence.

Teach me to recognize your presence in others.

Fill my heart with gratitude for the times your love has been shown to me through the care of others.

The Word

I read the Word of God slowly, a few times over, and I listen to what God is saying to me. (Please turn to the Scripture on the following pages. Inspiration points are provided should you need them. When you are ready, return here to continue.)

Conversation

What feelings are rising in me as I pray and reflect on God's Word?

I imagine Jesus himself sitting or standing near me, and I open my heart to him.

Conclusion

Glory be to the Father, and to the Son, and to the Holy Spirit,

as it was in the beginning, is now and ever shall be,

world without end. Amen.

Sunday 13th December
Third Sunday of Advent
Luke 3:10–18

The crowds asked John the Baptist, "What then should we do?" In reply he said to them, "Whoever has two coats must share with anyone who has none; and whoever has food must do likewise." Even tax collectors came to be baptized, and they asked him, "Teacher, what should we do?" He said to them, "Collect no more than the amount prescribed for you." Soldiers also asked him, "And we, what should we do?" He said to them, "Do not extort money from anyone by threats or false accusation, and be satisfied with your wages." As the people were filled with expectation, and all were questioning in their hearts concerning John, whether he might be the Messiah, John answered all of them by saying, "I baptize you with water; but one who is more powerful than I is coming; I am not worthy to untie the thong of his sandals. He will baptize you with the Holy Spirit and fire. His winnowing fork is in his hand, to clear his threshing floor and to gather the wheat into his granary; but the chaff he will burn with unquenchable fire." So, with many other exhortations, he proclaimed the good news to the people.

- For all the austerity of his life, John the Baptist spoke to people in words they could grasp. It was his austerity that drew people's respect and trust. Here was a man who cared nothing for comfort, money, or fame, who could not be bought, and who could speak the truth without fear.

- What does my lifestyle say about my faith in Christ? Do I hoard or share what I have with others, especially those who are poor and on the margins of society?

Monday 14th December
Matthew 21:23–27

When Jesus entered the temple, the chief priests and the elders of the people came to him as he was teaching, and said, "By what authority are you doing these things, and who gave you this authority?" Jesus said to them, "I will also ask you one question; if you tell me the answer, then I will also tell you by what authority I do these things. Did the baptism of John come from heaven, or was it of human origin?" And they argued with one another, "If we say, 'From heaven,' he will say to us, 'Why then did you not believe him?' But if we say, 'Of human origin,' we are afraid of the crowd; for all regard John as a prophet." So they answered Jesus, "We do not know." And he said to them, "Neither will I tell you by what authority I am doing these things."

- What authority does Jesus have? If he turned up today, would we want to see his qualifications before allowing him to preach? Or would his attitude, words, and deeds resonate deeply within us, so that we would say, "All that he says and does, and the way he does it, is just right"?

- God is busy in our world, trying to get people to see clearly. Like the priests and elders, do I sometimes evade the truth of what God is trying to tell me? I ask Jesus to help me be a truthful person. Even small lies and deceptions should have no place in my speech.

Tuesday 15th December
Matthew 21:28–32

Jesus said, "What do you think? A man had two sons; he went to the first and said, 'Son, go and work in the vineyard today.' He answered, 'I will not'; but later he changed his mind and went. The father went to the second and said the same; and he answered, 'I go, sir'; but he did not go. Which of the two did the will of his father?" They said, "The first." Jesus said to them, "Truly I tell you, the tax collectors and the prostitutes are going into the kingdom of God ahead of you. For John came to you in the way of righteousness and you did not believe him, but the tax collectors and the prostitutes believed him; and even after you saw it, you did not change your minds and believe him."

- Jesus asks us to think about whether our words and actions are in agreement. It is easy to talk—to pronounce and to make statements. It is more difficult to give time, effort, and attention. I profess my faith not only in Sunday words but also in the time I give to working for the reign of God during the week. Jesus values a few small acts more than many fine words.

- Jesus speaks this parable to me. I avoid applying it to others right now and simply accept Jesus' warmth as he sees how I have served. I listen for his invitation as he shows me where I hold back.

Wednesday 16th December
Luke 7:18b–23

At that time, John summoned two of his disciples and sent them to the Lord to ask, "Are you the one who is to come, or are we to wait for another?" When the men had come to him, they said, "John the Baptist has sent us to you to ask, 'Are you the one who is to come, or are we to wait for another?'" Jesus had just then cured many people of diseases, plagues, and evil spirits, and had given sight to many who were blind. And he answered them, "Go and tell John what you have seen and heard: the blind receive their sight, the lame walk, the lepers are cleansed, the deaf hear, the dead are raised, the poor have good news brought to them. And blessed is anyone who takes no offence at me."

- The readings before Christmas search my heart profoundly. Am I longing for Jesus to come more deeply into my life this Advent? Or am I waiting for God to come in some other form? Would I prefer a different kind of "good news" than the gospel about Jesus?

- Jesus wants to hearten me by pointing my attention to where the Spirit is at work. I review my current concerns with God, asking for light and hope.

Thursday 17th December
Matthew 1:1–17

An account of the genealogy of Jesus the Messiah, the son of David, the son of Abraham. Abraham was the father of Isaac, and Isaac the father of Jacob, and Jacob the father of Judah and his brothers, and Judah the father of Perez and Zerah by Tamar, and Perez the father of Hezron, and Hezron the father of Aram, and Aram the father of Aminadab, and Aminadab the father of Nahshon, and Nahshon the father of Salmon, and Salmon the father of Boaz by Rahab, and Boaz the father of Obed by Ruth, and Obed the father of Jesse, and Jesse the father of King David. And David was the father of Solomon by the wife of Uriah, and Solomon the father of Rehoboam, and Rehoboam the father of Abijah, and Abijah the father of Asaph, and Asaph the father of Jehoshaphat, and Jehoshaphat the father of Joram, and Joram the father of Uzziah, and Uzziah the father of Jotham, and Jotham the father of Ahaz, and Ahaz the father of Hezekiah, and Hezekiah the father of Manasseh, and Manasseh the father of Amos, and Amos the father of Josiah, and Josiah the father of Jechoniah and his brothers, at the time of the deportation to Babylon. And after the deportation to Babylon: Jechoniah was the father of Salathiel, and Salathiel the father of Zerubbabel, and Zerubbabel the father of Abiud, and Abiud the father of Eliakim, and Eliakim the father of Azor, and Azor the father of Zadok, and Zadok the father of Achim, and Achim the father of Eliud, and Eliud the father of Eleazar, and Eleazar the father of Matthan, and Matthan the father of Jacob, and Jacob the father of Joseph the husband of Mary, of whom Jesus was born, who is called the Messiah. So all the generations from Abraham to David are fourteen generations; and from David to the deportation to Babylon, fourteen generations; and from the deportation to Babylon to the Messiah, fourteen generations.

- Jesus' family tree is a colorful one. It includes a murderer and an adulterer, Jews and Gentiles, the famous and the nobodies. The powerful and the powerless find a place. So do females and males in odd relationships, as well as the upright and the good. All human life is here, to show that God includes everyone in divine planning. I marvel at this.

- Everyone in human history influences others. I think of people who have influenced me for good or for ill. Then I ask that through my prayer and my life I may be a good influence on others. With Jesus I reflect on my relationships.

Friday 18th December

Matthew 1:18–25

Now the birth of Jesus the Messiah took place in this way. When his mother Mary had been engaged to Joseph, but before they lived together, she was found to be with child from the Holy Spirit. Her husband Joseph, being a righteous man and unwilling to expose her to public disgrace, planned to dismiss her quietly. But just when he had resolved to do this, an angel of the Lord appeared to him in a dream and said, "Joseph, son of David, do not be afraid to take Mary as your wife, for the child conceived in her is from the Holy Spirit. She will bear a son, and you are to name him Jesus, for he will save his people from their sins." All this took place to fulfill what had been spoken by the Lord through the prophet: "Look, the virgin shall conceive and bear a son, and they shall name him Emmanuel," which means, "God is with us." When Joseph awoke from sleep, he did as the angel of the Lord commanded him; he took her as his wife but had no marital relations with her until she had borne a son, and he named him Jesus.

- Joseph is being taught a lesson about the surprising ways in which God works. Surely God is saying something here about the divine ability to bring good even out of situations the world thinks scandalous! "Nothing will be impossible with God."

- Emmanuel: "God is with us." There is never an instant when he is not with me. With him, I shape my own soul every day of my earthly life. I need have no fear of the changes of life. Instead, I see them for what they are: surprising stages along my journey home with him.

Saturday 19th December

Luke 1:5–25

In the days of King Herod of Judea, there was a priest named Zechariah, who belonged to the priestly order of Abijah. His wife was a descendant of Aaron, and her name was Elizabeth. Both of them were righteous before God, living blamelessly according to all the commandments and regulations of the Lord. But they had no children, because Elizabeth was barren, and both were getting on in years. Once when he was serving as priest before God and his section was on duty, he was chosen by lot, according to the custom of the priesthood, to enter the sanctuary of the Lord and offer incense. Now at the time of the incense-offering, the whole assembly of the people was praying outside. Then there appeared to him an angel of the Lord, standing at the right side of the altar of incense. When Zechariah saw him, he was terrified; and fear overwhelmed him. But the angel said to him, "Do not be afraid, Zechariah, for your prayer has been heard. Your wife Elizabeth will bear you a son, and you will name him John. You will have joy and gladness, and many will rejoice at his birth, for he will be great in the sight of the Lord. He must never drink wine or strong drink; even before his birth he will be filled with the Holy Spirit. He will turn many of the people of Israel to the Lord their God. With the spirit and power of Elijah, he will go before him, to turn the hearts of parents to their children, and the disobedient to the wisdom of the righteous, to make ready a people prepared for the Lord." Zechariah said to the angel, "How will I know that this is so? For I am an old man, and my wife is getting on in years." The angel replied, "I am Gabriel. I stand in the presence of God, and I have been sent to speak to you and to bring you this good news. But now, because you did not believe my words, which will be fulfilled in their time, you will become mute, unable to speak, until the day these things occur." Meanwhile, the people were waiting for Zechariah, and wondered at his delay in the sanctuary. When he did come out, he could not speak to them, and they realized that he had seen a vision in the sanctuary. He kept motioning to them and remained unable to speak. When his time of service was ended, he went to his home. After those days his wife Elizabeth conceived, and for five months she remained in seclusion. She said, "This is what the Lord has done for me when he looked favorably on me and took away the disgrace I have endured among my people."

• Zechariah, you lived a dedicated and blameless life. You served on that day as a priest before God, as on any other day. You attended scrupulously to the rites of purification. But nothing prepared you for a direct encounter with God. You never thought that your hope would be answered. Am I a bit like you?

- How much do we live life by simply doing what needs to be done or what is expected of us? Can we own our lives more, claiming the grace of the moment? Can we address our God as if we know that God can hear us? Can we love our dear ones as if we might never see them again? Poor Zechariah, if given a second chance, might have hugged the angel because the encounter promised him "joy and gladness."

December 20—December 26

Something to think and pray about each day this week:

Meeting God Within

When people succeed in coming home to themselves and glimpsing their own inner beauty, something amazing happens: they are blessed with a real compassion for who they themselves are, in all their vulnerabilities. This compassion in turn carves out a space where they can welcome God into their hearts. It is as if they must first become aware of the marvel of themselves, and only then are they ready to get in touch with the wonder of God. Their new relationship with themselves ushers in a nourishing friendship with the One who has always been calling them. This journey inward does not take place overnight. Although the heart is only fifteen inches from the head, it can take us years to arrive at our emotional core. I used to imagine that God didn't particularly like the world because it wasn't spiritual enough. Only later did it dawn on me that God had created the world in love and had passionately left clues to this fact everywhere. The persons and events of my daily life were already signs of God. Had I paid compassionate attention to my longings and my joys, I would have heard in them the symphony of God's own infinite joy. To find God, I did not have to leave the world, but come home to it—and to myself—and God would be there, waiting for me.

The Presence of God

God is with me, but more, God is within me.
Let me dwell for a moment on God's life-giving presence
in my body, in my mind, in my heart,
as I sit here, right now.

Freedom

"There are very few people
who realize what God would make of them
if they abandoned themselves into his hands
and let themselves be formed by his grace" (Saint Ignatius of Loyola).
I ask for the grace to trust myself totally to God's love.

Consciousness

I exist in a web of relationships—links to nature, people, God.
I trace out these links, giving thanks for the life that flows through them.
Some links are twisted or broken: I may feel regret, anger,
disappointment.
I pray for the gift of acceptance and forgiveness.

The Word

God speaks to each one of us individually. I listen attentively to hear
what he is saying to me. Read the text a few times, then listen. (Please
turn to the Scripture on the following pages. Inspiration points are
provided should you need them. When you are ready, return here to
continue.)

Conversation

Begin to talk to Jesus about the passage of Scripture you have just read.
What part of it strikes a chord in you? Perhaps the words of a friend—
or some story you have heard recently—will slowly rise to the surface
of your consciousness. If so, does the story throw light on what the
Scripture passage may be trying to say to you?

Conclusion

I thank God for these few moments we have spent alone together and
for any insights I may have been given concerning the text.

Sunday 20th December
Fourth Sunday of Advent
Luke 1:39–45

In those days Mary set out and went with haste to a Judean town in the hill country, where she entered the house of Zechariah and greeted Elizabeth. When Elizabeth heard Mary's greeting, the child leaped in her womb. And Elizabeth was filled with the Holy Spirit and exclaimed with a loud cry, "Blessed are you among women, and blessed is the fruit of your womb. And why has this happened to me, that the mother of my Lord comes to me? For as soon as I heard the sound of your greeting, the child in my womb leaped for joy. And blessed is she who believed that there would be a fulfillment of what was spoken to her by the Lord."

- Elizabeth is given the special grace of an intimate insight and appreciation of what is happening and who is really present. Do I always appreciate what is happening and who is really present?

- When I encounter someone for the first time, do I perceive and respect that person as a son or daughter of God? What about the people I meet on a day-to-day basis?

Monday 21st December
Luke 1:39–45

In those days Mary set out and went with haste to a Judean town in the hill country, where she entered the house of Zechariah and greeted Elizabeth. When Elizabeth heard Mary's greeting, the child leaped in her womb. And Elizabeth was filled with the Holy Spirit and exclaimed with a loud cry, "Blessed are you among women, and blessed is the fruit of your womb. And why has this happened to me, that the mother of my Lord comes to me? For as soon as I heard the sound of your greeting, the child in my womb leaped for joy. And blessed is she who believed that there would be a fulfillment of what was spoken to her by the Lord."

- Elizabeth is the first to bear witness to the Lord's presence in our world. We can bear witness and encourage one another along the way. Helping another to notice God brings hope and consolation way beyond our expectation.

- The Spirit of God in Elizabeth rejoiced in the presence of Mary. I pray for those who have been friends to me, for all whose companionship or example lift my heart.

Tuesday 22nd December
Luke 1:46–56

And Mary said, "My soul magnifies the Lord, and my spirit rejoices in God my Savior, for he has looked with favor on the lowliness of his servant. Surely, from now on all generations will call me blessed; for the Mighty One has done great things for me, and holy is his name. His mercy is for those who fear him from generation to generation. He has shown strength with his arm; he has scattered the proud in the thoughts of their hearts. He has brought down the powerful from their thrones, and lifted up the lowly; he has filled the hungry with good things, and sent the rich away empty. He has helped his servant Israel, in remembrance of his mercy, according to the promise he made to our ancestors, to Abraham and to his descendants forever." And Mary remained with Elizabeth about three months and then returned to her home.

- This glorious prayer, the *Magnificat*, is charged with dynamite. It points to a society in which nobody wants to have too much while others have too little. The hungry are fed and the lowly are raised up.

- Lord, give me Mary's confidence and generosity of spirit. I ask not only to listen to your voice and do your will, but to do it joyfully and fearlessly. Let me answer your call with an exultant "Yes!" because I know that my journey into the unknown will be made radiant by your transfiguring presence.

Wednesday 23rd December

Luke 1:57–66

Now the time came for Elizabeth to give birth, and she bore a son. Her neighbors and relatives heard that the Lord had shown his great mercy to her, and they rejoiced with her. On the eighth day they came to circumcise the child, and they were going to name him Zechariah after his father. But his mother said, "No; he is to be called John." They said to her, "None of your relatives has this name." Then they began motioning to his father to find out what name he wanted to give him. He asked for a writing tablet and wrote, "His name is John." And all of them were amazed. Immediately his mouth was opened and his tongue freed, and he began to speak, praising God. Fear came over all their neighbors, and all these things were talked about throughout the entire hill country of Judea. All who heard them pondered them and said, "What then will this child become?" For, indeed, the hand of the Lord was with him.

- I join in the excitement around the birth of Elizabeth's baby. I become aware that God is fulfilling his plans through human beings who collaborate. So, too, God wants the child to be called John, and this is what happens. In Luke's understanding of salvation, what God decides will eventually be fulfilled. I ask for faith to believe this and to be free of anxiety.

- How do I stay open to the God of Surprises, to the Spirit that moves at will? Is my comfort zone too well defended for me to be surprised by grace?

Thursday 24th December

Luke 1:67–79

His father Zechariah was filled with the Holy Spirit and spoke this prophecy: "Blessed be the Lord God of Israel, for he has looked favorably on his people and redeemed them. He has raised up a mighty savior for us in the house of his servant David, as he spoke through the mouth of his holy prophets from of old, that we would be saved from our enemies and from the hand of all who hate us. Thus he has shown the mercy promised to our ancestors, and has remembered his holy covenant, the oath that he swore to our ancestor Abraham, to grant us that we, being rescued from the hands of our enemies, might serve him without fear, in holiness and righteousness before him all our days. And you, child, will be called the prophet of the Most High; for you will go before the Lord to prepare his ways, to give knowledge of salvation to his people by the forgiveness of their sins. By the tender mercy of our God, the dawn from on high will break upon us, to give light to those who sit in darkness and in the shadow of death, to guide our feet into the way of peace."

- The *Benedictus* is a prayer of prophecy about the coming of the Savior. This "Most High" that Zechariah mentions comes not in a cloud of glory, but as a vulnerable child, with an ordinary family, in a cold stable. That is the kind of God we have.

- The prayer of Zechariah is a morning prayer for thousands every day. I read it slowly, letting the words reveal their meaning for me today.

Friday 25th December
The Nativity of the Lord
John 1:1–18

In the beginning was the Word, and the Word was with God, and the Word was God. He was in the beginning with God. All things came into being through him, and without him not one thing came into being. What has come into being in him was life, and the life was the light of all people. The light shines in the darkness, and the darkness did not overcome it. There was a man sent from God, whose name was John. He came as a witness to testify to the light, so that all might believe through him. He himself was not the light, but he came to testify to the light. The true light, which enlightens everyone, was coming into the world. He was in the world, and the world came into being through him; yet the world did not know him. He came to what was his own, and his own people did not accept him. But to all who received him, who believed in his name, he gave power to become children of God, who were born, not of blood or of the will of the flesh or of the will of man, but of God. And the Word became flesh and lived among us, and we have seen his glory, the glory as of a father's only son, full of grace and truth. (John testified to him and cried out, "This was he of whom I said, 'He who comes after me ranks ahead of me because he was before me.'") From his fullness we have all received, grace upon grace. The law indeed was given through Moses; grace and truth came through Jesus Christ. No one has ever seen God. It is God the only Son, who is close to the Father's heart, who has made him known.

• The Light of the World has come among us. He is born in the night, with his own star blazing above him. He lies in the dimness of a stable, that same Lord who, as a pillar of cloud by day and a pillar of fire by night, led the Israelites to freedom. He has come to bring his people from darkness into light. As we gaze into the manger, at the tiny creature who is given to us as a light to the nations, we can only whisper, "Come, let us adore him."

• Now that Jesus has arrived, I have a whole new meaning to my life. I am becoming a daughter or son of God! I have been adopted into God's own family. I am important to God! I can now feel happy about myself, no matter what difficulties may be in my life. Everyone else is important, too, so I ask to have great reverence from now on, for myself and for those around me.

Saturday 26th December
Matthew 10:17–22

Jesus said to his disciples, "Beware of them, for they will hand you over to councils and flog you in their synagogues; and you will be dragged before governors and kings because of me, as a testimony to them and the Gentiles. When they hand you over, do not worry about how you are to speak or what you are to say; for what you are to say will be given to you at that time; for it is not you who speak, but the Spirit of your

Father speaking through you. Brother will betray brother to death, and a father his child, and children will rise against parents and have them put to death; and you will be hated by all because of my name. But the one who endures to the end will be saved."

- It is a shock to read this gospel passage immediately after Christmas. But this is the world into which Jesus comes. He does not retreat from it in fear or disgust. He will wrap it in his love, and that will be enough to save humankind. I ask for Jesus' courage and love.

- Wisdom, it is said, is making peace with the unchangeable. Do I make peace with any suffering that comes my way?

December 27, 2015—January 2, 2016

Something to think and pray about each day this week:

What Shall I Say?

I work with homeless kids. They're tough, but sometimes one whom I have known for years will sit down in front of me and say, "Can I ask you something?" "Sure," I reply. The kid admits he has seriously offended society in some way, then says, "You won't give up on me, will you?" What shall I say? The conviction that everyone is to be loved infinitely and unconditionally is the foundation stone of a commitment to justice. Starting with myself, I believe that I am loved infinitely. What does love mean here? Love means wanting someone's happiness. Every loving parent wants to give their child all the happiness they can. And God, the Great Giver of Gifts, wishes me to have infinite happiness. That is why I can assert that I am loved infinitely. I am also valued beyond price. My value comes from the infinite love that the Giver of the Gifts has for me. So I am of infinite value. Western culture values people by their achievements, by what they do. We look up to those who succeed and look down on those who have not achieved. But if we have living faith, we value people instead by gospel values. I am valued and loved unconditionally. And so no one, nothing, not even my own sinfulness, can take away the value and dignity that God's love bestows on me.

The Presence of God

Dear Jesus, I come to you today longing for your presence.
I desire to love you as you love me.
May nothing ever separate me from you.

Freedom

"In these days, God taught me as a schoolteacher teaches a pupil" (Saint Ignatius of Loyola).

I remind myself that there are things God has to teach me yet and ask for the grace to hear them and let them change me.

Consciousness

Where do I sense hope, encouragement, and growth areas in my life?

By looking back over the last few months, I may be able to see which activities and occasions have produced rich fruit.

If I do notice such areas, I will determine to give those areas both time and space in the future.

The Word

The Word of God comes down to us through the Scriptures. May the Holy Spirit enlighten my mind and my heart to respond to the gospel teachings. (Please turn to the Scripture on the following pages. Inspiration points are provided should you need them. When you are ready, return here to continue.)

Conversation

Conversation requires talking and listening.

As I talk to Jesus, may I also learn to be still and listen.

I picture the gentleness in his eyes and his smile full of love as he gazes on me.

I can be totally honest with Jesus as I tell him of my worries and my cares. I will open up my heart to him as I tell him of my fears and my doubts. I will ask him to help me place myself fully in his care, to abandon myself to him, knowing that he always wants what is best for me.

Conclusion

Glory be to the Father, and to the Son, and to the Holy Spirit, as it was in the beginning, is now and ever shall be, world without end. Amen.

Sunday 27th December
The Holy Family of Jesus, Mary, and Joseph
Luke 2:41–52

Now every year his parents went to Jerusalem for the festival of the Passover. And when he was twelve years old, they went up as usual for the festival. When the festival was ended and they started to return, the boy Jesus stayed behind in Jerusalem, but his parents did not know it. Assuming that he was in the group of travelers, they went a day's journey. Then they started to look for him among their relatives and friends. When they did not find him, they returned to Jerusalem to search for him. After three days they found him in the temple, sitting among the teachers, listening to them and asking them questions. And all who heard him were amazed at his understanding and his answers. When his parents saw him they were astonished; and his mother said to him, "Child, why have you treated us like this? Look, your father and I have been searching for you in great anxiety." He said to them, "Why were you searching for me? Did you not know that I must be in my Father's house?" But they did not understand what he said to them. Then he went down with them and came to Nazareth, and was obedient to them. His mother treasured all these things in her heart. And Jesus increased in wisdom and in years, and in divine and human favor.

- "In my Father's house." Do I believe that the Father's house may be found within me? If I do, I can perhaps open myself to an even greater wonder: "Those who love me will keep my word, and my Father will love them, and we will come to them and make our home with them" (John 14:23).

- Let me take in this scene slowly. Jesus is coming of age, entering his teens, and is an eager student questioning his teachers. To his mother's query—"your father and I"—he points gently to another paternity: "I must be in my Father's house." No gospel scene shows more clearly the gradual process by which he grew into a sense of his mission. Let me savor it.

Monday 28th December
Matthew 2:13–18

Now after the wise men had left, an angel of the Lord appeared to Joseph in a dream and said, "Get up, take the child and his mother, and flee to Egypt, and remain there until I tell you; for Herod is about to search for the child, to destroy him." Then Joseph got up, took the child and his mother by night, and went to Egypt, and remained there until the death of Herod. This was to fulfill what had been spoken by the Lord through the prophet, "Out of Egypt I have called my son." When Herod saw that he had been tricked by the wise men, he was infuriated, and he sent and killed all the children in and around Bethlehem who were two years old or under, according to the time that he had learned from the wise men. Then was fulfilled what had been spoken through the prophet Jeremiah: "A voice was heard in Ramah, wailing and loud lamentation, Rachel weeping for her children; she refused to be consoled, because they are no more."

- There is something about the murder of children that shakes our faith. How could God allow the innocent and unprotected, whose whole lives lie before them, to be killed by evil people? We are driven back to the psalms of rage and protest:

  "Yahweh, how much longer are the wicked to triumph?
  Are these evil men to remain unsilenced,
  boasting and asserting themselves?
  No! Yahweh is still my citadel,
  my God is a rock where I take shelter.
  He will pay them back for all their sins,
  he will silence their wickedness,
  Yahweh our God will silence them." (Psalm 94)

- Lord, you have tasted human uncertainties and the difficulties of survival. Your mother, so blissfully happy when she prayed the *Magnificat*, had to adjust rapidly to homelessness and the life of asylum seekers. Let me be equally unsurprisable when you ask me to taste uncertainties and plans going awry.

Tuesday 29th December

Luke 2:22–35

When the time came for their purification according to the law of Moses, they brought him up to Jerusalem to present him to the Lord (as it is written in the law of the Lord, "Every firstborn male shall be designated as holy to the Lord"), and they offered a sacrifice according to what is stated in the law of the Lord, "a pair of turtledoves or two young pigeons." Now there was a man in Jerusalem whose name was Simeon; this man was righteous and devout, looking forward to the consolation of Israel, and the Holy Spirit rested on him. It had been revealed to him by the Holy Spirit that he would not see death before he had seen the Lord's Messiah. Guided by the Spirit, Simeon came into the temple; and when the parents brought in the child Jesus, to do for him what was customary under the law, Simeon took him in his arms and praised God, saying, "Master, now you are dismissing your servant in peace, according to your word; for my eyes have seen your salvation, which you have prepared in the presence of all peoples, a light for revelation to the Gentiles and for glory to your people Israel." And the child's father and mother were amazed at what was being said about him. Then Simeon blessed them and said to his mother Mary, "This child is destined for the falling and the rising of many in Israel, and to be a sign that will be opposed so that the inner thoughts of many will be revealed—and a sword will pierce your own soul too."

- Simeon was one of those known as the "quiet in the land"—Jews who did not look for a military Messiah. He had no dreams of armies or power but believed in a life of constant watchfulness and prayer until God should come. There is a double surprise here: the delight of Simeon at being able to welcome the Promised One and the astonishment of Mary and Joseph at what was being said about their boy.

- I watch Mary carefully handing over Jesus into Simeon's arms. I see the delight on the old man's face. The consolation he had waited for has come. Simeon hands the child back to me, and I ask that I may recognize in Jesus the consolation I need.

Wednesday 30th December
Luke 2:36–40

There was also a prophet, Anna the daughter of Phanuel, of the tribe of Asher. She was of a great age, having lived with her husband seven years after her marriage, then as a widow to the age of eighty-four. She never left the temple but worshipped there with fasting and prayer night and day. At that moment she came, and began to praise God and to speak about the child to all who were looking for the redemption of Jerusalem. When they had finished everything required by the law of the Lord, they returned to Galilee, to their own town of Nazareth. The child grew and became strong, filled with wisdom; and the favor of God was upon him.

- Anna, another of the "quiet in the land", had lived to a great age. All we know of her is this moment of recognition and blessing. That last sentence summarizes 90 percent of our knowledge of the biography of Jesus, a hidden life as he grew strong and wise. Lord, you are telling me that it is no harm to live quietly and to allow time for your favor to be upon me.

- Mary must have pondered endlessly in her heart about her baby son. He is so ordinary: he eats, sleeps, plays, laughs, and cries. He learns easily; he is a blessed child. But is the angel's promise true, that this is in reality the Son of God? How can it be? And yet there are the crumbs of confirmation: Elizabeth's blessing, the angels and the shepherds, the kings from the east, and now Simeon's and Anna's words. Mary is given enough to help her believe, and so are we.

Thursday 31st December
John 1:1–18

In the beginning was the Word, and the Word was with God, and the Word was God. He was in the beginning with God. All things came into being through him, and without him not one thing came into being. What has come into being in him was life, and the life was the light of all people. The light shines in the darkness, and the darkness did not overcome it. There was a man sent from God, whose name was John. He came as a witness to testify to the light, so that all might believe through him. He himself was not the light, but he came to testify to the light. The true light, which enlightens everyone, was coming into the world. He was in the world, and the world came into being through him; yet the world did not know him. He came to what was his own, and his own people did not accept him. But to all who received him, who believed in his name, he gave power to become children of God, who were born, not of blood or of the will of the flesh or of the will of man, but of God. And the Word became flesh and lived among us, and we have seen his glory, the glory as of a father's only son, full of grace and truth. (John testified to him and cried out, "This was he of whom I said, 'He who comes after me ranks ahead of me because he was before me.'") From his fullness we have all received, grace upon grace. The law indeed was given through Moses; grace and truth came through Jesus Christ. No one has ever seen God. It is God the only Son, who is close to the Father's heart, who has made him known.

- In this hymn that introduces the fourth Gospel, John proclaims the faith that marks us as Christians. We believe that Jesus is the Word of God, his perfect expression. "No one has ever seen God. It is God the only Son, who is close to the Father's heart, who has made him known."

- We often say that it is hard to pray because we cannot imagine God. But God has seen this problem and has painted a perfect self-portrait in Jesus. Now we know what God thinks about us and how much God loves us. I make a New Year's resolution: in the year ahead, I will give quality time to getting to know Jesus better.

Friday 1st January
Solemnity of Mary, the Holy Mother of God
Luke 2:16–21

So they went with haste and found Mary and Joseph, and the child lying in the manger. When they saw this, they made known what had been told them about this child; and all who heard it were amazed at what the shepherds told them. But Mary treasured all these words and pondered them in her heart. The shepherds returned, glorifying and praising God for all they had heard and seen, as it had been told them. After eight days had passed, it was time to circumcise the child; and he was called Jesus, the name given by the angel before he was conceived in the womb.

- The first day of the New Year is a fresh start in the following of Jesus. We could be anxious, but we are people of a great Promise and so we begin with trust and courage. In Mary's son we have the certain hope that the Word of God made flesh lives among us and takes on himself our fears and our heaviness.

- Lord, like Mary may I find room in my cluttered life simply to rest and be quiet in your presence. Mary's heart was a sacred space, and mine is also. Fill it with the joy of your presence.

Saturday 2nd January

John 1:19–28

This is the testimony given by John when the Jews sent priests and Levites from Jerusalem to ask him, "Who are you?" He confessed and did not deny it, but confessed, "I am not the Messiah." And they asked him, "What then? Are you Elijah?" He said, "I am not." "Are you the prophet?" He answered, "No." Then they said to him, "Who are you? Let us have an answer for those who sent us. What do you say about yourself?" He said, "I am the voice of one crying out in the wilderness, 'Make straight the way of the Lord,'" as the prophet Isaiah said. Now they had been sent from the Pharisees. They asked him, "Why then are you baptizing if you are neither the Messiah, nor Elijah, nor the prophet?" John answered them, "I baptize with water. Among you stands one whom you do not know, the one who is coming after me; I am not worthy to untie the thong of his sandal." This took place in Bethany across the Jordan where John was baptizing.

- There is a question for me: "Who are you? What do you say about yourself?" Lord, I think of you beside me, seeing the good and the promise in me. This is what I want to say about myself: I am called into being by God, who loves me.

- In prayer God speaks words of comfort and assurance into the wildernesses of our lives—our bad moments of guilt, fear, anxiety, and resentment. God speaks words that help us put ourselves into a bigger world, the world of the love of God. In prayer God also calls each of us to be voices in the wilderness for others in their search for love, for meaning, for faith, and for God.

January 3—January 9

Something to think and pray about each day this week:

The Christmas Story through a Contemplative Lens

The message of Christmas is simple: "You shall call him Emmanuel, which means 'God is with us.'" So says the angel to a bewildered Joseph, who must have spent the rest of his life pondering the implications of that statement.

If God is with us in this radical way, what is our response? Are we with God? What does it mean to be with God? The following reflection, from the Christian contemplative tradition, reveals two things: First, how simple it is to be with God; and second, the world-changing power of being with God.

> What each one is interiorly,
> face to face with God,
> unknown to anyone, is of vital consequence to all.
> And every act of love,
> every act of faith and adoration,
> every mute uplifting of the heart,
> raises the whole world nearer to God.
> From everyone who is in union with God
> there breathes a spiritual vitality, light, strength, and joy,
> which reach from end to end of the universe;
> a source of grace to those least worthy of it,
> even to those least conscious of it,
> and knowing nothing of how and whence it comes.

How about a New Year's resolution: That we would step out confidently into our chaotic world with the firm belief that simply by being with God we are helping to transform it. God, who sees our hearts, will bless us as we go.

The Presence of God
The more we call on God, the more we can feel God's presence. Day by day we are drawn closer to the loving heart of God.

Freedom
Lord, you created me to live in freedom. Mostly I take this gift for granted. Inspire me to live in the freedom you intended, with a heart untroubled and with complete trust in you.

Consciousness
In God's loving presence I unwind the past day, starting from now and looking back, moment by moment. I gather in all the goodness and light, in gratitude. I attend to the shadows and what they say to me, seeking healing, courage, forgiveness.

The Word
The Word of God comes down to us through the Scriptures. May the Holy Spirit enlighten my mind and my heart to respond to the gospel teachings. (Please turn to the Scripture on the following pages. Inspiration points are provided should you need them. When you are ready, return here to continue.)

Conversation
Do I notice myself reacting as I pray with the Word of God? Do I feel challenged, comforted, angry? Imagining Jesus sitting or standing by me, I speak out my feelings, as one trusted friend to another.

Conclusion
I thank God for these few moments we have spent alone together and for any insights I may have been given concerning the text.

Sunday 3rd January
The Epiphany of the Lord
Matthew 2:1–12

In the time of King Herod, after Jesus was born in Bethlehem of Judea, wise men from the East came to Jerusalem, asking, "Where is the child who has been born king of the Jews? For we observed his star at its rising, and have come to pay him homage." When King Herod heard this, he was frightened, and all Jerusalem with him; and calling together all the chief priests and scribes of the people, he inquired of them where the Messiah was to be born. They told him, "In Bethlehem of Judea; for so it has been written by the prophet: 'And you, Bethlehem, in the land of Judah, are by no means least among the rulers of Judah; for from you shall come a ruler who is to shepherd my people Israel.'" Then Herod secretly called for the wise men and learned from them the exact time when the star had appeared. Then he sent them to Bethlehem, saying, "Go and search diligently for the child; and when you have found him, bring me word so that I may also go and pay him homage." When they had heard the king, they set out; and there, ahead of them, went the star that they had seen at its rising, until it stopped over the place where the child was. When they saw that the star had stopped, they were overwhelmed with joy. On entering the house, they saw the child with Mary his mother; and they knelt down and paid him homage. Then, opening their treasure chests, they offered him gifts of gold, frankincense, and myrrh. And having been warned in a dream not to return to Herod, they left for their own country by another road.

- The wise men saw the star and steadily followed it. The people in Jerusalem did not. What star am I being called to follow this year? What gifts from my treasure chest will I offer Jesus in service of his mission? Lord, send me out each day to be a bearer of your love to all whom I encounter.

- Life is sometimes full of questions, seeking, and searching. I pray that I may always seek the truth and that I might recognize it when God puts it in my path.

Monday 4th January
Matthew 4:12–17, 23–25

Now when Jesus heard that John had been arrested, he withdrew to Galilee. He left Nazareth and made his home in Capernaum by the lake, in the territory of Zebulun and Naphtali, so that what had been spoken through the prophet Isaiah might be fulfilled: "Land of Zebulun, land of Naphtali, on the road by the sea, across the Jordan, Galilee of the Gentiles—the people who sat in darkness have seen a great light, and for those who sat in the region and shadow of death light has dawned." From that time Jesus began to proclaim, "Repent, for the kingdom of heaven has come near." Jesus went throughout Galilee, teaching in their synagogues and proclaiming the good news of the kingdom and curing every disease and every sickness among the people. So his fame spread throughout all Syria, and they brought to him all the sick, those who were afflicted with various diseases and pains, demoniacs, epileptics, and paralytics, and he cured them. And great crowds followed him from Galilee, the Decapolis, Jerusalem, Judea, and from beyond the Jordan.

- Jesus teaches, proclaims, and cures: What does he want me to learn today? What do I need to hear from him now? Where in my life does he wish to restore me to health?

- We think we know what busy means! Imagine what it was like for Jesus, beset by needs on every side. I pray that I might not be distracted by all the things I would like to do but that I might, with Jesus, bring life and truth to where I am.

Tuesday 5th January
Mark 6:34–44

As Jesus went ashore, he saw a great crowd; and he had compassion for them, because they were like sheep without a shepherd; and he began to teach them many things. When it grew late, his disciples came to him and said, "This is a deserted place, and the hour is now very late; send them away so that they may go into the surrounding country and villages and buy something for themselves to eat." But he answered them, "You give them something to eat." They said to him, "Are we to go and buy two hundred denarii worth of bread, and give it to them to eat?" And he said to them, "How many loaves have you? Go and see." When they had found out, they said, "Five, and two fish." Then he ordered them to get all the people to sit down in groups on the green grass. So they sat down in groups of hundreds and of fifties. Taking the five loaves and the two fish, he looked up to heaven, and blessed and broke the loaves, and gave them to his disciples to set before the people; and he divided the two fish among them all. And all ate and were filled; and they took up twelve baskets full of broken pieces and of the fish. Those who had eaten the loaves numbered five thousand men.

- The heart of Jesus went out to the people: It was as if they were part of him—unlike the disciples, who wanted to send them away. I consider how the heart of Jesus seeks me out, wanting to heal and nourish me, drawing me into relationship.

- Sometimes I seem to be in control but in secret am like a sheep without a shepherd. Help me, Lord, to hear your voice, and give me the humility to follow it.

Wednesday 6th January

Mark 6:45–52

Immediately Jesus made his disciples get into the boat and go on ahead to the other side, to Bethsaida, while he dismissed the crowd. After saying farewell to them, he went up on the mountain to pray. When evening came, the boat was out on the lake, and he was alone on the land. When he saw that they were straining at the oars against an adverse wind, he came towards them early in the morning, walking on the lake. He intended to pass them by. But when they saw him walking on the lake, they thought it was a ghost and cried out; for they all saw him and were terrified. But immediately he spoke to them and said, "Take heart, it is I; do not be afraid." Then he got into the boat with them and the wind ceased. And they were utterly astounded, for they did not understand about the loaves, but their hearts were hardened.

- This is a story about peace of soul. At the end of a long day surrounded by crowds, Jesus does not sleep but climbs a mountain to pray on his own. The bond with his Father was the source of his strength. We enjoy the same bond, the Holy Spirit in us; we can use the same strength.

- It is also a story about panic. With the waves breaking over the boat, the disciples cannot believe that the Lord has seen them and is approaching. I hear him say to me: Come.

Thursday 7th January

Luke 4:14–22a

Then Jesus, filled with the power of the Spirit, returned to Galilee, and a report about him spread through all the surrounding country. He began to teach in their synagogues and was praised by everyone. When he came to Nazareth, where he had been brought up, he went to the synagogue on the sabbath day, as was his custom. He stood up to read, and the scroll of the prophet Isaiah was given to him. He unrolled the scroll and found the place where it was written: "The Spirit of the Lord is upon me, because he has anointed me to bring good news to the poor. He has sent me to proclaim release to the captives and recovery of sight to the blind, to let the oppressed go free, to proclaim the year of the Lord's favor." And he rolled up the scroll, gave it back to the attendant, and sat down. The eyes of all in the synagogue were fixed on him. Then he began to say to them, "Today this Scripture has been fulfilled in your hearing." All spoke well of him and were amazed at the gracious words that came from his mouth.

- The details of this passage tell us much about the ordinary life of Jesus. It was his custom to go to the synagogue on the sabbath; though he took issue with details of the Law proclaimed there, he chose to join with his community in the worship of God. Though he wrote nothing (as far as we know), he read, and was chosen to read to the assembly. He read standing, and then sat down—the posture for serious teaching—and the eyes of all were fixed on him. It is a moment of grace and promise, as he brings the good news to his own people.

- In my imagination I join the synagogue congregation and hear this charismatic young man speaking the prophecy of Isaiah as his own mission statement. As I listen I sense with excitement that he is reaching out to me to join him. Lord, let me be part of that unending mission: to bring good news, vision, and freedom to those who need them.

Friday 8th January
Luke 5:12–16

Once, when Jesus was in one of the cities, there was a man covered with leprosy. When he saw Jesus, he bowed with his face to the ground and begged him, "Lord, if you choose, you can make me clean." Then Jesus stretched out his hand, touched him, and said, "I do choose. Be made clean." Immediately the leprosy left him. And he ordered him to tell no one. "Go," he said, "and show yourself to the priest, and, as Moses commanded, make an offering for your cleansing, for a testimony to them." But now more than ever the word about Jesus spread abroad; many crowds would gather to hear him and to be cured of their diseases. But he would withdraw to deserted places and pray.

- The demands on Jesus were great, the expectations many. Still he was able to keep his focus, to maintain his relationship with God. As I make this time to pray, I am doing as he did. Lord, let me never be too busy to give time to you, to us.

- Are there places I might go or conditions I might create to "withdraw to a deserted place"? What do I need to turn off—metaphorically or literally?

Saturday 9th January

John 3:22–30

Jesus and his disciples went into the Judean countryside, and he spent some time there with them and baptized. John also was baptizing at Aenon near Salim because water was abundant there; and people kept coming and were being baptized—John, of course, had not yet been thrown into prison. Now a discussion about purification arose between John's disciples and a Jew. They came to John and said to him, "Rabbi, the one who was with you across the Jordan, to whom you testified, here he is baptizing, and all are going to him." John answered, "No one can receive anything except what has been given from heaven. You yourselves are my witnesses that I said, 'I am not the Messiah, but I have been sent ahead of him.' He who has the bride is the bridegroom. The friend of the bridegroom, who stands and hears him, rejoices greatly at the bridegroom's voice. For this reason my joy has been fulfilled. He must increase, but I must decrease."

- My question as I grow older is not: "Am I qualified enough to show Jesus to people?" More and more it is: "Am I weak enough?" In witnessing to Jesus do I accept my failures and the wounds of life to be more important than my strengths? I am a wounded healer. Like my fellow human beings, I too am searching and struggling.

- Loving Father, you wake me from sleep today and call me into life and service. You want something of your goodness to shine through my frailty and brokenness. Bless this day!

The First Week of Ordinary Time
January 10—January 16

Something to think and pray about each day this week:

Thin Places

The early Celts had an affinity for the spirit world. Gifted with imagination, they found the threshold between this and the unseen world easy to cross. They used to say that heaven and earth are only three feet apart, and that in the thin places the distance is even smaller! The term "thin places" can put words on our own experiences of being drawn beyond ourselves into awesome yet kindly Mystery.

Creation, after all, is intense with divinity, which embraces us and reveals itself, unpredictably if we have eyes to see. The veil between God's world and "our world" is often drawn back for a moment to give us a glimpse of the "beyond." The monk Thomas Merton rightly says that the gate of heaven is everywhere. Places of beauty, wild landscapes, lonely mountains, magnificent sunsets, starry nights, or the roaring sea can enchant us. On other levels falling in love can open up a transfigured world. Or the divine breaks through in a smile, a baby's tiny finger, human beauty, a kind remark, a bar of music. The beggar's face, the eyes of a starving child, the hushed moment of the death of someone we loved can also break open the door of the heart. Be alert for such "thin places," for God can be found in all things. And our prayer points us daily to Jesus, in whom the human and divine blend perfectly.

The Presence of God

Lord, help me to be fully alive to your holy presence. Enfold me in your love. Let my heart become one with yours. My soul longs for your presence, Lord. When I turn my thoughts to you, I find peace and contentment.

Freedom

I am free. When I look at these words in writing they seem to create in me a feeling of awe. Yes, a wonderful feeling of freedom. Thank you, God.

Consciousness

To be conscious about something is to be aware of it. Dear Lord, help me to remember that you gave me life. Thank you for the gift of life. Teach me to slow down, to be still, and to enjoy the pleasures created for me. To be aware of the beauty that surrounds me. The marvel of mountains, the calmness of lakes, the fragility of a flower petal. I need to remember that all these things come from you.

The Word

I read the Word of God slowly, a few times over, and I listen to what God is saying to me. (Please turn to the Scripture on the following pages. Inspiration points are provided should you need them. When you are ready, return here to continue.)

Conversation

Jesus, you speak to me through the words of the gospels. May I respond to your call today. Teach me to recognize your hand at work in my daily living.

Conclusion

Glory be to the Father, and to the Son, and to the Holy Spirit, as it was in the beginning, is now and ever shall be, world without end. Amen.

Sunday 10th January
The Baptism of the Lord

Luke 3:15–16, 21–22

As the people were filled with expectation, and all were questioning in their hearts concerning John, whether he might be the Messiah, John answered all of them by saying, "I baptize you with water; but one who is more powerful than I is coming; I am not worthy to untie the thong of his sandals. He will baptize you with the Holy Spirit and fire." Now when all the people were baptized, and when Jesus also had been baptized and was praying, the heaven was opened, and the Holy Spirit descended upon him in bodily form like a dove. And a voice came from heaven, "You are my Son, the Beloved; with you I am well pleased."

- God always speaks to Jesus in an intimate and joyful fashion. He says: "You are my beloved Son; I am pleased with you. I love you deeply. Your whole being springs from me. I am your Father." Jesus answers, "Abba"—"beloved Father." His whole life reveals trust. He hands himself over unconditionally to his Father.

- God, I ponder on the love you have lavished also upon me, calling me your child. You are the tender and compassionate Mother of my life. You are the faithful Father, the rock on which I stand. Your love is everlasting. Your faithfulness is eternal.

Monday 11th January

Mark 1:14–20

Now after John was arrested, Jesus came to Galilee, proclaiming the good news of God, and saying, "The time is fulfilled, and the kingdom of God has come near; repent, and believe in the good news." As Jesus passed along the Sea of Galilee, he saw Simon and his brother Andrew casting a net into the sea—for they were fishermen. And Jesus said to them, "Follow me and I will make you fish for people." And immediately they left their nets and followed him. As he went a little farther, he saw James son of Zebedee and his brother John, who were in their boat mending the nets. Immediately he called them; and they left their father Zebedee in the boat with the hired men, and followed him.

- "Come, follow me": The ways of following Jesus are as varied as people themselves. But the ways always entail breaking free from what one was before. We are true disciples when we challenge ourselves with the question, "How would Jesus act in the situation I'm in right now?"

- Lord, you call the disciples to follow you and share in your mission. Their response is radical and immediate. May nothing hinder me from generously responding to your daily call to follow you.

Tuesday 12th January
Mark 1:21–28

They went to Capernaum; and when the sabbath came, Jesus entered the synagogue and taught. They were astounded at his teaching, for he taught them as one having authority, and not as the scribes. Just then there was in their synagogue a man with an unclean spirit, and he cried out, "What have you to do with us, Jesus of Nazareth? Have you come to destroy us? I know who you are, the Holy One of God." But Jesus rebuked him, saying, "Be silent, and come out of him!" And the unclean spirit, throwing him into convulsions and crying with a loud voice, came out of him. They were all amazed, and they kept on asking one another, "What is this? A new teaching—with authority! He commands even the unclean spirits, and they obey him." At once his fame began to spread throughout the surrounding region of Galilee.

- Saint Mark depicts Jesus engaged in a war against the cosmic forces of evil. Jesus overcomes the world's enemy, though in ways different to what we would expect. Do we believe he can do this, when we pray, "Deliver us from evil"?

- The teaching of Jesus is straight from his heart, from his relationship with God. I ask God to bless me so that all my words and actions profess my faith.

Wednesday 13th January
Mark 1:29–39

As soon as they left the synagogue, they entered the house of Simon and Andrew, with James and John. Now Simon's mother-in-law was in bed with a fever, and they told Jesus about her at once. He came and took her by the hand and lifted her up. Then the fever left her, and she began to serve them. That evening, at sundown, they brought to him all who were sick or possessed with demons. And the whole city was gathered around the door. And he cured many who were sick with various diseases, and cast out many demons; and he would not permit the demons to speak, because they knew him. In the morning, while it was still very dark, he got up and went out to a deserted place, and there he prayed. And Simon and his companions hunted for him. When they found him, they said to him, "Everyone is searching for you." He answered, "Let us go on to the neighboring towns, so that I may proclaim the message there also; for that is what I came out to do." And he went throughout Galilee, proclaiming the message in their synagogues and casting out demons.

- The first recorded hours of Jesus' ministry are a whirlwind of activity. We are meant to catch on to the fact that when Jesus enters human lives, things change fast and for the better for those who are open. A new creation is here! Everyone is meant to get in on it.

- What do I need from Jesus? Am I just a spectator, or am I fighting to get close to him? His presence brings wholeness—do I need that? People become more alive—do I need that? Simon's mother-in-law gets the energy to serve—do I need that?

Thursday 14th January
Mark 1:40–45

A leper came to him begging him, and kneeling he said to him, "If you choose, you can make me clean." Moved with pity, Jesus stretched out his hand and touched him, and said to him, "I do choose. Be made clean!" Immediately the leprosy left him, and he was made clean. After sternly warning him he sent him away at once, saying to him, "See that you say nothing to anyone; but go, show yourself to the priest, and offer for your cleansing what Moses commanded, as a testimony to them." But he went out and began to proclaim it freely, and to spread the word, so that Jesus could no longer go into a town openly, but stayed out in the country; and people came to him from every quarter.

- In this gospel passage we find Jesus moved with pity. Leprosy was a living death: the sufferer was isolated from family and community, and had to cry out, "Unclean, unclean!" when anyone approached. Touching the leper made Jesus ritually unclean also. There are no lengths to which Jesus will not go to help this man. He touches him, speaks to him, and gives him freedom to be fully human again. I spend a few moments with the leper before his cure and then meet him afterward. What might he say to me about faith in Jesus? About my pity for others in need? Whom do I touch?

- The leper knew his need and trusted that Jesus could help him. I pray with the same attitude—not hiding my neediness, not hesitant about bringing it before Jesus—listening for his encouraging response.

Friday 15th January

Mark 2:1–12

When Jesus returned to Capernaum after some days, it was reported that he was at home. So many gathered around that there was no longer room for them, not even in front of the door; and he was speaking the word to them. Then some people came, bringing to him a paralyzed man, carried by four of them. And when they could not bring him to Jesus because of the crowd, they removed the roof above him; and after having dug through it, they let down the mat on which the paralytic lay. When Jesus saw their faith, he said to the paralytic, "Son, your sins are forgiven." Now some of the scribes were sitting there, questioning in their hearts, "Why does this fellow speak in this way? It is blasphemy! Who can forgive sins but God alone?" At once Jesus perceived in his spirit that they were discussing these questions among themselves; and he said to them, "Why do you raise such questions in your hearts? Which is easier, to say to the paralytic, 'Your sins are forgiven,' or to say, 'Stand up and take your mat and walk'? But so that you may know that the Son of Man has authority on earth to forgive sins"—he said to the paralytic—"I say to you, stand up, take your mat and go to your home." And he stood up, and immediately took the mat and went out before all of them; so that they were all amazed and glorified God, saying, "We have never seen anything like this!"

- Two motifs intertwine in this scene: the curing of the paralytic and the forgiveness of his sins. The essential requirement for both events is faith in Jesus. Physical paralysis can make a person feel trapped in their body. The paralysis of sin thwarts a person in spirit and stunts their growth. The paralyzed man's friends have faith in the One who can make the blind able to see and the lame able to walk. They overcome every obstacle to present him for healing.

- Lord, I thank you for the many times when I was carried by others to you. Keep me sensitive to people and places in our world that need to be carried in faith. May your healing power of loving for-giveness enable me to stand up, to walk, and to glorify you.

Saturday 16th January
Mark 2:13–17

Jesus went out again beside the lake; the whole crowd gathered around him, and he taught them. As he was walking along, he saw Levi son of Alphaeus sitting at the tax booth, and he said to him, "Follow me." And he got up and followed him. And as he sat at dinner in Levi's house, many tax collectors and sinners were also sitting with Jesus and his disciples—for there were many who followed him. When the scribes of the Pharisees saw that he was eating with sinners and tax collectors, they said to his disciples, "Why does he eat with tax collectors and sinners?" When Jesus heard this, he said to them, "Those who are well have no need of a physician, but those who are sick; I have come to call not the righteous but sinners."

- I wonder how Jesus said the words, "Follow me." Like an order, an invitation, a whisper, a definite challenge? However it was said, it provoked a response.

- Allow Jesus to address you in your prayer. How do you hear his call to follow him—as a gentle invitation, or an urgent word? No matter how it is said, it is always spoken into the space of each person's interior freedom and deepest generosity.

The Second Week of Ordinary Time
January 17—January 23

Something to think and pray about each day this week:

Guests at the Wedding Feast

At the recent Feast of Epiphany (which means "manifestation"), the glory of God shines out for all the nations in Mary's little child. Then, at the Feast of the Baptism of the Lord, that light is manifest once more. Heaven opens and the Spirit comes down on Jesus. A voice is heard, "You are my Son, the Beloved" (Luke 3:22). Now, in this Sunday's gospel reading comes the wedding feast of Cana: Jesus transforms water into wine. He lets his glory be seen, and his disciples believe in him (John 2:11).

Note the setting: a wedding feast! Why? Because the prophets had already portrayed the ultimate transformation of our lives as being like a marriage union with God: "I shall betroth you to myself forever, betroth you with integrity and justice, with tenderness and love" (Hosea 2:19). And at the End, in God's radiant love "eternally there for us," we will shine out like the dawn. We shall be called "God's Delight" and our land shall be called "The Wedded," for the Lord takes delight in us (Isaiah 62:1–5). So, as we look to Jesus and contemplate him at the wedding feast, we can reflect on all these promises that his radiant presence holds out for us. As his disciples we can ask for the grace to believe in him and entrust ourselves completely to him who is Light.

The Presence of God

Dear Jesus, as I call on you today I realize that I often come asking for favors. Today I'd like just to be in your presence. Let my heart respond to your love.

Freedom

God is not foreign to my freedom. Instead the Spirit breathes life into my most intimate desires, gently nudging me toward all that is good. I ask for the grace to let myself be enfolded by the Spirit.

Consciousness

In the presence of my loving Creator, I look honestly at my feelings over the past day—the highs, the lows, and the level ground. Can I see where the Lord has been present?

The Word

God speaks to each one of us individually. I listen attentively to hear what he is saying to me. Read the text a few times, then listen. (Please turn to the Scripture on the following pages. Inspiration points are provided should you need them. When you are ready, return here to continue.)

Conversation

Begin to talk to Jesus about the piece of Scripture you have just read. What part of it strikes a chord in you? Perhaps the words of a friend—or some story you have heard recently—will slowly rise to the surface of your consciousness. If so, does the story throw light on what the Scripture passage may be trying to say to you?

Conclusion

I thank God for these few moments we have spent alone together and for any insights I may have been given concerning the text.

Sunday 17th January
Second Sunday in Ordinary Time
John 2:1–11

On the third day there was a wedding in Cana of Galilee, and the mother of Jesus was there. Jesus and his disciples had also been invited to the wedding. When the wine gave out, the mother of Jesus said to him, "They have no wine." And Jesus said to her, "Woman, what concern is that to you and to me? My hour has not yet come." His mother said to the servants, "Do whatever he tells you." Now standing there were six stone water jars for the Jewish rites of purification, each holding twenty or thirty gallons. Jesus said to them, "Fill the jars with water." And they filled them up to the brim. He said to them, "Now draw some out, and take it to the chief steward." So they took it. When the steward tasted the water that had become wine, and did not know where it came from (though the servants who had drawn the water knew), the steward called the bridegroom and said to him, "Everyone serves the good wine first, and then the inferior wine after the guests have become drunk. But you have kept the good wine until now." Jesus did this, the first of his signs, in Cana of Galilee, and revealed his glory; and his disciples believed in him.

- Jesus reveals his glory, but not through a TV campaign or e-mails. He goes to a wedding. He likes to celebrate God's wonderful gift of marriage. He also takes the opportunity to reveal the abundance of God's grace. He is saying, "My wedding gift to you is 200 gallons of God's love!"

- Lord, we thank you for good marriages. We thank you for the wonder of faithful, unconditional love shown by husband and wife, parents and grandparents. This fidelity powerfully reflects the quality of your love for us all.

Monday 18th January
Mark 2:18–22

Now John's disciples and the Pharisees were fasting; and people came and said to him, "Why do John's disciples and the disciples of the Pharisees fast, but your disciples do not fast?" Jesus said to them, "The wedding guests cannot fast while the bridegroom is with them, can they? As long as they have the bridegroom with them, they cannot fast. The days will come when the bridegroom is taken away from them, and then they will fast on that day. No one sews a piece of unshrunk cloth on an old cloak; otherwise, the patch pulls away from it, the new from the old, and a worse tear is made. And no one puts new wine into old wineskins; otherwise, the wine will burst the skins, and the wine is lost, and so are the skins; but one puts new wine into fresh wineskins."

• Jesus does not want my life to be a patchwork of pieces of my choosing. Instead, he invites me to be made anew. I pray for the vision, hope, and courage that I need.

• I ask God for the humility to accept the wisdom of the gospel instead of replacing it with my own.

Tuesday 19th January
Mark 2:23–28

One sabbath Jesus was going through the cornfields; and as they made their way his disciples began to pluck heads of grain. The Pharisees said to him, "Look, why are they doing what is not lawful on the sabbath?" And he said to them, "Have you never read what David did when he and his companions were hungry and in need of food? He entered the house of God, when Abiathar was high priest, and ate the bread of the Presence, which it is not lawful for any but the priests to eat, and he gave some to his companions." Then he said to them, "The sabbath was made for humankind, and not humankind for the sabbath; so the Son of Man is lord even of the sabbath."

- The Pharisees were skillful at pointing out deficiencies in others. Before God I review my thoughts and words to take care that I do not measure the world by my own small scale.

- Forgiveness, mercy, and compassion are at the heart of true religion. Without these, only heartlessness and empty performance remain. Lord, would others see me as a truly religious person?

Wednesday 20th January
Mark 3:1–6

Jesus entered the synagogue, and a man was there who had a withered hand. They watched him to see whether he would cure him on the sabbath, so that they might accuse him. And he said to the man who had the withered hand, "Come forward." Then he said to them, "Is it lawful to do good or to do harm on the sabbath, to save life or to kill?" But they were silent. He looked around at them with anger; he was grieved at their hardness of heart and said to the man, "Stretch out your hand." He stretched it out, and his hand was restored. The Pharisees went out and immediately conspired with the Herodians against him, how to destroy him.

- Jesus' anger grows out of his passion for life. I let myself imagine how Jesus wants to brush away whatever it is that holds me back from living fully, as he calls me to do. For my part I ask for the strength I need to "stretch out" whatever ails me for healing.

- I watch Jesus in this scene. What would I have done in regard to the man with the withered hand? Is my heart strengthened? Am I rightly angry when people are despised? Do I channel my anger into healing?

Thursday 21st January
Mark 3:7–12

Jesus departed with his disciples to the lake, and a great multitude from Galilee followed him; hearing all that he was doing, they came to him in great numbers from Judea, Jerusalem, Idumea, beyond the

Jordan, and the region around Tyre and Sidon. He told his disciples to have a boat ready for him because of the crowd, so that they would not crush him; for he had cured many, so that all who had diseases pressed upon him to touch him. Whenever the unclean spirits saw him, they fell down before him and shouted, "You are the Son of God!" But he sternly ordered them not to make him known.

- Jesus is at ease in open spaces: near lakesides, hills, and the sky, unprotected by institutional walls. People converge on him from unexpected places, seeking healing and good news. Lord, I come to you seeking to be healed and to hear good news. No place is too far that we cannot come to you.

- The magnetism of Jesus is revealed here. Ordinary, unimportant people offer him an enthusiastic reception. They approach him with one desire: to touch him and be healed. Loving energy flows from Jesus. Am I easy about joining this enthusiastic crowd of poor people? Can I admit that I, too, need the healing touch of the Son of God? Do I radiate healing to others?

Friday 22nd January

Mark 3:13–19

Jesus went up the mountain and called to him those whom he wanted, and they came to him. And he appointed twelve, whom he also named apostles, to be with him, and to be sent out to proclaim the message, and to have authority to cast out demons. So he appointed the twelve: Simon (to whom he gave the name Peter); James son of Zebedee and John the brother of James (to whom he gave the name Boanerges, that is, Sons of Thunder); and Andrew, and Philip, and Bartholomew, and Matthew, and Thomas, and James son of Alphaeus, and Thaddaeus, and Simon the Cananaean, and Judas Iscariot, who betrayed him. Then he went home.

- As I read this list of names, I consider how my name, too, is called by Jesus. He knows who I am, loves me, and believes that I am ready to work by his side.

- Jesus did not choose people because of what they were. He chose them for what they could become under his direction and power. Lord, I am nothing remarkable, yet you call me to be with you. Give me courage to serve you with generous commitment.

Saturday 23rd January
Mark 3:20–21

The crowd came together again, so that they could not even eat. When the family of Jesus heard it, they went out to restrain him, for people were saying, "He has gone out of his mind."

- Why did people think Jesus was out of his mind? Because he had abandoned a secure trade as a carpenter for a wandering life; had run into trouble with the authorities in what seemed like a deliberate way; had gathered an odd group of disciples around him. He seemed indifferent to social and financial security and the opinion of others. Lord, you ask me to take risks as you did. This is not a comfortable prayer when I think about what you have in store for me. Give me courage.

- Those who knew Jesus well seemed surprised by how he lived and acted. I pray for the freedom that I need not to be hemmed in by my habits or by the expectations of others. To live freely is to challenge those who accept constraints. I pray for the courage I may need to let the spirit of God lead me even more.

The Third Week of Ordinary Time
January 24—January 30

Something to think and pray about each day this week:

Witnesses to God's Graciousness

This year, on the Sundays of Ordinary Time, the Gospel of Luke is proclaimed. In it Jesus is portrayed as displaying the graciousness of God. He is shown as especially the friend of people on the margins of society, namely those who are poor, who are considered of little account, and who are often termed "sinners" because they don't keep the Law. And that graciousness is very noticeable in our gospel text for this Sunday. We see Jesus in the synagogue at Nazareth, as he unrolls the scroll of the prophet Isaiah. He reads out from it to the people "and applies to himself" the words about the humble Servant: "The spirit of the Lord has been given to me, for he has anointed me. He has sent me to bring the good news to the poor, and to heal the broken-hearted. He has sent me to proclaim liberty to captives, sight to the blind, to let the oppressed go free, to proclaim the Lord's year of favor" (Luke 4:18–19).

This is the way Jesus sees himself as he sets out on his public ministry! So we might simply look at him this week, and hear him, over and over, as he proclaims these words of gracious care for the oppressed and marginalized. May we become the "graciousness" of God in our place and time.

The Presence of God

I pause for a moment and reflect on God's life-giving presence in every part of my body, in everything around me, in the whole of my life. I remind myself that I am in your presence, O Lord. I will take refuge in your loving heart. You are my strength in times of weakness. You are my comforter in times of sorrow.

Freedom

Lord, you gave me life and the gift of freedom. Through your love I exist in this world. May I never take the gift of life for granted. May I always respect the right to life of others.

Consciousness

Help me, Lord, to be more conscious of your presence. Teach me to recognize your presence in others. Fill my heart with gratitude for the times your love has been shown to me through the care of others.

The Word

I take my time to read the Word of God slowly, a few times, allowing myself to dwell on anything that strikes me. (Please turn to the Scripture on the following pages. Inspiration points are provided should you need them. When you are ready, return here to continue.)

Conversation

I know with certainty there were times when you carried me, Lord. When it was through your strength I got through the dark times in my life.

Conclusion

Glory be to the Father, and to the Son, and to the Holy Spirit, as it was in the beginning, is now and ever shall be, world without end. Amen.

Sunday 24th January
Third Sunday in Ordinary Time

Luke 1:1–4; 4:14–21

Since many have undertaken to set down an orderly account of the events that have been fulfilled among us, just as they were handed on to us by those who from the beginning were eyewitnesses and servants of the word, I too decided, after investigating everything carefully from the very first, to write an orderly account for you, most excellent Theophilus, so that you may know the truth concerning the things about which you have been instructed. Jesus, filled with the power of the Spirit, returned to Galilee, and a report about him spread through all the surrounding country. He began to teach in their synagogues and was praised by everyone. When he came to Nazareth, where he had been brought up, he went to the synagogue on the sabbath day, as was his custom. He stood up to read, and the scroll of the prophet Isaiah was given to him. He unrolled the scroll and found the place where it was written: "The Spirit of the Lord is upon me, because he has anointed me to bring good news to the poor. He has sent me to proclaim release to the captives and recovery of sight to the blind, to let the oppressed go free, to proclaim the year of the Lord's favor." And he rolled up the scroll, gave it back to the attendant, and sat down. The eyes of all in the synagogue were fixed on him. Then he began to say to them, "Today this Scripture has been fulfilled in your hearing."

- I must take personally what God says here: "You are the one I choose today to bring good news to the poor and oppressed. The Holy Spirit is upon you. I am sending you!" Jesus saw these statements as giving him his identity. Do they give me mine?

- Holy Spirit of God, you are the living force in the words of the gospel we proclaim. You are the wind on which the message about Jesus is borne to others. Our agenda is to proclaim you. This is worth all the trouble this life can bring.

Monday 25th January

Mark 16:15–18

Jesus said to the apostles, "Go into all the world and proclaim the good news to the whole creation. The one who believes and is baptized will be saved; but the one who does not believe will be condemned. And these signs will accompany those who believe: by using my name they will cast out demons; they will speak in new tongues; they will pick up snakes in their hands, and if they drink any deadly thing, it will not hurt them; they will lay their hands on the sick, and they will recover."

- Lord Jesus, we leave the frailty that is in us open to your touch. We commit the joy and the failures of our life to you. Use them to bring good to others.

- I pray for healing for those parts of creation that are wounded and damaged, that have yet to learn of the good news that Jesus sends us to proclaim. I proclaim the good news to the whole of creation by the way I live, by being a blessing to the world that God has made.

Tuesday 26th January

Mark 3:31–35

Jesus' mother and his brothers came, and standing outside, they sent in a message asking for him. A crowd was sitting around him; and they said to him, "Your mother and brothers and sisters are outside asking for you." And he replied, "Who are my mother and my brothers?" And looking at those who sat around him, he said, "Here are my mother and my brothers. Whoever does the will of God is my brother and sister and mother."

- Jesus does not put limits on belonging; instead his embrace takes in all who do God's will. I ask God to help me broaden my horizons, not to let me be limited by a narrow scope of what is comfortable. Jesus invites me to call God my father, and he recognizes me as one of his family. What more assurance do I need that Jesus walks with me?

- The essence of being a Christian is to widen our relationships—of trust, affection, commitment, loyalty, faithfulness, kindness, thoughtfulness, compassion, mercy, helpfulness, encouragement, support, strength, protection—all the qualities that bind people together in mutual love and unity.

Wednesday 27th January

Mark 4:1–20

Again Jesus began to teach beside the sea. Such a very large crowd gathered around him that he got into a boat on the sea and sat there, while the whole crowd was beside the sea on the land. He began to teach them many things in parables, and in his teaching he said to them: "Listen! A sower went out to sow. And as he sowed, some seed fell on the path, and the birds came and ate it up. Other seed fell on rocky ground, where it did not have much soil, and it sprang up quickly, since it had no depth of soil. And when the sun rose, it was scorched; and since it had no root, it withered away. Other seed fell among thorns, and the thorns grew up and choked it, and it yielded no grain. Other seed fell into good soil and brought forth grain, growing up and increasing and yielding thirty and sixty and a hundredfold." And he said, "Let anyone with ears to hear listen!" When he was alone, those who were around him along with the twelve asked him about the parables. And he said to them, "To you has been given the secret of the kingdom of God, but for those outside, everything comes in parables; in order that 'they may indeed look, but not perceive, and may indeed listen, but not understand; so that they may not turn again and be forgiven.'" And he said to them, "Do you not understand this parable? Then how will you understand all the parables? The sower sows the word. These are the ones on the path where the word is sown: when they hear, Satan immediately comes and takes away the word that is sown in them. And these are the ones sown on rocky ground: when they hear the word, they immediately receive it with joy. But they have no root, and endure only for a while; then, when trouble or persecution arises on account of the word, immediately they fall away. And others are those sown among the thorns: these are the ones who hear the word, but the cares of the world, and the lure of wealth, and the desire for other things come in and choke the word, and it yields nothing. And these are the ones sown on the good soil: they hear the word and accept it and bear fruit, thirty and sixty and a hundredfold."

- If your word is like a seed, Lord, then it is an organism, with a life of its own. My part is to receive it, give it roots and depth so that it survives hardships, and protect it from the thorns of multiple cares and desires. If I allow your word some space in my life, there is no limit to the fruit it may bear.

- The sower knows that not all seed will flourish. I pray for forgiveness and healing for the rocky, bare places I observe in my life. I pray that I may not neglect where there is growth but that I may grow in gratitude and hope.

Thursday 28th January
Mark 4:21–25

Jesus said to them, "Is a lamp brought in to be put under the bushel basket, or under the bed, and not on the lampstand? For there is nothing hidden, except to be disclosed; nor is anything secret, except to come to light. Let anyone with ears to hear listen!" And he said to them, "Pay attention to what you hear; the measure you give will be the measure you get, and still more will be given you. For to those who have, more will be given; and from those who have nothing, even what they have will be taken away."

- "Listen!" "Pay attention!" Jesus knows it is easy for people to become inattentive even to the very things that bring them life. I take this time to be attuned to my life and circumstances, listening for what God is saying to me.

- Jesus' saying about "the measure you give" seems like a variation on "you only get as good as you give." What Jesus means is that the person who seeks to gain some spiritual insight into what he is saying will have that insight increased by exposure to his parables, whereas whoever does not listen to Jesus will end up in spiritual ignorance. In listening to and following Jesus, I grow in familiarity with his voice and hear more about what it is I have, and more is added. I give thanks and I pray for those who have nothing, that they might take time with God, who has such time for them.

Friday 29th January
Mark 4:26–34

Jesus said, "The kingdom of God is as if someone would scatter seed on the ground, and would sleep and rise night and day, and the seed would sprout and grow, he does not know how. The earth produces of itself, first the stalk, then the head, then the full grain in the head. But when the grain is ripe, at once he goes in with his sickle, because the harvest has come." He also said, "With what can we compare the kingdom of God, or what parable will we use for it? It is like a mustard seed, which, when sown upon the ground, is the smallest of all the seeds on earth; yet when it is sown it grows up and becomes the greatest of all shrubs, and puts forth large branches, so that the birds of the air can make nests in its shade." With many such parables he spoke the word to them, as they were able to hear it; he did not speak to them except in parables, but he explained everything in private to his disciples.

• Thank you, Lord, for this most consoling of images. I was not brought into this world to help you out of a mess. You above all are the one who is working. Your dynamism, active in nature from the beginning of time, should humble me. You are the force of growth, and if you privilege me with the chance to add incrementally to that growth, that is your gift to me, not mine to you.

• The reign of God is in hopeful activity, in patient waiting and inspired observation. Show me, Lord, how I already inhabit your kingdom.

Saturday 30th January
Mark 4:35–41

On that day, when evening had come, Jesus said to the disciples, "Let us go across to the other side." And leaving the crowd behind, they took him with them in the boat, just as he was. Other boats were with him. A great gale arose, and the waves beat into the boat, so that the boat was already being swamped. But he was in the stern, asleep on the cushion; and they woke him up and said to him, "Teacher, do you not care that we are perishing?" He woke up and rebuked the wind, and said to the sea, "Peace! Be still!" Then the wind ceased, and there was a dead calm. He said to them, "Why are you afraid? Have you still no faith?" And they were filled with great awe and said to one another, "Who then is this, that even the wind and the sea obey him?"

- Mark's Gospel challenges the disciples to grow into a more mature faith. Pitched and tossed on the raging sea, they fear shipwreck. In desperation, they wake Jesus up. He had been asleep, but they had been asleep also! They had been asleep to who he really is.

- Jesus did not directly answer the question the apostles asked. Instead, he acted for the good. Perhaps I can see how God sometimes answers my prayer and shows care for me by acting for my good, too?

January 31—February 6

Something to think and pray about each day this week:

Recognizing and Accepting Anger

If I have been badly hurt, I will be angry. This can cause me fear because I know I may not be able to control my anger. I may also feel guilty because I may have been taught that I should not feel angry. But what am I supposed to do with these feelings if others expect me always to be polite, gentle, and mild? People do not like to listen to my anger, perhaps because they cannot cope well with their own anger, much less with someone else's.

Anger and revengeful feelings are natural reactions to hurt. I want the persons who wronged me to know what my pain feels like. I want to give them a dose of their own medicine so that they understand what they did. This is a primitive and normal response to have when one is wronged. It would help so much if my family and friends could accept that my anger is natural and appropriate. Without that I turn the anger on to myself, so that it burns me inside and leads to depression. Or I try to get the burning coals of anger out of my system by aggressive behavior.

In his Passion, Jesus experienced anger and surely also a desire for revenge. We watch how he coped with them, and we learn. The advice, "Be angry but do not sin" (Ephesians 4:26) gets the balance right.

The Presence of God

Dear Lord, as I come to you today, fill my heart and my whole being with the wonder of your presence. Help me to be open to you for this time as I put aside the cares of this world. Fill my mind with your peace, your love.

Freedom

I will ask God's help to be free from my own preoccupations, to be open to God in this time of prayer, and to come to know, love, and serve God more.

Consciousness

I ask how I am within myself today. Am I particularly tired, stressed, or off-form? If any of these characteristics apply, can I try to let go of the concerns that disturb me?

The Word

The Word of God comes down to us through the Scriptures. May the Holy Spirit enlighten my mind and my heart to respond to the gospel teachings. (Please turn to the Scripture on the following pages. Inspiration points are provided should you need them. When you are ready, return here to continue.)

Conversation

How has God's Word moved me? Has it left me cold? Has it consoled me or moved me to act in a new way? I imagine Jesus standing or sitting beside me. I turn and share my feelings with him.

Conclusion

I thank God for these few moments we have spent alone together and for any insights I may have been given concerning the text.

Sunday 31st January
Fourth Sunday in Ordinary Time
Luke 4:21–30

Jesus began to say to those in the synagogue, "Today this Scripture has been fulfilled in your hearing." All spoke well of him and were amazed at the gracious words that came from his mouth. They said, "Is not this Joseph's son?" He said to them, "Doubtless you will quote to me this proverb, 'Doctor, cure yourself!' And you will say, 'Do here also in your hometown the things that we have heard you did at Capernaum.'" And he said, "Truly I tell you, no prophet is accepted in the prophet's hometown. But the truth is, there were many widows in Israel in the time of Elijah, when the heaven was shut up three years and six months, and there was a severe famine over all the land; yet Elijah was sent to none of them except to a widow at Zarephath in Sidon. There were also many lepers in Israel in the time of the prophet Elisha, and none of them was cleansed except Naaman the Syrian." When they heard this, all in the synagogue were filled with rage. They got up, drove him out of the town, and led him to the brow of the hill on which their town was built, so that they might hurl him off the cliff. But he passed through the midst of them and went on his way.

- "Is this not Joseph's son?" His townspeople begrudged Jesus his success and the fact that "all spoke well of him." How do I feel when someone I know well is successful? Am I a begrudging person?

- "He passed through the midst of them." Jesus was fully human, yet he was also in control of his life. He is a mysterious person. No one could take his life from him: he would lay it down freely. I make myself a companion to Jesus as he walks sadly away from Nazareth.

Monday 1st February
Mark 5:1–20

They came to the other side of the sea, to the country of the Gerasenes. And when he had stepped out of the boat, immediately a man out of the tombs with an unclean spirit met him. He lived among the tombs;

and no one could restrain him any more, even with a chain; for he had often been restrained with shackles and chains, but the chains he wrenched apart, and the shackles he broke in pieces; and no one had the strength to subdue him. Night and day among the tombs and on the mountains he was always howling and bruising himself with stones. When he saw Jesus from a distance, he ran and bowed down before him; and he shouted at the top of his voice, "What have you to do with me, Jesus, Son of the Most High God? I adjure you by God, do not torment me." For he had said to him, "Come out of the man, you unclean spirit!" Then Jesus asked him, "What is your name?" He replied, "My name is Legion; for we are many." He begged him earnestly not to send them out of the country. Now there on the hillside a great herd of swine was feeding; and the unclean spirits begged him, "Send us into the swine; let us enter them." So he gave them permission. And the unclean spirits came out and entered the swine; and the herd, numbering about two thousand, rushed down the steep bank into the lake, and were drowned in the sea. The swineherds ran off and told it in the city and in the country. Then people came to see what it was that had happened. They came to Jesus and saw the demoniac sitting there, clothed and in his right mind, the very man who had had the legion; and they were afraid. Those who had seen what had happened to the demoniac and to the swine reported it. Then they began to beg Jesus to leave their neighborhood. As he was getting into the boat, the man who had been possessed by demons begged him that he might be with him. But Jesus refused, and said to him, "Go home to your friends, and tell them how much the Lord has done for you, and what mercy he has shown you." And he went away and began to proclaim in the Decapolis how much Jesus had done for him; and everyone was amazed.

- I take some time to notice how much the Lord has done for me. I ask God to help me to grow in a sense of gratitude and trust.

- Not everyone is sent to be a missionary overseas. Jesus sent this man back home to his friends to witness to the work of God. Perhaps this is where he sends me, too.

Tuesday 2nd February
The Presentation of the Lord

Luke 2:22–32

When the time came for their purification according to the law of Moses, Mary and Joseph brought him up to Jerusalem to present him to the Lord (as it is written in the law of the Lord, "Every firstborn male shall be designated as holy to the Lord"), and they offered a sacrifice according to what is stated in the law of the Lord, "a pair of turtledoves or two young pigeons." Now there was a man in Jerusalem whose name was Simeon; this man was righteous and devout, looking forward to the consolation of Israel, and the Holy Spirit rested on him. It had been revealed to him by the Holy Spirit that he would not see death before he had seen the Lord's Messiah. Guided by the Spirit, Simeon came into the temple; and when the parents brought in the child Jesus, to do for him what was customary under the law, Simeon took him in his arms and praised God, saying, "Master, now you are dismissing your servant in peace, according to your word; for my eyes have seen your salvation, which you have prepared in the presence of all peoples, a light for revelation to the Gentiles and for glory to your people Israel."

- Simeon spent many years waiting in the temple, trusting that God would show him a sign of hope. I take some time to notice the signs of hope that God has given me in these days. I ask God's Holy Spirit to direct my attention and to enlighten me.

- Lord, may I, too, open my eyes in grateful amazement when I see your interventions in my life.

Wednesday 3rd February

Mark 6:1–6

Jesus came to his hometown, and his disciples followed him. On the sabbath he began to teach in the synagogue, and many who heard him were astounded. They said, "Where did this man get all this? What is this wisdom that has been given to him? What deeds of power are being done by his hands! Is not this the carpenter, the son of Mary and brother of James and Joses and Judas and Simon, and are not his sisters here with us?" And they took offence at him. Then Jesus said to them, "Prophets are not without honor, except in their hometown, and among their own kin, and in their own house." And he could do no deed of power there, except that he laid his hands on a few sick people and cured them. And he was amazed at their unbelief. Then he went about among the villages teaching.

- Jesus "was amazed at their unbelief." Do I sometimes amaze God by my unbelief? Do I bring God down to my own small size, so that I am no longer open to wonder? And do I diminish other people? The Irish poet Patrick Kavanagh wrote the challenging line, "He had the knack of making men feel as small as they really were, which meant, as great as God had made them." Can I do that? Or do I diminish myself, so that I am afraid to use my gifts, afraid to respond when the Holy Spirit prompts me to be kind, to speak out, or to intervene in awkward situations?

- Lord, save me from spoiling the lives of others or my own. Let me amaze you a little by responding more often to the gentle calls of grace!

Thursday 4th February
Mark 6:7–13

Jesus called the twelve and began to send them out two by two, and gave them authority over the unclean spirits. He ordered them to take nothing for their journey except a staff; no bread, no bag, no money in their belts; but to wear sandals and not to put on two tunics. He said to them, "Wherever you enter a house, stay there until you leave the place. If any place will not welcome you and they refuse to hear you, as you leave, shake off the dust that is on your feet as a testimony against them." So they went out and proclaimed that all should repent. They cast out many demons, and anointed with oil many who were sick and cured them.

- Here is the embryonic church taking its first baby steps! The story of human salvation is getting under way. We can learn much from it. The group is centered on Jesus—they are to carry his message to an unprepared world; they are being sent out on a mission. They have to let go of their securities—a fixed abode, workplace, possessions, money. They must trust that Jesus knows what he is doing; they also need the good will of those they visit. In return Jesus shares with them his authority over evil and his power to heal. Is that a fair exchange?

- Jesus' trust in us is breathtaking. I, too, am being sent out each day to bring good news to those I engage with. Jesus, make me aware that you are with me wherever I go.

Friday 5th February
Mark 6:14–29

King Herod heard of it, for Jesus' name had become known. Some were saying, "John the baptizer has been raised from the dead; and for this reason these powers are at work in him." But others said, "It is Elijah." And others said, "It is a prophet, like one of the prophets of old." But when Herod heard of it, he said, "John, whom I beheaded, has been raised." For Herod himself had sent men who arrested John, bound him, and put him in prison on account of Herodias, his brother Philip's wife, because Herod had married her. For John had been telling Herod, "It is not lawful for you to have your brother's wife." And Herodias had a grudge against him, and wanted to kill him. But she could not, for Herod feared John, knowing that he was a righteous and holy man, and he protected him. When he heard him, he was greatly perplexed; and yet he liked to listen to him. But an opportunity came when Herod on his birthday gave a banquet for his courtiers and officers and for the leaders of Galilee. When the daughter of this same Herodias came in and danced, she pleased Herod and his guests; and the king said to the girl, "Ask me for whatever you wish, and I will give it." And he solemnly swore to her, "Whatever you ask me, I will give you, even half of my kingdom." She went out and said to her mother,

"What should I ask for?" She replied, "The head of John the baptizer." Immediately she rushed back to the king and requested, "I want you to give me at once the head of John the Baptist on a platter." The king was deeply grieved; yet out of regard for his oaths and for the guests, he did not want to refuse her. Immediately the king sent a soldier of the guard with orders to bring John's head. He went and beheaded him in the prison, brought his head on a platter, and gave it to the girl. Then the girl gave it to her mother. When his disciples heard about it, they came and took his body, and laid it in a tomb.

- This is one of the most dramatic stories in world literature. John the Baptist is the helpless and innocent one, standing for the truth. He will suffer and die because of a weak ruler, Herod. He is laid in a tomb and disappears from human history. This all points to Jesus: he is also a great prophet, innocent, and doomed to suffer and die because of the weakness of Pontius Pilate. We are being warned not to lose faith in Jesus: he, too, will be laid in a tomb, but through his resurrection he will change the story of humankind.

- Discipleship is demanding. Like Jesus, each of us in our own way is called to serve and to give our lives for the sake of others (Mark 10:45). Lord, do not let me lose courage when things go wrong. Let me keep on trying to do good.

Saturday 6th February
Mark 6:30–34

The apostles gathered around Jesus, and told him all that they had done and taught. He said to them, "Come away to a deserted place all by yourselves and rest a while." For many were coming and going, and they had no leisure even to eat. And they went away in the boat to a deserted place by themselves. Now many saw them going and recognized them, and they hurried there on foot from all the towns and arrived ahead of them. As he went ashore, he saw a great crowd; and he had compassion for them, because they were like sheep without a shepherd; and he began to teach them many things.

- The apostles were concerned about their doings, their words; Jesus seems to say to them, "Stand back a little. Perhaps it's not all about you but is about what God is doing in and through you."
- Jesus does not say, "Go away to a quiet place," but he invites us to be with him—to be in relationship, in dialogue.

The Fifth Week of Ordinary Time
February 7—February 13

Something to think and pray about each day this week:

Christ's "Disturbing Freshness"

If we are to nourish faith for tomorrow, we are challenged today to imagine a different quality of Christian commitment than existed before. Sixty years ago Henri de Lubac described Christ as "the great disturber" but also as the new image of God and of humanity, who brings refreshing novelty into a tired world. He was asking how we had arrived at a situation where Christianity was seen either as the enemy of full humanity, or, worse still, as a boring and empty legend. These same accusations are alive today, though in a different cultural context.

Our lived culture is nine-tenths invisible: it contains meanings and values that underlie a whole way of life. We live by unstated and unexamined perceptions. But this world of images and values has immense, if often unconscious, impact on our capacity for life decisions, including, of course, the decision about faith in God.

It is a liberation to realize, with Cardinal John Henry Newman, that existential truth can only be found when the whole person is involved: some forms of knowledge are accessible only through love. Many are now seeking a spiritual consciousness beyond the confusion and fragmentation of our day. There is a hunger, less shy or silent than it was a generation back, for something more, which Christians may identify as the "disturbing freshness of Christ."

The Presence of God

Be still and know that I am God. Lord, may your spirit guide me to seek your loving presence more and more. For it is there I find rest and refreshment from this busy world.

Freedom

Everything has the potential to draw forth from me a fuller love and life. Yet my desires are often fixed, caught on illusions of fulfillment. I ask that God through my freedom may orchestrate my desires in a vibrant, loving melody rich in harmony.

Consciousness

At this moment, Lord, I turn my thoughts to you. I will set aside my chores and preoccupations. I will take rest and refreshment in your presence, Lord.

The Word

I read the Word of God slowly, a few times over, and I listen to what God is saying to me. (Please turn to the Scripture on the following pages. Inspiration points are provided should you need them. When you are ready, return here to continue.)

Conversation

Sometimes I wonder what I might say if I were to meet you in person, Lord. I think I might say, "Thank you, Lord" for always being there for me.

Conclusion

Glory be to the Father, and to the Son, and to the Holy Spirit, as it was in the beginning, is now and ever shall be, world without end. Amen.

Sunday 7th February
Fifth Sunday in Ordinary Time

Luke 5:1–11

Once while Jesus was standing beside the lake of Gennesaret, and the crowd was pressing in on him to hear the Word of God, he saw two boats there at the shore of the lake; the fishermen had gone out of them and were washing their nets. He got into one of the boats, the one belonging to Simon, and asked him to put out a little way from the shore. Then he sat down and taught the crowds from the boat. When he had finished speaking, he said to Simon, "Put out into the deep water and let down your nets for a catch." Simon answered, "Master, we have worked all night long but have caught nothing. Yet if you say so, I will let down the nets." When they had done this, they caught so many fish that their nets were beginning to break. So they signaled to their partners in the other boat to come and help them. And they came and filled both boats, so that they began to sink. But when Simon Peter saw it, he fell down at Jesus' knees, saying, "Go away from me, Lord, for I am a sinful man!" For he and all who were with him were amazed at the catch of fish that they had taken; and so also were James and John, sons of Zebedee, who were partners with Simon. Then Jesus said to Simon, "Do not be afraid; from now on you will be catching people." When they had brought their boats to shore, they left everything and followed him.

• Peter recognized who Jesus was and realized that being close to Jesus would make demands on him. Jesus recognized who Peter was and saw that Peter had the capacity to respond to what he might ask of him. Jesus invited Peter to use his practiced skill in a new way, for the good of the gospel. I lay my skills and talents before Jesus, asking him to show me how I might use them for God and others.

• God uses the ordinary experiences of life to draw people to him. The gate of heaven is always open, to everyone. Why then should I ever become despondent about people—perhaps in my own family circle—who do not practice their religion?

Monday 8th February
Mark 6:53–56

When Jesus and the disciples had crossed over, they came to land at Gennesaret and moored the boat. When they got out of the boat, people at once recognized him, and rushed about that whole region and began to bring the sick on mats to wherever they heard he was. And wherever he went, into villages or cities or farms, they laid the sick in the marketplaces, and begged him that they might touch even the fringe of his cloak; and all who touched it were healed.

- The magnetism of Jesus is extraordinary. Do I share the enthusiasm of the crowds, or do I miss the action? What difficulties do I overcome to get to him—like rising earlier to pray, or going to visit the sick, or taking quality time in a busy day to sit with him?

- Imagine that Jesus shows up in your marketplace! What would the reaction be? Does Mark intend us to see that the marketplaces of the world could be a center for divine power and healing if the gospel were alive in them? We are, after all, God's ambassadors (2 Corinthians 5:20)!

Tuesday 9th February
Mark 7:1–13

Now when the Pharisees and some of the scribes who had come from Jerusalem gathered around him, they noticed that some of his disciples were eating with defiled hands, that is, without washing them. (For the Pharisees, and all the Jews, do not eat unless they thoroughly wash their hands, thus observing the tradition of the elders; and they do not eat anything from the market unless they wash it; and there are also many other traditions that they observe, the washing of cups, pots, and bronze kettles.) So the Pharisees and the scribes asked him, "Why do your disciples not live according to the tradition of the elders, but eat with defiled hands?" He said to them, "Isaiah prophesied rightly about you hypocrites, as it is written, 'This people honors me with their lips, but their hearts are far from me; in vain do they worship me, teaching human precepts as doctrines.' You abandon the commandment of God and hold to human tradition." Then he said to them, "You have a fine way of rejecting the commandment of God in order to keep your tradition! For Moses said, 'Honor your father and your mother'; and, 'Whoever speaks evil of father or mother must surely die.' But you say that if anyone tells father or mother, 'Whatever support you might have had from me is Corban' (that is, an offering to God)—then you no longer permit doing anything for a father or mother, thus making void the Word of God through your tradition that you have handed on. And you do many things like this."

- The Pharisees brought a "policing" attitude to their practice of faith; they compared themselves to others, looking down on those who lived differently. I let Jesus speak to me about any similar attitude he might notice in me.

- Faced with a religious question, Jesus turned to the tradition of his people. What life does God have to offer me as I consider my roots and heritage?

Wednesday 10th February
Ash Wednesday
Matthew 6:1–6, 16–18

"Beware of practicing your piety before others in order to be seen by them; for then you have no reward from your Father in heaven. 'So whenever you give alms, do not sound a trumpet before you, as the hypocrites do in the synagogues and in the streets, so that they may be praised by others. Truly I tell you, they have received their reward. But when you give alms, do not let your left hand know what your right hand is doing, so that your alms may be done in secret; and your Father who sees in secret will reward you. 'And whenever you pray, do not be like the hypocrites; for they love to stand and pray in the synagogues and at the street corners, so that they may be seen by others. Truly I tell you, they have received their reward. But whenever you pray, go into your room and shut the door and pray to your Father who is in secret;

and your Father who sees in secret will reward you. 'And whenever you fast, do not look dismal, like the hypocrites, for they disfigure their faces so as to show others that they are fasting. Truly I tell you, they have received their reward. But when you fast, put oil on your head and wash your face, so that your fasting may be seen not by others but by your Father who is in secret; and your Father who sees in secret will reward you."

- Today, Ash Wednesday, Christians all over the world begin the penitential but joyous season of Lent. Whatever we do in Lent should bring us ever closer to Jesus and prepare us to celebrate his resurrection at Easter.

- The beginning of Lent is good news: God is near and nothing can keep us from God. Jesus will find that himself later on. Anything we do in Lent is intended to bring us to God and believe the good news. Fasting, prayers, and almsgiving are ways to God, not to misery. But they can be motivated by selfishness or generosity. Key to our choices is where our hearts are. Is my heart set on God alone? Do I sometimes set out to get praise and admiration?

Thursday 11th February
Luke 9:22–25

Jesus said to his disciples: "The Son of Man must undergo great suffering, and be rejected by the elders, chief priests, and scribes, and be killed, and on the third day be raised." Then he said to them all, "If any want to become my followers, let them deny themselves and take up their cross daily and follow me. For those who want to save their life will lose it, and those who lose their life for my sake will save it. What does it profit them if they gain the whole world, but lose or forfeit themselves?"

- Jesus states clearly that his project to save the world will end in earthly disaster for himself. I sit with him in silence and gratitude that he does not simply give up and abandon humankind to its malice.

- Let me also chat with him about the things I endure. He is not saying that suffering is good, but that I can either accept it patiently or try to reject it. He looks hard at me and says, "You could spend your life just looking after yourself and trying to avoid pain and hurt. Or you can embrace the world with love and risk failure, betrayal, and disappointment from those you try to serve. Of course you will get hurt, but an eternal blessing will be yours at the End." I respond: "Lord, let me live my life as you lived yours." He thanks me.

Friday 12th February
Matthew 9:14–15

The disciples of John came to Jesus, saying, "Why do we and the Pharisees fast often, but your disciples do not fast?" And Jesus said to them, "The wedding guests cannot mourn as long as the bridegroom is with them, can they? The days will come when the bridegroom is taken away from them, and then they will fast."

- We can often feel like John's disciples, confused and unsure about what to do. The divisions in the church upset us. But Jesus is saying, "With my coming, a wedding has started; a new creation is under way. Be joyful!"

- John's disciples are waiting in the wrong place. I must stop living in no-man's land. I must wake up—the savior of the world has come, and I must join him.

Saturday 13th February
Luke 5:27–32

Jesus went out and saw a tax collector named Levi, sitting at the tax booth; and he said to him, "Follow me." And he got up, left everything, and followed him. Then Levi gave a great banquet for him in his house; and there was a large crowd of tax collectors and others sitting at the table with them. The Pharisees and their scribes were complaining to his disciples, saying, "Why do you eat and drink with tax collectors and sinners?" Jesus answered, "Those who are well have no need of a physician, but those who are sick; I have come to call not the righteous but sinners to repentance."

- Tax collectors were despised; they were social and religious outcasts. Why then does Jesus choose Levi out of all possible candidates? Because he is determined to break down dramatically the barriers that fragment human community.

- The banquet points to "table fellowship": eating and drinking together shows that the guests accept one another. Because Jesus is the main guest, we are shown that if we want to be with him at the table, we must accept the companionship of people we previously despised. At the Eucharist Jesus invites everyone to participate, not simply as individuals but as fellow disciples who are both sinners and forgiven. Do I "complain" about this?

February 14—February 20

Something to think and pray about each day this week:

The Joyful Season

The season of Lent has begun. Lent originally meant "springtime," and so we can view it as a springtime for the spirit. It is a time also to spring clean the cave of our hearts!

Whatever the variations in the practice of Lent over the last 2,000 years, the main issue is whether Lent helps me to become more aware of how I stand in relation to God and my neighbor. The ancient practices designed to achieve these goals were fasting, almsgiving, and prayer. The call to fast makes me focus on the affairs of the spirit rather than of the body. The call to almsgiving makes me more alert to my needy neighbor. The call to prayer nourishes my relationship with God, and especially with Jesus in his Passion. What about fasting? There are many little things I can perhaps do without. The point is that the shock to the system should lead to a deeper sense of what God may want of me!

Jesus warns us against trying to attract notice when we fast or pray or give alms (Matthew 6). The simple act of washing off the ashes on Ash Wednesday is understood in some Christian circles as a reminder of Jesus' admonition to look joyous! Lent is a "joyful season."

The Presence of God

At any time of the day or night we can call on Jesus. He is always waiting, listening for our call. What a wonderful blessing. No phone needed, no e-mails, just a whisper.

Freedom

If God were trying to tell me something, would I know? If God were reassuring me or challenging me, would I notice? I ask for the grace to be free of my own preoccupations and open to what God may be saying to me.

Consciousness

How do I find myself today? Where am I with God? With others? Do I have something to be grateful for? Then I give thanks. Is there something I am sorry for? Then I ask forgiveness.

The Word

God speaks to each one of us individually. I listen attentively to hear what he is saying to me. Read the text a few times, then listen. (Please turn to the Scripture on the following pages. Inspiration points are provided should you need them. When you are ready, return here to continue.)

Conversation

What is stirring in me as I pray? Am I consoled, troubled, left cold? I imagine Jesus himself standing or sitting at my side, and I share my feelings with him.

Conclusion

I thank God for these few moments we have spent alone together and for any insights I may have been given concerning the text.

Sunday 14th February
First Sunday of Lent
Luke 4:1–13

Jesus, full of the Holy Spirit, returned from the Jordan and was led by the Spirit in the wilderness, where for forty days he was tempted by the devil. He ate nothing at all during those days, and when they were over, he was famished. The devil said to him, "If you are the Son of God, command this stone to become a loaf of bread." Jesus answered him, "It is written, 'One does not live by bread alone.'" Then the devil led him up and showed him in an instant all the kingdoms of the world. And the devil said to him, "To you I will give their glory and all this authority; for it has been given over to me, and I give it to anyone I please. If you, then, will worship me, it will all be yours." Jesus answered him, "It is written, 'Worship the Lord your God, and serve only him.'" Then the devil took him to Jerusalem, and placed him on the pinnacle of the temple, saying to him, "If you are the Son of God, throw yourself down from here, for it is written, 'He will command his angels concerning you, to protect you,' and 'On their hands they will bear you up, so that you will not dash your foot against a stone.'" Jesus answered him, "It is said, 'Do not put the Lord your God to the test.'" When the devil had finished every test, he departed from him until an opportune time.

- In the wilderness Jesus did not engage the devil's temptations. He simply quoted the Word of God in Scripture. God's Word has power, even over demons.

- Jesus' experience teaches us that there is nothing wrong with being tempted; it's how we react to the temptation that matters. A short prayer or a quote from God's Word will help us let it go. For example: "Lead me not into temptation" or "I must forgive, not once but seventy times."

Monday 15th February

Matthew 25:31–46

Jesus said to his disciples, "When the Son of Man comes in his glory, and all the angels with him, then he will sit on the throne of his glory. All the nations will be gathered before him, and he will separate people one from another as a shepherd separates the sheep from the goats, and he will put the sheep at his right hand and the goats at the left. Then the king will say to those at his right hand, 'Come, you that are blessed by my Father, inherit the kingdom prepared for you from the foundation of the world; for I was hungry and you gave me food, I was thirsty and you gave me something to drink, I was a stranger and you welcomed me, I was naked and you gave me clothing, I was sick and you took care of me, I was in prison and you visited me.' Then the righteous will answer him, 'Lord, when was it that we saw you hungry and gave you food, or thirsty and gave you something to drink? And when was it that we saw you a stranger and welcomed you, or naked and gave you clothing? And when was it that we saw you sick or in prison and visited you?' And the king will answer them, 'Truly I tell you, just as you did it to one of the least of these who are members of my family, you did it to me.' Then he will say to those at his left hand, 'You that are accursed, depart from me into the eternal fire prepared for the devil and his angels; for I was hungry and you gave me no food, I was thirsty and you gave me nothing to drink, I was a stranger and you did not welcome me, naked and you did not give me clothing, sick and in prison and you did not visit me.' Then they also will answer, 'Lord, when was it that we saw you hungry or thirsty or a stranger or naked or sick or in prison, and did not take care of you?' Then he will answer them, 'Truly I tell you, just as you did not do it to one of the least of these, you did not do it to me.' And these will go away into eternal punishment, but the righteous into eternal life."

- This long and exciting parable has a simple message: "Minister to the needy around you, or else you are missing the whole point of living!" Saint Matthew's hearers had difficulty with what would happen to non-Jews, since they themselves were the Chosen People. Jesus says that with his coming into the world, everyone is a "chosen person." Everyone is to be treated with limitless respect. This is the way to get ready for God's final community of love. Jesus is already present but in disguise, in every person. Only at the End will he and they be revealed "in glory."

- What do I see when I see the needy? Do I focus on the hidden glory of others? How would I fare if human history were to be terminated today?

Tuesday 16th February
Matthew 6:7–15

Jesus said, "When you are praying, do not heap up empty phrases as the Gentiles do; for they think that they will be heard because of their many words. Do not be like them, for your Father knows what you need before you ask him. Pray then in this way: Our Father in heaven, hallowed be your name. Your kingdom come. Your will be done, on earth as it is in heaven. Give us this day our daily bread. And forgive us our debts, as we also have forgiven our debtors. And do not bring us to the time of trial, but rescue us from the evil one. For if you forgive others their trespasses, your heavenly Father will also forgive you; but if you do not forgive others, neither will your Father forgive your trespasses."

- As you pray now, is God a distant figure with little interest in your affairs? And what about your day: is God around or are you alone? The good news is that God is indescribably close to us as we go about our affairs. "Your Father knows what you need before you ask him." We might say that God is infinite awareness, and that his focus is on us. "God is closer to me than I am to myself," says Saint Augustine.

- Try to imagine that God is with you every moment of this day. He is with you as someone who loves you and who knows all you need.

He is always helping you, especially as you try to bring God's values into your everyday life.

Wednesday 17th February
Luke 11:29–32

When the crowds were increasing, Jesus began to say, "This generation is an evil generation; it asks for a sign, but no sign will be given to it except the sign of Jonah. For just as Jonah became a sign to the people of Nineveh, so the Son of Man will be to this generation. The queen of the South will rise at the judgment with the people of this generation and condemn them, because she came from the ends of the earth to listen to the wisdom of Solomon, and see, something greater than Solomon is here! The people of Nineveh will rise up at the judgment with this generation and condemn it, because they repented at the proclamation of Jonah, and see, something greater than Jonah is here!"

- Jesus uses imagination in trying to help his audience catch on to the mystery of who he is. So he reminds them of famous characters in stories they already know well. He then tries to open their minds further by saying twice that "something greater" is here in his person. This is a mysterious assertion. But God is mysterious, so coming closer to the truth about God means being led along the path of mystery. Do I cultivate my capacity for mystery, or do I live on the surface of life? Do I reduce the wonders of nature and the cosmos to mere facts, or do I allow myself to ponder what their author must be like?

- Everything is a divine mystery since all comes from God. Let me sit with Jesus and ask him to enliven the mystical dimension that may be dormant in me.

Thursday 18th February
Matthew 7:7–12

Jesus said, "Ask, and it will be given to you; search, and you will find; knock, and the door will be opened for you. For everyone who asks receives, and everyone who searches finds, and for everyone who knocks, the door will be opened. Is there anyone among you who, if your child asks for bread, will give a stone? Or if the child asks for a fish, will give a snake? If you then, who are evil, know how to give good gifts to your children, how much more will your Father in heaven give good things to those who ask him! In everything do to others as you would have them do to you; for this is the law and the prophets.

• Is this gospel true? So often, our prayers seem to go unheard or unanswered. But good things happen in God's own time. A woman had a son who was very troubled since childhood. He had an inner rage that showed itself in destructive behavior. Often she bore the brunt of his anger. Not surprisingly, he lurched from one disaster to the next. He lost a number of jobs and a number of partners. Currently he has few prospects. But now in his forties, he has become reflective, and his style is changing. He is gentler, and though he is unemployed, last Christmas he scraped up some money and bought thoughtful little gifts for the important people in his life. He and his mother have begun to chat about things in ways that were never possible before. Thirty-five years of prayer are being answered.

• Jesus does not say that we will be given precisely what we ask for; or that we will find exactly what we are looking for; or that the particular door we want will be opened to us. But we will receive "good things"!

Friday 19th February

Matthew 5:20–26

Jesus said, "For I tell you, unless your righteousness exceeds that of the scribes and the Pharisees, you will never enter the kingdom of heaven. You have heard that it was said to those of ancient times, 'You shall not murder'; and 'whoever murders shall be liable to judgment.' But I say to you that if you are angry with a brother or sister, you will be liable to judgment; and if you insult a brother or sister, you will be liable to the council; and if you say, 'You fool,' you will be liable to the hell of fire.

So when you are offering your gift at the altar, if you remember that your brother or sister has something against you, leave your gift there before the altar and go; first be reconciled to your brother or sister, and then come and offer your gift. Come to terms quickly with your accuser while you are on the way to court with him, or your accuser may hand you over to the judge, and the judge to the guard, and you will be thrown into prison. Truly I tell you, you will never get out until you have paid the last penny."

- Scribes and Pharisees were righteous and were people of the law. Jesus asks for more—for the compassion that sees beyond the law and people's weaknesses to the glory and love of God in each and all.

- The standards operating in the kingdom of heaven are high! Jesus does not dismiss Old Testament teaching, but he goes to the root of things. We can be smug and content with our conventional good behavior. Jesus, however, says to us: "But what about your anger? What about insulting someone? Do you despise anyone, ever? Such behavior won't do anymore."

Saturday 20th February
Matthew 5:43–48

Jesus said to his disciples, "You have heard that it was said, 'You shall love your neighbor and hate your enemy.' But I say to you, Love your enemies and pray for those who persecute you, so that you may be children of your Father in heaven; for he makes his sun rise on the evil and on the good, and sends rain on the righteous and on the unrighteous. For if you love those who love you, what reward do you have? Do not even the tax collectors do the same? And if you greet only your brothers and sisters, what more are you doing than others? Do not even the Gentiles do the same? Be perfect, therefore, as your heavenly Father is perfect."

- Again Jesus shows how high the standards are in the new community he is establishing. This new community is no mere human one: at the heart of it is God. So all its relationships will have a divine quality. If we want to be "children of our Father in heaven," our hearts must embrace our enemies in genuine love.

- Before Jesus came, God was portrayed as destroying the wicked. But Jesus portrays God as pouring out good things on wicked as well as good people. This seems like extravagant madness. But when we come to the Passion, we find Jesus doing what he talks about here. He pours out divine love on everyone, bad and good. He prays for his enemies. On the world scene today, we have plenty of people to love and to pray for!

The Second Week of Lent
February 21—February 27

Something to think and pray about each day this week:

God at Work in the World

A long tradition in spirituality identified union with God as being found solely in contemplative prayer. In that tradition it was understood that we can only unite ourselves with God through uniting our spirit with God, who is Spirit.

This means leaving behind this material, messy, chaotic world and climbing the mountain, as Jesus did with Peter, James, and John. There, at the top of the mountain, far distant from the cares of this world, in contemplative prayer we enter into an intimate relationship with God. Like Peter, James, and John, we wish to remain there and enjoy the intimacy of union with God.

Saint Ignatius of Loyola, however, had a more complex understanding of how some of us may find union with God. Yes, he would say, climb the mountain. But you may perhaps instead be told to go back down the mountain, to this material, messy, violent world, and to find union with God through union of your will with God's will. God, he would say, labors in our world and can be found there as fully as on the mountain. Doing what God wants is what ultimately matters either for you or for the contemplative.

If we work in the world we must, again and again, climb to the top of the mountain, to be alone with God and with ourselves, our memories and desires. There we renew our strength to continue the struggle for a more just world.

The Presence of God

God is with me, but more, God is within me. Let me dwell for a moment on God's life-giving presence in my body, in my mind, and in my heart, as I sit here, right now.

Freedom

By God's grace I was born to live in freedom. Free to enjoy the pleasures he created for me. Dear Lord, grant that I may live as you intended, with complete confidence in your loving care.

Consciousness

Where do I sense hope, encouragement, and growth areas in my life? By looking back over the last few months, I may be able to see which activities and occasions have produced rich fruit. If I do notice such areas, I will determine to give those areas both time and space in the future.

The Word

I take my time to read the Word of God slowly, a few times, allowing myself to dwell on anything that strikes me. (Please turn to the Scripture on the following pages. Inspiration points are provided should you need them. When you are ready, return here to continue.)

Conversation

What feelings are rising in me as I pray and reflect on God's Word? I imagine Jesus himself sitting or standing near me, and I open my heart to him.

Conclusion

Glory be to the Father, and to the Son, and to the Holy Spirit, as it was in the beginning, is now and ever shall be, world without end. Amen.

Sunday 21st February
Second Sunday of Lent

Luke 9:28b–36

Jesus took with him Peter and John and James, and went up on the mountain to pray. And while he was praying, the appearance of his face changed, and his clothes became dazzling white. Suddenly they saw two men, Moses and Elijah, talking to him. They appeared in glory and were speaking of his departure, which he was about to accomplish at Jerusalem. Now Peter and his companions were weighed down with sleep; but since they had stayed awake, they saw his glory and the two men who stood with him. Just as they were leaving him, Peter said to Jesus, "Master, it is good for us to be here; let us make three dwellings, one for you, one for Moses, and one for Elijah"—not knowing what he said. While he was saying this, a cloud came and overshadowed them; and they were terrified as they entered the cloud. Then from the cloud came a voice that said, "This is my Son, my Chosen; listen to him!" When the voice had spoken, Jesus was found alone. And they kept silent and in those days told no one any of the things they had seen.

- "On the mountain" the three apostles had a favored glimpse of Jesus' prayer and glory. His prayer here is a conversation with Moses and Elijah. They talked about his Passion and death. This was a down-to-earth conversation about the shape of Jesus' life. Is my prayer like that?

- The appearance of Jesus' face was "changed." Even his clothing is made radiant. We know that, if we are faithful, we shall be transfigured in Jesus' glory. As Saint Paul says: "Christ in you, your hope of glory" (Colossians 1:27).

Monday 22nd February

Matthew 16:13–19

Now when Jesus came into the district of Caesarea Philippi, he asked his disciples, "Who do people say that the Son of Man is?" And they said, "Some say John the Baptist, but others Elijah, and still others

Jeremiah or one of the prophets." He said to them, "But who do you say that I am?" Simon Peter answered, "You are the Messiah, the Son of the living God." And Jesus answered him, "Blessed are you, Simon son of Jonah! For flesh and blood has not revealed this to you, but my Father in heaven. And I tell you, you are Peter, and on this rock I will build my church, and the gates of Hades will not prevail against it. I will give you the keys of the kingdom of heaven, and whatever you bind on earth will be bound in heaven, and whatever you loose on earth will be loosed in heaven.'

- The traditional setting for this memorable encounter in Caesarea Philippi is a lovely riverbank under a huge rocky cliff. Jesus asks: Who do people say that I am? Impetuous Peter, always ready to speak out and take risks, confesses Jesus as the Messiah. It is an inspired confession. This uneducated fisherman, who was to prove so shaky when Jesus was arrested, is rewarded with a new name, suggested by the great solid rock above them, and also with a new role, leading the people of God. Lord, you did not leave us orphans.

- The motley band of the twelve with Peter as leader would guide the future community of Jesus. They believed that Jesus was the Son of God. Our community today is somewhat similar—the motley group who are saintly and sinful but who with firm faith believe that Jesus is the Son of God. Peter is praised today within the church for his belief and faith in Jesus as the Son of the living God. This faith would lead him into times of doubt and unfaithfulness, and eventually to martyrdom. The first call in his following of Jesus was to grow in the faith that would sustain his life. May our faith do the same.

Tuesday 23rd February
Matthew 23:1–12

Jesus said to the crowds and to his disciples, "The scribes and the Pharisees sit on Moses' seat; therefore, do whatever they teach you and follow it; but do not do as they do, for they do not practice what they teach. They tie up heavy burdens, hard to bear, and lay them on the shoulders of others; but they themselves are unwilling to lift a finger to move them. They do all their deeds to be seen by others; for they make their phylacteries broad and their fringes long. They love to have the place of honor at banquets and the best seats in the synagogues, and to be greeted with respect in the marketplaces, and to have people call them rabbi. But you are not to be called rabbi, for you have one teacher, and you are all students. And call no one your father on earth, for you have one Father—the one in heaven. Nor are you to be called instructors, for you have one instructor, the Messiah. The greatest among you will be your servant. All who exalt themselves will be humbled, and all who humble themselves will be exalted."

- In Jesus people saw a whole person. He did not bother about appearing generous, or courageous, or truthful—people quickly saw that he was these things. Lord, I have only to see the history of the church to realize how easily these words are forgotten. Ecclesiastics have exalted themselves, looked for titles, and exercised leadership by domination rather than service. I need to come back to the memory of you washing your disciples' feet. Blessed are those who clean the toilets, put out the garbage, and care for the old and incontinent. We are never as close to God as when we are serving.

- Hypocrisy means play-acting, being untrue to oneself. Jesus' harshest words are reserved for this vice. He sums it up very succinctly as, "Hey, do not practice what they preach." Do I?

Wednesday 24th February
Matthew 20:17–28

While Jesus was going up to Jerusalem, he took the twelve disciples aside by themselves, and said to them on the way, "See, we are going up to Jerusalem, and the Son of Man will be handed over to the chief priests and scribes, and they will condemn him to death; then they will hand him over to the Gentiles to be mocked and flogged and crucified; and on the third day he will be raised." Then the mother of the sons of Zebedee came to him with her sons, and kneeling before him, she asked a favor of him. And he said to her, "What do you want?" She said to him, "Declare that these two sons of mine will sit, one at your right hand and one at your left, in your kingdom." But Jesus answered, "You do not know what you are asking. Are you able to drink the cup that I am about to drink?" They said to him, "We are able." He said to them, "You will indeed drink my cup, but to sit at my right hand and at my left, this is not mine to grant, but it is for those for whom it has been prepared by my Father." When the ten heard it, they were angry with the two brothers. But Jesus called them to him and said, "You know that the rulers of the Gentiles lord it over them, and their great ones are tyrants over them. It will not be so among you; but whoever wishes to be great among you must be your servant, and whoever wishes to be first among you must be your slave; just as the Son of Man came not to be served but to serve, and to give his life a ransom for many."

- There is a sense of doom and destiny in Jesus' words. The anticipation of personal catastrophe chills the heart. When Jesus foretells the Passion, he mentions not just the handover but the flogging and mocking. It is hard to imagine the terror that must have shadowed his heart in those last weeks.

- This walk to Jerusalem is heavy with foreboding. Jesus tries to tell the twelve of the fears that fill his soul: he will be betrayed by friends and delivered to his enemies; he will hear the death sentence read over him; he will suffer injustice, mockery, humiliation, insults; he will undergo the torture of scourging and finally face a horrific death on a gallows. That is the cup you drank, Lord. If you ask me to share it, give me the strength.

Thursday 25th February
Luke 16:19–31

Jesus said to the Pharisees, "There was a rich man who was dressed in purple and fine linen and who feasted sumptuously every day. And at his gate lay a poor man named Lazarus, covered with sores, who longed to satisfy his hunger with what fell from the rich man's table; even the dogs would come and lick his sores. The poor man died and was carried away by the angels to be with Abraham. The rich man also died and was buried. In Hades, where he was being tormented, he looked up and saw Abraham far away with Lazarus by his side. He called out, 'Father Abraham, have mercy on me, and send Lazarus to dip the tip of his finger in water and cool my tongue; for I am in agony in these flames.' But Abraham said, 'Child, remember that during your lifetime you received your good things, and Lazarus in like manner evil things; but now he is comforted here, and you are in agony. Besides all this, between you and us a great chasm has been fixed, so that those who might want to pass from here to you cannot do so, and no one can cross from there to us.' He said, 'Then, father, I beg you to send him to my father's house—for I have five brothers—that he may warn them, so that they will not also come into this place of torment.' Abraham replied, 'They have Moses and the prophets; they should listen to them.' He said, 'No, father Abraham; but if someone goes to them from the dead, they will repent.' He said to him, 'If they do not listen to Moses and the prophets, neither will they be convinced even if someone rises from the dead.'"

- This is a parable of startling contrasts, but its central message is simple: be alert to the needs under your nose. It is not concerned with patterns of good living on the part of Lazarus, nor of evildoing on the part of the rich man. But the latter closed his eyes to the needy at his gate. And without an eye for the needy around us, our life becomes self-centered and callous. Jesus is asking his listeners to open their eyes to what is around them and to open their ears to the simple commands of the gospel: love your neighbor.

- We can move too quickly through this parable—we know it and its ending well. Stay in prayer with its beginning. Nobody should be covered in sores and hungry; nobody should be comforted only by dogs. In a world of homelessness, hunger, and loneliness, should anyone be dressed so well and feast so well? One had no choice but to fast, the other had a choice to help. Saint Ignatius wrote for each day, "Who will I help today?"

Friday 26th February
Matthew 21:33–43, 45–46

Jesus said, "Listen to another parable. There was a landowner who planted a vineyard, put a fence around it, dug a wine press in it, and built a watchtower. Then he leased it to tenants and went to another country. When the harvest time had come, he sent his slaves to the tenants to collect his produce. But the tenants seized his slaves and beat one, killed another, and stoned another. Again he sent other slaves, more than the first; and they treated them in the same way. Finally he sent his son to them, saying, 'They will respect my son.' But when the tenants saw the son, they said to themselves, 'This is the heir; come, let us kill him and get his inheritance.' So they seized him, threw him out of the vineyard, and killed him. Now when the owner of the vineyard comes, what will he do to those tenants?" They said to him, "He will put those wretches to a miserable death, and lease the vineyard to other tenants who will give him the produce at the harvest time." Jesus said to them, "Have you never read in the Scriptures: 'The stone that the builders rejected has become the cornerstone; this was the Lord's doing, and it is amazing in our eyes'? Therefore I tell you, the kingdom of God will be taken away from you and given to a people that produces the fruits of the kingdom." When the chief priests and the Pharisees heard his parables, they realized that he was speaking about them. They wanted to arrest him, but they feared the crowds, because they regarded him as a prophet.

• Lord, this parable is about those who rejected Jesus, but also about me. I am the tenant of your vineyard. For me you have planted and protected a crop, and from me you expect some harvest. The fruit is for you, not for me. I may feel annoyed when you ask, but you are right to expect something of me.

- The Pharisees feared his words, because they feared how others were reacting. They were fearful because they lacked faith that deep down they were loved. Prayer is enjoying moments of being loved, and then I am happy that Jesus is speaking about me.

Saturday 27th February
Luke 15:1–3, 11–32

Now all the tax collectors and sinners were coming near to listen to him. And the Pharisees and the scribes were grumbling and saying, "This fellow welcomes sinners and eats with them." So he told them this parable: "There was a man who had two sons. The younger of them said to his father, 'Father, give me the share of the property that will belong to me.' So he divided his property between them. A few days later the younger son gathered all he had and traveled to a distant country, and there he squandered his property in dissolute living. When he had spent everything, a severe famine took place throughout that country, and he began to be in need. So he went and hired himself out to one of the citizens of that country, who sent him to his fields to feed the pigs. He would gladly have filled himself with the pods that the pigs were eating; and no one gave him anything. But when he came to himself he said, 'How many of my father's hired hands have bread enough and to spare, but here I am dying of hunger! I will get up and go to my father, and I will say to him, "Father, I have sinned against heaven and before you; I am no longer worthy to be called your son; treat me like one of your hired hands."' So he set off and went to his father. But while he was still far off, his father saw him and was filled with compassion; he ran and put his arms around him and kissed him. Then the son said to him, 'Father, I have sinned against heaven and before you; I am no longer worthy to be called your son.' But the father said to his slaves, 'Quickly, bring out a robe—the best one—and put it on him; put a ring on his finger and sandals on his feet. And get the fatted calf and kill it, and let us eat and celebrate; for this son of mine was dead and is alive again; he was lost and is found!' And they began to celebrate. Now his elder son was in the field; and when he came and approached the house, he heard music and dancing. He called one of the slaves and asked what was going on. He replied, 'Your brother has come, and your father has killed the fatted calf, because he has got him back safe and sound.' Then he became angry and refused to go in. His father came out and began to plead with him. But he answered his father, 'Listen! For all these years I have been working like a slave for you, and I have never disobeyed your command; yet you have never given me even a young goat so that I might celebrate with my friends. But when this son of yours came back, who has devoured your property with prostitutes, you killed the fatted calf for him!' Then the father said to him, 'Son, you are always with me, and all that is mine is yours. But we had to celebrate and rejoice, because this brother of yours was dead and has come to life; he was lost and has been found.'"

- In different cultures over the centuries God has been pictured in all sorts of images and imaginations. In this parable we have Jesus' image, which is astonishing: a fond father who does not stop his wastrel son from bringing shame on himself and the family, and who not merely forgives him but embraces him, interrupts his apology, and throws a big party to express his own joy. Dear Lord, whatever happens to me, let me never forget or doubt this picture of you.

- At his lowest point the younger son "came to himself." He realized the person he had become was not his real self. This story tells us that conversion is possible; we can return to our best—our truest—selves, and when we do we will find our loving God ready to welcome us home with open arms.

February 28—March 5

Something to think and pray about each day this week:

Cleansed by tears

The famous sermon on hell in James Joyce's *A Portrait of the Artist as a Young Man* exposes a schoolboy's soul tortured by sins of lust, the boy convinced that his sins are beyond forgiveness because God is great and stern.

He has, however, a glimmer of hope: his failure has not offended Our Lady. So he prays, in the words of Cardinal John Henry Newman: "God once had meant to come on earth in heavenly glory, but we sinned; and then he could not safely visit us but with a shrouded majesty and a bedimmed radiance, for he was God. So he came himself in weakness, not in power, and he sent thee, a creature, in his stead, with a creature's comeliness and luster, suited to our state. And now thy very face and form, dear Mother, speak to us of the eternal: not like earthly beauty, dangerous to look upon, but like the morning star which is thy emblem, bright and musical, breathing purity, telling of heaven and infusing peace. O harbinger of day! O light of the pilgrim! Lead us still as thou hast led. In the dark night, across the bleak wilderness, guide us on to our Lord Jesus, guide us home."

His eyes dimmed with tears, he looks humbly up to heaven and weeps for the innocence he has lost. Later he finds a chapel and emerges from the confessional, a contrite young man of sixteen now at peace with God.

The Presence of God
God is with me, but more, God is within me, giving me existence. Let me dwell for a moment on God's life-giving presence in my body, my mind, my heart, and in the whole of my life.

Freedom
"In these days, God taught me as a schoolteacher teaches a pupil" (Saint Ignatius of Loyola). I remind myself that there are things God has to teach me yet and ask for the grace to hear them and let them change me.

Consciousness
I exist in a web of relationships—links to nature, people, God. I trace out these links, giving thanks for the life that flows through them. Some links are twisted or broken: I may feel regret, anger, disappointment. I pray for the gift of acceptance and forgiveness.

The Word
The Word of God comes down to us through the Scriptures. May the Holy Spirit enlighten my mind and my heart to respond to the gospel teachings. (Please turn to the Scripture on the following pages. Inspiration points are provided should you need them. When you are ready, return here to continue.)

Conversation
Conversation requires talking and listening. As I talk to Jesus may I also learn to be still and listen. I picture the gentleness in his eyes and the smile full of love as he gazes on me. I can be totally honest with Jesus as I tell him of my worries and my cares. I will open up my heart to him as I tell him of my fears and my doubts. I will ask him to help me to place myself fully in his care, to abandon myself to him, knowing that he always wants what is best for me.

Conclusion
I thank God for these few moments we have spent alone together and for any insights I may have been given concerning the text.

Sunday 28th February
Third Sunday of Lent
Luke 13:1–9

At that very time there were some present who told him about the Galileans whose blood Pilate had mingled with their sacrifices. He asked them, "Do you think that because these Galileans suffered in this way they were worse sinners than all other Galileans? No, I tell you; but unless you repent, you will all perish as they did. Or those eighteen who were killed when the tower of Siloam fell on them—do you think that they were worse offenders than all the others living in Jerusalem? No, I tell you; but unless you repent, you will all perish just as they did." Then he told this parable: "A man had a fig tree planted in his vineyard; and he came looking for fruit on it and found none. So he said to the gardener, 'See here! For three years I have come looking for fruit on this fig tree, and still I find none. Cut it down! Why should it be wasting the soil?' He replied, 'Sir, let it alone for one more year, until I dig round it and put manure on it. If it bears fruit next year, well and good; but if not, you can cut it down.'"

- Jesus comments on the news stories of his time. Just as in our time, narratives of destruction and distress capture the attention. As always, Jesus is telling us not only to look outward but to look inward as well; he is concerned with what is going on in our heads and what is happening in our hearts. We can ask ourselves how God is opening us to compassion, prompting us to repentance and leading us to life.

- Jesus often speaks of the need to repent. This means turning away from anything that is not of God. I ask to be brought more and more into the world of goodness and love, of light and truth. I want to be a genuine disciple.

Monday 29th February

Luke 4:24–30

Jesus said, "Truly I tell you, no prophet is accepted in the prophet's hometown. But the truth is, there were many widows in Israel in the time of Elijah, when the heaven was shut up three years and six months, and there was a severe famine over all the land; yet Elijah was sent to none of them except to a widow at Zarephath in Sidon. There were also many lepers in Israel in the time of the prophet Elisha, and none of them was cleansed except Naaman the Syrian." When they heard this, all in the synagogue were filled with rage. They got up, drove him out of the town, and led him to the brow of the hill on which their town was built, so that they might hurl him off the cliff. But he passed through the midst of them and went on his way.

- The people in question here were jealous of their community of faith. Jesus was including all nationalities in the care and the saving love of God. They were jealous of their own relationship with God, and used it in many ordinary ways to keep others out of favor and off of land and to deny human rights to anyone outside their circle. Jesus is the one of universal welcome, his heart open in prayer and life to all, no matter their creed, nation, gender, age, or any of the categories with which we are divided from each other.

- When I hear things that hurt my pride, do I attack the speakers and drive them away? Lord, let me be more humble. Let me seek to know the truth about myself, even though it may be painful. Only the truth will set me free.

Tuesday 1st March

Matthew 18:21–35

Peter came and said to him, "Lord, if another member of the church sins against me, how often should I forgive? As many as seven times?" Jesus said to him, "Not seven times, but, I tell you, seventy-seven times. For this reason the kingdom of heaven may be compared to a king who wished to settle accounts with his slaves. When he began the reckoning, one who owed him ten thousand talents was brought to him; and, as he could not pay, his lord ordered him to be sold, together with his wife and children and all his possessions, and payment to be made. So the slave fell on his knees before him, saying, 'Have patience with me, and I will pay you everything.' And out of pity for him, the lord of that slave released him and forgave him the debt. But that same slave, as he went out, came upon one of his fellow slaves who owed him a hundred denarii; and seizing him by the throat, he said, 'Pay what you owe.' Then his fellow slave fell down and pleaded with him, 'Have patience with me, and I will pay you.' But he refused; then he went and threw him into prison until he would pay the debt. When his fellow slaves saw what had happened, they were greatly distressed, and they went and reported to their lord all that had taken place. Then his lord summoned him and said to him, 'You wicked slave! I forgave you all that debt because you pleaded with me. Should you not have had mercy on your fellow slave, as I had mercy on you?' And in anger his lord handed him over to be tortured until he would pay his entire debt. So my heavenly Father will also do to every one of you, if you do not forgive your brother or sister from your heart."

- I should take some time to try and see how the call to forgiveness affects me. This is a hard one: Forgive and go on forgiving. It means letting go of my treasured grievances and resentments. They are a burden on me, not on the one I resent. In the Lord's Prayer, Jesus makes forgiveness as central as our daily bread. Nothing sets apart the spirit of Christ from other spirits more clearly than this.

- If we must be prepared to forgive seventy-seven times, then we must also be ready to ask for forgiveness—and believe we are forgiven—seventy-seven times. Does forgiveness flow back and forth in my dealings with others, or is it rare in my life?

Wednesday 2nd March
Matthew 5:17–19

Jesus said to his disciples, "Do not think that I have come to abolish the law or the prophets; I have come not to abolish but to fulfill. For truly I tell you, until heaven and earth pass away, not one letter, not one stroke of a letter, will pass from the law until all is accomplished. Therefore, whoever breaks one of the least of these commandments, and teaches others to do the same, will be called least in the kingdom of heaven; but whoever does them and teaches them will be called great in the kingdom of heaven. For I tell you, unless your righteousness exceeds that of the scribes and Pharisees, you will never enter the kingdom of heaven."

- Jesus is not careless about the requirements of the law. He wants us, too, to be attentive and careful and asks us to bring all aspects of our lives before God. I pray that I might respect the voice of my conscience as I try to hear how God is speaking to me.

- I am often told who are the winners and losers; I hear about the great, and I am taught to ignore the small. Jesus shows me a different way of thinking about who is great in his sight. I think of the people I admire and ask Jesus to show me who really deserves my attention.

Thursday 3rd March
Luke 11:14–23

Now Jesus was casting out a demon that was mute; when the demon had gone out, the one who had been mute spoke, and the crowds were amazed. But some of them said, "He casts out demons by Beelzebul, the ruler of the demons." Others, to test him, kept demanding from him a sign from heaven. But he knew what they were thinking and said to them, "Every kingdom divided against itself becomes a desert, and house falls on house. If Satan also is divided against himself, how will his kingdom stand?—for you say that I cast out the demons by Beelzebul. Now if I cast out the demons by Beelzebul, by whom do your exorcists cast them out? Therefore they will be your judges. But if it is by the finger of God that I cast out the demons, then the kingdom of God has come to you. When a strong man, fully armed, guards his castle, his property is safe. But when one stronger than he attacks him and overpowers him, he takes away his armor in which he trusted and divides his plunder. Whoever is not with me is against me, and whoever does not gather with me scatters."

- Some of the original listeners to this story, who have just witnessed Jesus curing a man who was mute, refuse to think well of him and invent a slanderous story. It prods me: Do I think ill of others more readily than I credit them with good? Lord, give me the grace to see the best in others, as I'd wish them to see the best in me.

- Am I divided against myself—sometimes listening to Jesus, sometimes listening to evil? Have I a discerning heart?

Friday 4th March
Mark 12:28–34

One of the scribes came near and heard them disputing with one another, and seeing that Jesus answered them well, he asked him, "Which commandment is the first of all?" Jesus answered, "The first is, 'Hear, O Israel: the Lord our God, the Lord is one; you shall love the Lord your God with all your heart, and with all your soul, and with all your mind, and with all your strength.' The second is this, 'You shall love your neighbor as yourself.' There is no other commandment greater than these." Then the scribe said to him, "You are right, Teacher; you have truly said that 'he is one, and besides him there is no other'; and 'to love him with all the heart, and with all the understanding, and with all the strength,' and 'to love one's neighbor as oneself'—this is much more important than all whole burnt offerings and sacrifices." When Jesus saw that he answered wisely, he said to him, "You are not far from the kingdom of God." After that no one dared to ask him any question.

- Real prayer brings us into the kingdom of God; in prayer the kingdom or reign of God grows within us. Prayer that does not reach the heart can leave us dry, unenthusiastic about the things of God, and dissatisfied.

- "The Lord our God, the Lord is one . . ." As I hear Jesus' answer to the scribe, I think how a Muslim would agree warmly with all that he hears and how Jesus might well say of many a Muslim, Jew, and Christian equally: "You are not far from the kingdom of God." Lord, let me not put barriers where you put windows.

Saturday 5th March
Luke 18:9–14

Jesus also told this parable to some who trusted in themselves that they were righteous and regarded others with contempt: "Two men went up to the temple to pray, one a Pharisee and the other a tax collector. The Pharisee, standing by himself, was praying thus, 'God, I thank you that I am not like other people: thieves, rogues, adulterers, or even like this tax collector. I fast twice a week; I give a tenth of all my income.' But the tax collector, standing far off, would not even look up to heaven, but was beating his breast and saying, 'God, be merciful to me, a sinner!' I tell you, this man went down to his home justified rather than the other; for all who exalt themselves will be humbled, but all who humble themselves will be exalted."

- The contrast between the Pharisee and tax collector has entered so deeply into our culture that it is sometimes reversed, and people are more anxious to hide at the back of the church than to be in the front pews.

- How does the story strike me? I would hate to be the object of people's contempt. But Lord, if they knew me as you do, they might be right to feel contempt. And I have no right to look down on those whose sins are paraded in the media. Be merciful to me.

March 6—March 12

Something to think and pray about each day this week:

Indiscriminate Loving

"God is love in the same way as an emerald is green." So says Simone Weil. What does this mean? It means that God *is* love through and through. There isn't something else hidden behind God's love. Nothing I do could make God love me more—or less! Jesus compares his Father to the sun, which simply shines, so that both the just and the unjust are warmed by it. Every time I see the sun, I can say, "God is a bit like that!"

The task of the Son is to reveal the generous nature of divine loving and then to show people a new way of relating. "Be loving, as my Father and I are loving!" he says. Jesus illustrates in word and deed this new way of relating. His parables jolted and disconcerted his hearers. What a shock that the good neighbor to the injured man was a Samaritan! And surely the good father should have disowned his wayward son? Surely again those who labored all day should get more than the last-minute arrivals?

Jesus had a well-integrated personality. He could be gentle but also challenging and angry. So he clashed head-on with the religious leaders of the day and threw the moneylenders out of the temple. Wise love takes many forms: it is not timid and passive; it can be demanding as well as long-suffering.

The Presence of God

I pause for a moment and think of the love and the grace that God showers on me: I am created in the image and likeness of God; I am God's dwelling place.

Freedom

Lord, you granted me the great gift of freedom. In these times grant that I may be free from any form of racism or intolerance. Remind me, Lord, that we are all equal in your loving eyes.

Consciousness

Knowing that God loves me unconditionally, I can afford to be honest about how I am. How has the past day been, and how do I feel now? I share my feelings openly with the Lord.

The Word

I read the Word of God slowly, a few times over, and I listen to what God is saying to me. (Please turn to the Scripture on the following pages. Inspiration points are provided should you need them. When you are ready, return here to continue.)

Conversation

Jesus, you always welcomed little children when you walked on this earth. Teach me to have a childlike trust in you, to live in the knowledge that you will never abandon me.

Conclusion

Glory be to the Father, and to the Son, and to the Holy Spirit, as it was in the beginning, is now and ever shall be, world without end. Amen.

Sunday 6th March
Fourth Sunday of Lent
Luke 15:1–3, 11–32

Now all the tax collectors and sinners were coming near to listen to him. And the Pharisees and the scribes were grumbling and saying, "This fellow welcomes sinners and eats with them." So he told them this parable: "There was a man who had two sons. The younger of them said to his father, 'Father, give me the share of the property that will belong to me.' So he divided his property between them. A few days later the younger son gathered all he had and traveled to a distant country, and there he squandered his property in dissolute living. When he had spent everything, a severe famine took place throughout that country, and he began to be in need. So he went and hired himself out to one of the citizens of that country, who sent him to his fields to feed the pigs. He would gladly have filled himself with the pods that the pigs were eating; and no one gave him anything. But when he came to himself he said, 'How many of my father's hired hands have bread enough and to spare, but here I am dying of hunger! I will get up and go to my father, and I will say to him, "Father, I have sinned against heaven and before you; I am no longer worthy to be called your son; treat me like one of your hired hands."' So he set off and went to his father. But while he was still far off, his father saw him and was filled with compassion; he ran and put his arms around him and kissed him. Then the son said to him, 'Father, I have sinned against heaven and before you; I am no longer worthy to be called your son.' But the father said to his slaves, 'Quickly, bring out a robe—the best one—and put it on him; put a ring on his finger and sandals on his feet. And get the fatted calf and kill it, and let us eat and celebrate; for this son of mine was dead and is alive again; he was lost and is found!' And they began to celebrate. Now his elder son was in the field; and when he came and approached the house, he heard music and dancing. He called one of the slaves and asked what was going on. He replied, 'Your brother has come, and your father has killed the fatted calf, because he has got him back safe and sound.' Then he became angry and refused to go in. His father came out and began to plead with him. But he answered his father, 'Listen! For all these years I have been working like a slave for you, and I have never disobeyed your command; yet you have never given me even a young goat so that I might celebrate with my friends. But when this son of yours came back, who has devoured your property with prostitutes, you killed the fatted calf for him!' Then the father said to him, 'Son, you are always with me, and all that is mine is yours. But we had to celebrate and rejoice, because this brother of yours was dead and has come to life; he was lost and has been found.'"

- So many of Jesus' parables, like this one, startle their hearers with their shocking picture of God's inclusive love—which seeks out one lost sheep, turns a house upside down to find a single coin, and pays those who have worked the least the same as those who have worked the most. Every single person is important to God. Do you feel that way about yourself? Do you treat others with that same awareness?

- The Pharisees and scribes resented Jesus when he dared to welcome sinners. Like the older son in the story, they were insiders, the faithful ones who felt they had earned God's favor. Now they were being asked not to exclude those who had sinned but to rejoice over their repentance. God calls us to look for opportunities to overcome our prejudices and desire to exclude and instead to embrace God's mercy.

Monday 7th March
John 4:43–54

When the two days were over, he went from that place to Galilee (for Jesus himself had testified that a prophet has no honor in the prophet's own country). When he came to Galilee, the Galileans welcomed him, since they had seen all that he had done in Jerusalem at the festival; for they too had gone to the festival. Then he came again to Cana in Galilee where he had changed the water into wine. Now there was a royal official whose son lay ill in Capernaum. When he heard that Jesus had come from Judea to Galilee, he went and begged him to come down and heal his son, for he was at the point of death. Then

Jesus said to him, "Unless you see signs and wonders you will not believe." The official said to him, "Sir, come down before my little boy dies." Jesus said to him, "Go; your son will live." The man believed the word that Jesus spoke to him and started on his way. As he was going down, his slaves met him and told him that his child was alive. So he asked them the hour when he began to recover, and they said to him, "Yesterday at one in the afternoon the fever left him." The father realized that this was the hour when Jesus had said to him, "Your son will live." So he himself believed, along with his whole household. Now this was the second sign that Jesus did after coming from Judea to Galilee.

- At first Jesus recoils when the official begs him to cure his son: "Unless you see signs and wonders you will not believe." He is exposed to countless requests for help, but what he treasures most is the company of those—like Martha's sister Mary—who want to know God for himself, not for what he can deliver. After the child is healed, and the father returns in gratitude and faith, Jesus welcomes him.

- Lord, forgive me for the times I have treated you like a messenger. I turn to you in a crisis, begging for a favor. When the crisis passes, I easily go back to living as though you did not exist. I want to find time for you, to live in your presence.

Tuesday 8th March
John 5:1–16

There was a festival of the Jews, and Jesus went up to Jerusalem. Now in Jerusalem by the Sheep Gate there is a pool, called in Hebrew Beth-zatha, which has five porticoes. In these lay many invalids—blind, lame, and paralyzed. One man was there who had been ill for thirty-eight years. When Jesus saw him lying there and knew that he had been there a long time, he said to him, "Do you want to be made well?" The sick man answered him, "Sir, I have no one to put me into the pool when the water is stirred up; and while I am making my way, someone else steps down ahead of me." Jesus said to him, "Stand up, take your mat and walk." At once the man was made well, and he took up his mat and began to walk. Now that day was a sabbath. So the Jews said to the man who had been cured, "It is the sabbath; it is not lawful for you to carry your mat." But he answered them, "The man who made me well said to me, 'Take up your mat and walk.'" They asked him, "Who is the man who said to you, 'Take it up and walk'?" Now the man who had been healed did not know who it was, for Jesus had disappeared in the crowd that was there. Later Jesus found him in the temple and said to him, "See, you have been made well! Do not sin any more, so that nothing worse happens to you." The man went away and told the Jews that it was Jesus who had made him well. Therefore the Jews started persecuting Jesus, because he was doing such things on the sabbath.

- I can wait all my life for the stirring of the water. How safe it is not to see, not to have to move! No one can blame me for my inaction because there's nobody to lift me. When Jesus asks, "Do you want to be made well?" I don't really answer the question. I am not sure. If I were healed I would have to move on from the familiar place in which I have been lying all these years. God, stir my heart!

- The man by the pool is waiting for healing from the stirring of the waters. He does not know that Jesus, source of all healing, is standing beside him. Do I look for healing in the wrong places?

Wednesday 9th March
John 5:17–30

Jesus answered them, "My Father is still working, and I also am working." For this reason the Jews were seeking all the more to kill him, because he was not only breaking the sabbath, but was also calling God his own Father, thereby making himself equal to God. Jesus said to them, "Very truly, I tell you, the Son can do nothing on his own, but only what he sees the Father doing; for whatever the Father does, the Son does likewise. The Father loves the Son and shows him all that he himself is doing; and he will show him greater works than these, so that you will be astonished. Indeed, just as the Father raises the dead and gives them life, so also the Son gives life to whomsoever he wishes. The Father judges no one but has given all judgment to the Son, so that all may honor the Son just as they honor the Father. Anyone who does not honor the Son does not honor the Father who sent him. Very truly, I tell you, anyone who hears my word and believes him who sent me has eternal life, and does not come under judgment, but has passed from death to life. Very truly, I tell you, the hour is coming, and is now here, when the dead will hear the voice of the Son of God, and those who hear will live. For just as the Father has life in himself, so he has granted the Son also to have life in himself; and he has given him authority to execute judgment, because he is the Son of Man. Do not be astonished at this; for the hour is coming when all who are in their graves will hear his voice and will come out—those who have done good, to the resurrection of life, and those who have done evil, to the resurrection of condemnation. I can do nothing on my own. As I hear, I judge; and my judgment is just, because I seek to do not my own will but the will of him who sent me."

- Jesus is utterly attentive to the Father. This attention allows the Father's creative, life-giving love to flow through Christ to those around him. Perfect love demands perfect attention. How attentive will I be to the people in my life today?

- The relationship between the Father and Son is perfect. The Father is reflected in all that the Son does. Do I bear witness to God's work in what I say and do?

Thursday 10th March
John 5:31–47

Jesus said, "If I testify about myself, my testimony is not true. There is another who testifies on my behalf, and I know that his testimony to me is true. You sent messengers to John, and he testified to the truth. Not that I accept such human testimony, but I say these things so that you may be saved. He was a burning and shining lamp, and you were willing to rejoice for a while in his light. But I have a testimony greater than John's. The works that the Father has given me to complete, the very works that I am doing, testify on my behalf that the Father has sent me. And the Father who sent me has himself testified on my behalf. You have never heard his voice or seen his form, and you do not have his word abiding in you, because you do not believe him whom he has sent. You search the Scriptures because you think that in them you have eternal life; and it is they that testify on my behalf. Yet you refuse to come to me to have life. I do not accept glory from human beings. But I know that you do not have the love of God in you. I have come in my Father's name, and you do not accept me; if another comes in his own name, you will accept him. How can you believe when you accept glory from one another and do not seek the glory that comes from the one who alone is God? Do not think that I will accuse you before the Father; your accuser is Moses, on whom you have set your hope. If you believed Moses, you would believe me, for he wrote about me. But if you do not believe what he wrote, how will you believe what I say?"

- The biblical rule of evidence required two witnesses. Jesus calls on John the Baptist and Moses to testify to his identity and mission. What would a person of integrity say about me?

- John the Baptist fulfilled Isaiah's prophecy that a voice would cry, "In the wilderness prepare the way of the Lord; make straight in the desert a highway for our God" (Isaiah 40:3). As we make our Lenten journey, let us reflect on what we are doing to make our own crooked ways straight.

Friday 11th March
John 7:1–2, 10, 25–30

Jesus went about in Galilee. He did not wish to go about in Judea because the Jews were looking for an opportunity to kill him. Now the Jewish festival of Booths was near. But after his brothers had gone to the festival, then he also went, not publicly but as it were in secret. Now some of the people of Jerusalem were saying, "Is not this the man whom they are trying to kill? And here he is, speaking openly, but they say nothing to him! Can it be that the authorities really know that this is the Messiah? Yet we know where this man is from; but when the Messiah comes, no one will know where he is from." Then Jesus cried out as he was teaching in the temple, "You know me, and you know where I am from. I have not come on my own. But the one who sent me is true, and you do not know him. I know him, because I am from him, and he sent me." Then they tried to arrest him, but no one laid hands on him, because his hour had not yet come.

- This gospel passage describes the struggle in Jesus: how to reveal himself to his people when many of them were seeking an excuse to kill him. Because they know he is from Nazareth, they write him off—it is too ordinary a place to produce a Messiah.

- Lord, you show yourself to me in the ordinary. Let me recognize you there today.

Saturday 12th March

John 7:40–53

When they heard Jesus' words, some in the crowd said, "This is really the prophet." Others said, "This is the Messiah." But some asked, "Surely the Messiah does not come from Galilee, does he? Has not the Scripture said that the Messiah is descended from David and comes from Bethlehem, the village where David lived?" So there was a division in the crowd because of him. Some of them wanted to arrest him, but no one laid hands on him. Then the temple police went back to the chief priests and Pharisees, who asked them, "Why did you not arrest him?" The police answered, "Never has anyone spoken like this!" Then the Pharisees replied, "Surely you have not been deceived too, have you? Has any one of the authorities or of the Pharisees believed in him? But this crowd, which does not know the law—they are accursed." Nicodemus, who had gone to Jesus before, and who was one of them, asked, "Our law does not judge people without first giving them a hearing to find out what they are doing, does it?" They replied, "Surely you are not also from Galilee, are you? Search and you will see that no prophet is to arise from Galilee." Then each of them went home.

- Here are two ways of approaching Jesus: some hear him, see how he lives, and love and enjoy him; others go back to their books and argue about his pedigree.

- Lord, save me from losing you in the babble of books and arguments. May I meet and know and enjoy you.

March 13—March 19

Something to think and pray about each day this week:

Wanting to Forgive

If I refuse absolutely even to want to forgive, I cannot pray the Our Father. It makes no sense. But if I have problems with forgiving, then I can pray it. In effect I am saying: "Lord, I have great problems with what you call me to. Please help me. You are better at forgiving than I am, so please forgive me fully, no matter how I hurt you. I accept that you want me to keep on trying to forgive, and I will try."

So the divine call to forgive is addressed to me as I am, in my actual situation. I am called to do what I can, no more, no less. But I know that the love of Christ is always inviting me beyond where I am. On that difficult journey toward loving our enemy, we have a friend in our Lord, not another enemy throwing even more burdens on us. Because he is our friend, he is not going to be shocked at our feelings of anger or revenge. He will understand these, because he shares our anger and horror at what has been done to us. He will walk with us as we move slowly toward freedom, where we are no longer dominated by what has happened to us.

The Presence of God

Come to me all you who are burdened, and I will give you rest. Here I am, Lord. I come to seek your presence. I long for your healing power.

Freedom

Lord grant me the grace to have freedom of the spirit. Cleanse my heart and soul so I may live joyously in your love.

Consciousness

Knowing that God loves me unconditionally, I look honestly over the last day, its events and my feelings. Do I have something to be grateful for? Then I give thanks. Is there something I am sorry for? Then I ask forgiveness.

The Word

God speaks to each one of us individually. I listen attentively to hear what he is saying to me. Read the text a few times, then listen. (Please turn to the Scripture on the following pages. Inspiration points are provided should you need them. When you are ready, return here to continue.)

Conversation

Remembering that I am still in God's presence, I imagine Jesus himself standing or sitting beside me, and I say whatever is on my mind, whatever is in my heart, speaking as one friend to another.

Conclusion

I thank God for these few moments we have spent alone together and for any insights I may have been given concerning the text.

Sunday 13th March
Fifth Sunday of Lent
John 8:1–11

Early in the morning Jesus came again to the temple. All the people came to him and he sat down and began to teach them. The scribes and the Pharisees brought a woman who had been caught in adultery; and making her stand before all of them, they said to him, "Teacher, this woman was caught in the very act of committing adultery. Now in the law Moses commanded us to stone such women. Now what do you say?" They said this to test him, so that they might have some charge to bring against him. Jesus bent down and wrote with his finger on the ground. When they kept on questioning him, he straightened up and said to them, "Let anyone among you who is without sin be the first to throw a stone at her." And once again he bent down and wrote on the ground. When they heard it, they went away, one by one, beginning with the elders; and Jesus was left alone with the woman standing before him. Jesus straightened up and said to her, "Woman, where are they? Has no one condemned you?" She said, "No one, sir." And Jesus said, "Neither do I condemn you. Go your way, and from now on do not sin again.'"

• Where do I stand in this scene? Like the woman standing before her accusers? Like a silent sympathizer hoping that something will happen to save her? Like the skulking male adulterer who got her into this trouble? Like the bystanders already collecting the best stones with a view to a killing? Like one of the elders who slinks away, unable to cast the first stone? What goes through my head as Jesus is doodling in the sand?

• Sometimes we are overwhelmed by a sense of our own guilt. The voices of accusation roar in our ears. Frozen with fear, we wait for condemnation. Lord, like the woman in the reading, may we hear the damning voices fade until there is only your voice left, telling us to move on and sin no more.

Monday 14th March

John 8:12–20

Again Jesus spoke to them, saying, "I am the light of the world. Whoever follows me will never walk in darkness but will have the light of life." Then the Pharisees said to him, "You are testifying on your own behalf; your testimony is not valid." Jesus answered, "Even if I testify on my own behalf, my testimony is valid because I know where I have come from and where I am going, but you do not know where I come from or where I am going. You judge by human standards; I judge no one. Yet even if I do judge, my judgment is valid; for it is not I alone who judge, but I and the Father who sent me. In your law it is written that the testimony of two witnesses is valid. I testify on my own behalf, and the Father who sent me testifies on my behalf." Then they said to him, "Where is your Father?" Jesus answered, "You know neither me nor my Father. If you knew me, you would know my Father also." He spoke these words while he was teaching in the treasury of the temple, but no one arrested him, because his hour had not yet come.

- On the first day of creation God flooded the heavens and the earth with divine radiance by uttering the mighty words: "Let there be light." No matter how dark things may seem, I remind myself that darkness can never overpower light. I turn to Christ, the light of the world.

- I pray in the words of Saint Benedict: "O gracious and Holy Father, give us wisdom to perceive you, diligence to seek you, patience to wait for you, eyes to behold you, a heart to meditate upon you, and a life to proclaim you; through the power of the Spirit of Jesus Christ our Lord."

Tuesday 15th March

John 8:21–30

Jesus said to them, "I am going away, and you will search for me, but you will die in your sin. Where I am going, you cannot come." Then the Jews said, "Is he going to kill himself? Is that what he means by saying, 'Where I am going, you cannot come'?" He said to them, "You are from below, I am from above; you are of this world, I am not of this world. I told you that you would die in your sins, for you will die in your sins unless you believe that I am he." They said to him, "Who are you?" Jesus said to them, "Why do I speak to you at all? I have much to say about you and much to condemn; but the one who sent me is true, and I declare to the world what I have heard from him." They did not understand that he was speaking to them about the Father. So Jesus said, "When you have lifted up the Son of Man, then you will realize that I am he, and that I do nothing on my own, but I speak these things as the Father instructed me. And the one who sent me is with me; he has not let me alone, for I always do what is pleasing to him." As he was saying these things, many believed in him.

- In the days of Jesus' Passion we hear him crying out to God in doubt. He might remember these words he spoke, that God does not leave him alone. We, too, are never alone; the love, grace, and help of God are always with us. Give thanks in prayer for these gifts or ask for what you need just now.

- It is when we see Jesus lifted up on the cross that we realize who he is and why he lived. The rest of the gospels are like a preface to the Passion. On the cross we see the triumph of love over evil, and our best help in coping with the reality of evil.

Wednesday 16th March
John 8:31–42

Then Jesus said to the Jews who had believed in him, "If you continue in my word, you are truly my disciples; and you will know the truth, and the truth will make you free." They answered him, "We are descendants of Abraham and have never been slaves to anyone. What do you mean by saying, 'You will be made free'?" Jesus answered them, "Very truly, I tell you, everyone who commits sin is a slave to sin. The slave does not have a permanent place in the household; the Son has a place there forever. So if the Son makes you free, you will be free indeed. I know that you are descendants of Abraham; yet you look for an opportunity to kill me, because there is no place in you for my word. I declare what I have seen in the Father's presence; as for you, you should do what you have heard from the Father." They answered him, "Abraham is our father." Jesus said to them, "If you were Abraham's children, you would be doing what Abraham did, but now you are trying to kill me, a man who has told you the truth that I heard from God. This is not what Abraham did. You are indeed doing what your father does." They said to him, "We are not illegitimate children; we have one father, God himself." Jesus said to them, "If God were your Father, you would love me, for I came from God and now I am here. I did not come on my own, but he sent me."

- Jesus' promise is that the truth will make us free. Lord, I do want to be free, so let me listen to those who tell me the truth about myself. Let me listen also to your word, which tries to reach into my heart and liberate me. Let me start with the great truth of which you try to convince me: that I am endlessly loved by you.

- When in my life have I had an experience that made me truly see Jesus as the one sent by God?

Thursday 17th March
John 8:51–59

Jesus said, "Very truly, I tell you, whoever keeps my word will never see death." The Jews said to him, "Now we know that you have a demon. Abraham died, and so did the prophets; yet you say, 'Whoever keeps my word will never taste death.' Are you greater than our father Abraham, who died? The prophets also died. Who do you claim to be?" Jesus answered, "If I glorify myself, my glory is nothing. It is my Father who glorifies me, he of whom you say, 'He is our God,' though you do not know him. But I know him; if I were to say that I do not know him, I would be a liar like you. But I do know him and I keep his word. Your ancestor Abraham rejoiced that he would see my day; he saw it and was glad." Then the Jews said to him, "You are not yet fifty years old, and have you seen Abraham?" Jesus said to them, "Very truly, I tell you, before Abraham was, I am." So they picked up stones to throw at him, but Jesus hid himself and went out of the temple.

- The Jews had no doubt that Jesus was claiming a divine nature. As son of Mary he was born in Bethlehem in time; but as God he is outside time—the same yesterday, today, and forever.

- Lord I am praying here on the edge of what I can grasp, reaching for the eternal Now. What matters to me is that you are as much my contemporary as you were of Pilate and the stone-throwing enemies of Jesus.

Friday 18th March
John 10:31–42

The Jews took up stones again to stone him. Jesus replied, "I have shown you many good works from the Father. For which of these are you going to stone me?" The Jews answered, "It is not for a good work that we are going to stone you, but for blasphemy, because you, though only a human being, are making yourself God." Jesus answered, "Is it not written in your law, 'I said, you are gods'? If those to whom the Word of God came were called 'gods'—and the Scripture cannot be annulled—can you say that the one whom the Father has sanctified and sent into the world is blaspheming because I said, 'I am God's Son'? If I am not doing the works of my Father, then do not believe me. But if I do them, even though you do not believe me, believe the works, so that you may know and understand that the Father is in me and I am in the Father." Then they tried to arrest him again, but he escaped from their hands. He went away again across the Jordan to the place where John had been baptizing earlier, and he remained there. Many came to him, and they were saying, "John performed no sign, but everything that John said about this man was true." And many believed in him there.

- The works of Jesus are the works of love. This is the love of him we know—love unto death. What we see in Jesus we can see of the Father. What the Father sees in Jesus, he sees and loves in us. We pray that our hearts may be made like the heart of Jesus.

- Some believed in Jesus, and some did not. In a way that's the basic question the gospel puts to us, too. Do we really believe that in Jesus we see God? And if we believe in Jesus, can others recognize Jesus in us?

Saturday 19th March
Saint Joseph, Spouse of the Blessed Virgin Mary
Matthew 1:16, 18–21, 24a

Jacob [was] the father of Joseph the husband of Mary, of whom Jesus was born, who is called the Messiah. Now the birth of Jesus the Messiah took place in this way. When his mother Mary had been engaged to Joseph, but before they lived together, she was found to be with child from the Holy Spirit. Her husband Joseph, being a righteous man and unwilling to expose her to public disgrace, planned to dismiss her quietly. But just when he had resolved to do this, an angel of the Lord appeared to him in a dream and said, "Joseph, son of David, do not be afraid to take Mary as your wife, for the child conceived in her is from the Holy Spirit. She will bear a son, and you are to name him Jesus, for he will save his people from their sins." When Joseph awoke from sleep, he did as the angel of the Lord commanded him; he took her as his wife.

- What do we know about Saint Joseph? That he loved Mary so much that he suppressed his doubts about her chastity and allowed himself to be regarded as the father of her child, knowing that he wasn't; that he brought up that child as his own, despite great difficulties and dangers, particularly at the start; that he taught him his trade; that he loved him; and that his parenting, evident in Jesus' virile health as an adult (physical stamina, courage, strength of purpose, and appeal to women, men, and children), was good and successful. Joseph is the obvious patron of adoptive fathers of all kinds.

- God, you give your help and guidance to those who trust in you. Where do I need your help and guidance today?

Holy Week
March 20—March 26

Something to think and pray about each day this week:

Suffering and Joy

In the culture of Jesus' time, crucifixion was a disgraceful way to die. So it took time for the disciples to see in this dreadful event the supreme revelation of God's love for us. We must never trivialize or domesticate this enduring shock. The cross remains, to convert us to God's way of seeing the appalling damage caused by sin and evil. We learn how demanding reconciliation is. Amazing grace is revealed, but it is costly grace, too. It seemed to Jesus that only the cross would break open our hearts, so it was worth it. That hope brought him joy.

We are asked to suffer, if necessary, in order to foster the values of the kingdom. As followers of Jesus we, too, must be in solidarity with a wounded humanity. This may mean living simply for the sake of others; or working with the sick; or spending time with life's victims. For all of us it means enduring with patience the day-to-day difficulties of life.

Suffering is often unearned and always undesired: often we can't change it, but Jesus shows us how to bear it with love. Such love radiates and inspires others. You know such people, and perhaps you are this way yourself without feeling in any way heroic. Mysteriously, joy is possible even in suffering, perhaps because suffering brings us so close to God.

The Presence of God

The more we call on God, the more we can feel God's presence. Day by day we are drawn closer to the loving heart of God.

Freedom

Your death on the cross has set me free. I can live joyously and freely without fear of death. Your mercy knows no bounds.

Consciousness

I remind myself that I am in the presence of the Lord. I will take refuge in his loving heart. He is my strength in times of weakness. He is my comforter in times of sorrow.

The Word

I take my time to read the Word of God slowly, a few times, allowing myself to dwell on anything that strikes me. (Please turn to the Scripture on the following pages. Inspiration points are provided should you need them. When you are ready, return here to continue.)

Conversation

Do I notice myself reacting as I pray with the Word of God? Do I feel challenged, comforted, angry? Imagining Jesus sitting or standing by me, I speak out my feelings, as one trusted friend to another.

Conclusion

Glory be to the Father, and to the Son, and to the Holy Spirit, as it was in the beginning, is now and ever shall be, world without end. Amen.

Sunday 20th March
Palm Sunday of the Passion of the Lord
Luke 23:1–49

Then the assembly rose as a body and brought Jesus before Pilate. They began to accuse him, saying, "We found this man perverting our nation, forbidding us to pay taxes to the emperor, and saying that he himself is the Messiah, a king." Then Pilate asked him, "Are you the king of the Jews?" He answered, "You say so." Then Pilate said to the chief priests and the crowds, "I find no basis for an accusation against this man." But they were insistent and said, "He stirs up the people by teaching throughout all Judea, from Galilee where he began even to this place." When Pilate heard this, he asked whether the man was a Galilean. And when he learned that he was under Herod's jurisdiction, he sent him off to Herod, who was himself in Jerusalem at that time. When Herod saw Jesus, he was very glad, for he had been wanting to see him for a long time, because he had heard about him and was hoping to see him perform some sign. He questioned him at some length, but Jesus gave him no answer. The chief priests and the scribes stood by, vehemently accusing him. Even Herod with his soldiers treated him with contempt and mocked him; then he put an elegant robe on him, and sent him back to Pilate. That same day Herod and Pilate became friends with each other; before this they had been enemies. Pilate then called together the chief priests, the leaders, and the people, and said to them, "You brought me this man as one who was perverting the people; and here I have examined him in your presence and have not found this man guilty of any of your charges against him. Neither has Herod, for he sent him back to us. Indeed, he has done nothing to deserve death. I will therefore have him flogged and release him." Then they all shouted out together, "Away with this fellow! Release Barabbas for us!" (This was a man who had been put in prison for an insurrection that had taken place in the city, and for murder.) Pilate, wanting to release Jesus, addressed them again; but they kept shouting, "Crucify, crucify him!" A third time he said to them, "Why, what evil has he done? I have found in him no ground for the sentence of death; I will therefore have him flogged and then release him." But they kept urgently demanding with loud shouts that he should be crucified; and their voices prevailed. So Pilate gave his verdict that their demand should be granted. He released the man they asked for, the one who had been put in prison for insurrection and murder, and he handed Jesus over as they wished. As they led him away, they seized a man, Simon of Cyrene, who was coming from the country, and they laid the cross on him, and made him carry it behind Jesus. A great number of the people followed him, and among them were women who were beating their breasts and wailing for him. But Jesus turned to them and said, "Daughters of Jerusalem, do not weep for me, but weep for yourselves and for your children. For the days are surely coming when they will say, 'Blessed are the barren, and the wombs that never bore, and the breasts that never nursed.' Then they will begin to say to the mountains, 'Fall on us'; and to the hills, 'Cover us.' For if they do this when the wood is green, what will happen when it is dry?" Two others also, who were criminals, were led away to be put to death with him. When they came to the place that is called the Skull, they crucified Jesus there with the criminals, one on his right and one on his left. Then Jesus said, "Father, forgive them; for they do not know what they are doing." And they cast lots to divide his clothing. And the people stood by, watching; but the leaders scoffed at him, saying, "He saved others; let him save himself if he is the Messiah of God, his chosen one!" The soldiers also mocked him, coming up and offering him sour wine, and saying, "If you are the King of the Jews, save yourself!" There was also an inscription over him, "This is the King of the Jews." One of the criminals who were hanged there kept deriding him and saying, "Are you not the Messiah? Save yourself and us!" But the other rebuked him, saying, "Do you not fear God, since you are under the same sentence of condemnation? And we indeed have been condemned justly, for we are getting what we deserve for our deeds, but this man has done nothing wrong." Then he said, "Jesus, remember me when you come into your kingdom." He replied, "Truly I tell you, today you will be with me in Paradise." It was now about noon, and darkness came over the whole land until three in the afternoon, while the sun's light failed; and the curtain of the temple was torn in two. Then Jesus, crying with a loud voice, said, "Father, into your hands I commend my spirit." Having said this, he breathed his last. When the centurion saw what had taken place, he praised God and said, "Certainly this man was innocent." And when all the crowds who had gathered there for this spectacle saw what had taken place, they returned home, beating their breasts. But all his acquaintances, including the women who had followed him from Galilee, stood at a distance, watching these things.

- We need to train ourselves to look for signs of Jesus' reign. His real identity can be seen only by the humble. The "good thief" saw things as they were: he knew his own sinfulness; he recognized Jesus' character; he asked for little yet was rewarded for his honesty. Humility brings a true perspective and is the ground for meeting God. I pray for humility.

- In the extraordinary mystery of the Eucharist, Lord, you become part of me and I of you. I celebrate this Eucharist in memory of you: slake my hunger and thirst on the bread and wine and through this come closest to meeting my deepest desire, for union with God.

Monday 21st March
John 12:1–11

Six days before the Passover Jesus came to Bethany, the home of Lazarus, whom he had raised from the dead. There they gave a dinner for him. Martha served, and Lazarus was one of those at the table with him. Mary took a pound of costly perfume made of pure nard, anointed Jesus' feet, and wiped them with her hair. The house was filled with the fragrance of the perfume. But Judas Iscariot, one of his disciples (the one who was about to betray him), said, "Why was this perfume not sold for three hundred denarii and the money given to the poor?" (He said this not because he cared about the poor, but because he was a thief; he kept the common purse and used to steal what was put into it.) Jesus said, "Leave her alone. She bought it so that she might keep it for the day of my burial. You always have the poor with you, but you do not always have me." When the great crowd of the Jews learned that he was there, they came not only because of Jesus but also to see Lazarus, whom he had raised from the dead. So the chief priests planned to put Lazarus to death as well, since it was on account of him that many of the Jews were deserting and were believing in Jesus.

- The gift of Mary: the most costly gift she could find. Jesus was open-hearted enough to receive her gift even though others would need the money spent on it. What is my gift to give him this day as I pray? Offer the gift of your loving heart.

- Lord, when I find myself critical of others, it may be my own warped vision that needs to be corrected.

Tuesday 22nd March
John 13:21–33, 36–38

Jesus was troubled in spirit, and declared, "Very truly, I tell you, one of you will betray me." The disciples looked at one another, uncertain of whom he was speaking. One of his disciples—the one whom Jesus loved—was reclining next to him; Simon Peter therefore motioned to him to ask Jesus of whom he was speaking. So while reclining next to Jesus, he asked him, "Lord, who is it?" Jesus answered, "It is the one to whom I give this piece of bread when I have dipped it in the dish." So when he had dipped the piece of bread, he gave it to Judas son of Simon Iscariot. After he received the piece of bread, Satan entered into him. Jesus said to him, "Do quickly what you are going to do." Now no one at the table knew why he said this to him. Some thought that, because Judas had the common purse, Jesus was telling him, "Buy what we need for the festival"; or, that he should give something to the poor. So, after receiving the piece of bread, he immediately went out. And it was night. When he had gone out, Jesus said, "Now the Son of Man has been glorified, and God has been glorified in him. If God has been glorified in him, God will also glorify him in himself and will glorify him at once. Little children, I am with you only a little longer. You will look for me; and as I said to the Jews so now I say to you, "Where I am going, you cannot come." Simon Peter said to him, "Lord, where are you going?" Jesus answered, "Where I am going, you cannot follow me now; but you will follow afterward." Peter said to him, "Lord, why can I not follow you now? I will lay down my life for you." Jesus answered, "Will you lay down your life for me? Very truly, I tell you, before the cock crows, you will have denied me three times."

- God is glorified in all sorts of ways. He is glorified in the Passion of Jesus, as all that is done is done from love. Even in sending out Judas there is the beginning of the journey of passion—love that will result in the love of the cross.

- Peter hit deep points of his life here. His sureness of following Jesus was challenged by Jesus himself. He would later find himself weak and failing in this following. We oscillate in our following of the Lord; these days let us know in the certainty of Jesus' love that there is always another day, another chance, another joy in our following of Jesus.

Wednesday 23rd March
Matthew 26:14–25

Then one of the twelve, who was called Judas Iscariot, went to the chief priests and said, "What will you give me if I betray him to you?" They paid him thirty pieces of silver. And from that moment he began to look for an opportunity to betray him. On the first day of Unleavened Bread the disciples came to Jesus, saying, "Where do you want us to make the preparations for you to eat the Passover?" He said, "Go into the city to a certain man, and say to him, 'The Teacher says, My time is near; I will keep the Passover at your house with my disciples.'" So the disciples did as Jesus had directed them, and they prepared the Passover meal. When it was evening, he took his place with the twelve; and while they were eating, he said, "Truly I tell you, one of you will betray me." And they became greatly distressed and began to say to him one after another, "Surely not I, Lord?" He answered, "The one who has dipped his hand into the bowl with me will betray me. The Son of Man goes as it is written of him, but woe to that one by whom the Son of Man is betrayed! It would have been better for that one not to have been born." Judas, who betrayed him, said, "Surely not I, Rabbi?" He replied, "You have said so."

- Holy Week is an invitation to walk closely with Jesus: we fix our gaze on him and accompany him in his suffering; we let him look closely at us and see us as we really are. We do not have to present a brave face to him but can tell him about where we have been disappointed, let down—perhaps even betrayed. We avoid getting stuck in our own misfortune by seeing as he sees, by learning from his heart.

- Help me to see, Jesus, how you do not condemn. You invite each of us to recognize the truth of our own discipleship. You invite us to follow you willingly, freely, forgiven.

Thursday 24th March
Holy Thursday
John 13:1–15

Now before the festival of the Passover, Jesus knew that his hour had come to depart from this world and go to the Father. Having loved his own who were in the world, he loved them to the end. The devil had already put it into the heart of Judas son of Simon Iscariot to betray him. And during supper Jesus, knowing that the Father had given all things into his hands, and that he had come from God and was going to God, got up from the table, took off his outer robe, and tied a towel around himself. Then he poured water into a basin and began to wash the disciples' feet and to wipe them with the towel that was tied around him. He came to Simon Peter, who said to him, "Lord, are you going to wash my feet?" Jesus answered, "You do not know now what I am doing, but later you will understand." Peter said to him, "You will never wash my feet." Jesus answered, "Unless I wash you, you have no share with me." Simon Peter said to him, "Lord, not my feet only but also my hands and my head!" Jesus said to him, "One who has bathed does not need to wash, except for the feet, but is entirely clean. And you are clean, though not all of you." For he knew who was to betray him; for this reason he said, "Not all of you are clean." After he had washed their feet, had put on his robe, and had returned to the table, he said to them, "Do you know what I have done to you? You call me Teacher and Lord—and you are right, for that is what I am. So if I, your Lord and Teacher, have washed your feet, you also ought to wash one another's feet. For I have set you an example, that you also should do as I have done to you."

• Can you watch this scene and allow Jesus to wash your feet? Imagine him looking at you, pouring water, and drying your feet. This is what he wants to do. Allow him! And then maybe you might imagine yourself doing the same for others. As you do this, pray for them.

• Jesus says, "Later you will understand." Sometimes that's not enough for me! I want to understand now. Help me, Jesus, to live as you did even when I don't fully comprehend what you are asking of me.

Friday 25th March
Friday of the Passion of the Lord (Good Friday)
John 18:1—19:24

Pilate handed Jesus over to them to be crucified. So they took Jesus; and carrying the cross by himself, he went out to what is called the Place of the Skull, which in Hebrew is called Golgotha. There they crucified him, and with him two others, one on either side, with Jesus between them. Pilate also had an inscription written and put on the cross. It read, "Jesus of Nazareth, the King of the Jews." Many of the Jews read this inscription, because the place where Jesus was crucified was near the city; and it was written in Hebrew, in Latin, and in Greek. Then the chief priests of the Jews said to Pilate, "Do not write, 'The King of the Jews,' but, 'This man said, I am King of the Jews.'" Pilate answered, "What I have written I have written." When the soldiers had crucified Jesus, they took his clothes and divided them into four parts, one for each soldier. They also took his tunic; now the tunic was seamless, woven in one piece from the top. So they said to one another, "Let us not tear it, but cast lots for it to see who will get it." This was to fulfill what the Scripture says, "They divided my clothes among themselves, and for my clothing they cast lots."

- Can you look at the cross and allow Jesus to die for you? Notice how you feel and what you would like to say. Maybe the questions of Saint Ignatius of Loyola in looking at the crucified Christ come to mind: "What have I done for Christ? What am I doing for Christ? What ought I to do for Christ?"

- Good Friday puts the cross before me and challenges me not to look away. If I have followed Jesus' footsteps to Calvary, I do not have to fear because I, like him, am confident in God's enduring presence. Wherever there is suffering or pain, I look again, seeking the face of Jesus. I ask him for the strength I need to be a sign of hope wherever there is despair, to be a presence of love wherever it is most needed.

Saturday 26th March
Holy Saturday
Luke 24:1–12

On the first day of the week, at early dawn, they came to the tomb, taking the spices that they had prepared. They found the stone rolled away from the tomb, but when they went in, they did not find the body. While they were perplexed about this, suddenly two men in dazzling clothes stood beside them. The women were terrified and bowed their faces to the ground, but the men said to them, "Why do you look for the living among the dead? He is not here, but has risen. Remember how he told you, while he was still in Galilee, that the Son of Man must be handed over to sinners, and be crucified, and on the third day rise again." Then they remembered his words, and returning from the tomb, they told all this to the eleven and to all the rest. Now it was Mary Magdalene, Joanna, Mary the mother of James, and the other women with them who told this to the apostles. But these words seemed to them an idle tale, and they did not believe them. But Peter got up and ran to the tomb; stooping and looking in, he saw the linen cloths by themselves; then he went home, amazed at what had happened.

- We can picture the women moving through the garden with heavy hearts, oblivious to the dawning spring morning. They are oblivious above all to the glorious presence of the risen Christ not a stone's throw away. Lord, help me to realize that when I am weighed down with sorrow, anxiety, or hopelessness, you are no farther from me than you were from the women in that dawn garden.

- Women are the first witnesses to the resurrection. They reveal the qualities of good disciples in their capacity to believe. I ask not to treat the resurrection as an idle tale but as the message that transforms our world and gives hope to everyone.

March 27—April 2

Something to think and pray about each day this week:

The Joy of Freedom

We belong to God's own family. How then can we act as if we are still slaves? We can move beyond lives of quiet desperation; we can stop feeling burdened, hopeless, dull, and passive. Our liberation was Jesus' agenda: "The Spirit has sent me to proclaim release to the captives . . . to let the oppressed go free" (Luke 4:18). The liberation of humankind is his great achievement.

Our freedom is God's primary gift to us. In fact it makes us like God. We need not be afraid to claim it and exercise it. Even when we misuse our free will, God does not take it away but works to undo the damage we cause. We learn from Jesus how to use our freedom well. He makes us a free people, a chosen race, sons and daughters of God. How should such people live? Not as slaves or sheep, surely, but as people who had been imprisoned but have just been let out into the open air and the sunlight that the free enjoy.

Of course I have to struggle to grow in freedom. It doesn't happen all at once. But I can make a fresh start every day. I pray: "God, thank you for my freedom. Let me live it out well today. Give me joy, energy, enthusiasm, and commitment for all that is worthwhile."

The Presence of God

God is with me, but more, God is within me, giving me existence. Let me dwell for a moment on God's life-giving presence in my body, my mind, my heart, and in the whole of my life.

Freedom

Lord, may I never take the gift of freedom for granted. You gave me the great blessing of freedom of spirit. Fill my spirit with your peace and your joy.

Consciousness

How am I really feeling? Lighthearted? Heavyhearted? I may be very much at peace, happy to be here. Equally, I may be frustrated, worried, or angry. I acknowledge how I really am. It is the real me that the Lord loves.

The Word

The Word of God comes down to us through the Scriptures. May the Holy Spirit enlighten my mind and my heart to respond to the gospel teachings. (Please turn to the Scripture on the following pages. Inspiration points are provided should you need them. When you are ready, return here to continue.)

Conversation

Jesus, you speak to me through the words of the gospels. May I respond to your call today. Teach me to recognize your hand at work in my daily living.

Conclusion

I thank God for these few moments we have spent alone together and for any insights I may have been given concerning the text.

Sunday 27th March
Easter Sunday of the Resurrection of the Lord
Luke 24:13–35

Now on that same day two of them were going to a village called Emmaus, about seven miles from Jerusalem, and talking with each other about all these things that had happened. While they were talking and discussing, Jesus himself came near and went with them, but their eyes were kept from recognizing him. And he said to them, "What are you discussing with each other while you walk along?" They stood still, looking sad. Then one of them, whose name was Cleopas, answered him, "Are you the only stranger in Jerusalem who does not know the things that have taken place there in these days?" He asked them, "What things?" They replied, "The things about Jesus of Nazareth, who was a prophet mighty in deed and word before God and all the people, and how our chief priests and leaders handed him over to be condemned to death and crucified him. But we had hoped that he was the one to redeem Israel. Yes, and besides all this, it is now the third day since these things took place. Moreover, some women of our group astounded us. They were at the tomb early this morning, and when they did not find his body there, they came back and told us that they had indeed seen a vision of angels who said that he was alive. Some of those who were with us went to the tomb and found it just as the women had said; but they did not see him." Then he said to them, "Oh, how foolish you are, and how slow of heart to believe all that the prophets have declared! Was it not necessary that the Messiah should suffer these things and then enter into his glory?" Then beginning with Moses and all the prophets, he interpreted to them the things about himself in all the Scriptures. As they came near the village to which they were going, he walked ahead as if he were going on. But they urged him strongly, saying, "Stay with us, because it is almost evening and the day is now nearly over." So he went in to stay with them. When he was at the table with them, he took bread, blessed and broke it, and gave it to them. Then their eyes were opened, and they recognized him; and he vanished from their sight. They said to each other, "Were not our hearts burning within us while he was talking to us on the road, while he was opening the Scriptures to us?" That same hour they got up and returned to Jerusalem; and they found the eleven and their companions gathered together. They were saying, "The Lord has risen indeed, and he has appeared to Simon!" Then they told what had happened on the road, and how he had been made known to them in the breaking of the bread.

- The trudging disciples had turned their backs on Jerusalem and were picking over the story as they knew it. So it was that Jesus found them, coming near and walking with them. I let him fall in step with me now.

- Jesus, find me where I am. Draw near and walk with me. Help me to recognize how my story comes to life as I listen to yours. Let me so hear your good news that my heart may glow. Let me forget myself and receive your Spirit. You bring me the message of Life, and you trust me to do for others what you want to do for me.

Monday 28th March
Matthew 28:8–15

The women left the tomb quickly with fear and great joy, and ran to tell his disciples. Suddenly Jesus met them and said, "Greetings!" And they came to him, took hold of his feet, and worshipped him. Then Jesus said to them, "Do not be afraid; go and tell my brothers to go to Galilee; there they will see me." While they were going, some of the guard went into the city and told the chief priests everything that had happened. After the priests had assembled with the elders, they devised a plan to give a large sum of money to the soldiers, telling them, "You must say, 'His disciples came by night and stole him away while we were asleep.' If this comes to the governor's ears, we will satisfy him and keep you out of trouble." So they took the money and did as they were directed. And this story is still told among the Jews to this day.

- The women left the tomb with joy, interpreting the emptiness posi-tively; having gone to care for the dead, they realized their task was to announce the living. So it was that they were able to meet Jesus and receive from him a new mission. I pray that I may have the same space in my life—that, by laying aside my own preoccupations, I might be free to proclaim good news.

• Help us, O God, to do what we can as we remain alert, noticing the movement of your Spirit. May we receive life as you offer it to us—even if in unexpected ways.

Tuesday 29th March
John 20:11–18

Mary stood weeping outside the tomb. As she wept, she bent over to look into the tomb; and she saw two angels in white, sitting where the body of Jesus had been lying, one at the head and the other at the feet. They said to her, "Woman, why are you weeping?" She said to them, "They have taken away my Lord, and I do not know where they have laid him." When she had said this, she turned around and saw Jesus standing there, but she did not know that it was Jesus. Jesus said to her, "Woman, why are you weeping? Whom are you looking for?" Supposing him to be the gardener, she said to him, "Sir, if you have carried him away, tell me where you have laid him, and I will take him away." Jesus said to her, "Mary!" She turned and said to him in Hebrew, "Rabbouni!" (which means Teacher). Jesus said to her, "Do not hold on to me, because I have not yet ascended to the Father. But go to my brothers and say to them, 'I am ascending to my Father and your Father, to my God and your God.'" Mary Magdalene went and announced to the disciples, "I have seen the Lord"; and she told them that he had said these things to her.

• Mary went to do her best, to tend to Jesus' mortal remains. She accepted the reality as she saw it but was determined to do what she could to bring dignity and honor.

• Mary weeps for what she sees as missing, her tears making it difficult for her to see who is present. Easter rescues us not only from our sin but calls us beyond our dutiful habits, our worthy projects, and our personal values. Jesus asks us, "Whom are you looking for?" and invites us to let our hopes find true life. He wants to enrich us and to help us to recognize where his Spirit is moving in our lives.

Wednesday 30th March

Luke 24:13–35

Now on that same day two of them were going to a village called Emmaus, about seven miles from Jerusalem, and talking with each other about all these things that had happened. While they were talking and discussing, Jesus himself came near and went with them, but their eyes were kept from recognizing him. And he said to them, "What are you discussing with each other while you walk along?" They stood still, looking sad. Then one of them, whose name was Cleopas, answered him, "Are you the only stranger in Jerusalem who does not know the things that have taken place there in these days?" He asked them, "What things?" They replied, "The things about Jesus of Nazareth, who was a prophet mighty in deed and word before God and all the people, and how our chief priests and leaders handed him over to be condemned to death and crucified him. But we had hoped that he was the one to redeem Israel. Yes, and besides all this, it is now the third day since these things took place. Moreover, some women of our group astounded us. They were at the tomb early this morning, and when they did not find his body there, they came back and told us that they had indeed seen a vision of angels who said that he was alive. Some of those who were with us went to the tomb and found it just as the women had said; but they did not see him." Then he said to them, "Oh, how foolish you are, and how slow of heart to believe all that the prophets have declared! Was it not necessary that the Messiah should suffer these things and then enter into his glory?" Then beginning with Moses and all the prophets, he interpreted to them the things about himself in all the Scriptures. As they came near the village to which they were going, he walked ahead as if he were going on. But they urged him strongly, saying, "Stay with us, because it is almost evening and the day is now nearly over." So he went in to stay with them. When he was at the table with them, he took bread, blessed and broke it, and gave it to them. Then their eyes were opened, and they recognized him; and he vanished from their sight. They said to each other, "Were not our hearts burning within us while he was talking to us on the road, while he was opening the Scriptures to us? That same hour they got up and returned to Jerusalem; and they found the eleven and their companions gathered together. They were saying, "The Lord has risen indeed, and he has appeared to Simon!" Then they told what had happened on the road, and how he had been made known to them in the breaking of the bread.

- Jesus has never really vanished. In the blessing and breaking of bread he is present; every altar is Emmaus, the place of this story. Maybe every time we share a family meal or friendship we are at Emmaus. Pray for those we break bread with—Eucharistic or ordinary bread. Maybe now all bread is holy, and every meal a holy meal.

- Jesus, find me where I am. Draw near and walk with me. Help me to recognize how my story comes to life as I listen to yours. Let me so hear your good news that my heart may glow. Let me forget myself and receive your Spirit. You bring me the message of life and you trust me to do for others what you want to do for me.

Thursday 31st March
Luke 24:35–48

Then they told what had happened on the road, and how he had been made known to them in the breaking of the bread. While they were talking about this, Jesus himself stood among them and said to them, "Peace be with you." They were startled and terrified, and thought that they were seeing a ghost. He said to them, "Why are you frightened, and why do doubts arise in your hearts? Look at my hands and my feet; see that it is I myself. Touch me and see; for a ghost does not have flesh and bones as you see that I have." And when he had said this, he showed them his hands and his feet. While in their joy they were disbelieving and still wondering, he said to them, "Have you anything here to eat?" They gave him a piece of broiled fish, and he took it and ate in their presence. Then he said to them, "These are my words that I spoke to you while I was still with you—that everything written about me in the law of Moses, the prophets, and the psalms must be fulfilled." Then he opened their minds to understand the Scriptures, and he said to them, "Thus it is written, that the Messiah is to suffer and to rise from the dead on the third day, and that repentance and forgiveness of sins is to be proclaimed in his name to all nations, beginning from Jerusalem. You are witnesses of these things."

- The big word of Easter is "peace." It is the greeting of Jesus—like the signature tune of a radio show. We know with the greeting of peace that Jesus is near. Allow that word to flow through the silence and the words of your prayer this day.

- The disciples received another report of Jesus' presence and were talking about it, yet they were not ready to receive his own message, "Peace be with you." I pray that, in these Easter days, I may not only receive the reports but that I might accept Jesus' gift of peace in my heart.

Friday 1st April
John 21:1–14

After these things Jesus showed himself again to the disciples by the Sea of Tiberias; and he showed himself in this way. Gathered there together were Simon Peter, Thomas called the Twin, Nathanael of Cana in Galilee, the sons of Zebedee, and two others of his disciples. Simon Peter said to them, "I am going fishing." They said to him, "We will go with you." They went out and got into the boat, but that night they caught nothing. Just after daybreak, Jesus stood on the beach; but the disciples did not know that it was Jesus. Jesus said to them, "Children, you have no fish, have you?" They answered him, "No." He said to them, "Cast the net to the right side of the boat, and you will find some." So they cast it, and now they were not able to haul it in because there were so many fish. That disciple whom Jesus loved said to Peter, "It is the Lord!" When Simon Peter heard that it was the

Lord, he put on some clothes, for he was naked, and jumped into the sea. But the other disciples came in the boat, dragging the net full of fish, for they were not far from the land, only about a hundred yards off. When they had gone ashore, they saw a charcoal fire there, with fish on it, and bread. Jesus said to them, "Bring some of the fish that you have just caught." So Simon Peter went aboard and hauled the net ashore, full of large fish, a hundred fifty-three of them; and though there were so many, the net was not torn. Jesus said to them, "Come and have breakfast." Now none of the disciples dared to ask him, "Who are you?" because they knew it was the Lord. Jesus came and took the bread and gave it to them, and did the same with the fish. This was now the third time that Jesus appeared to the disciples after he was raised from the dead.

- The breakfast on the beach is a surprise for the disciples. Maybe they expected some rebuke—instead they got fed! And whatever way Jesus fed them, they recognized him. The invitation to them is to all of us; every time of prayer is an invitation to breakfast!

- Peter was not the first to recognize Jesus but was the first to respond. I pray that I might hear good news spoken to me by those around me.

Saturday 2nd April
Mark 16:9–15

Now after Jesus rose early on the first day of the week, he appeared first to Mary Magdalene, from whom he had cast out seven demons. She went out and told those who had been with him, while they were mourning and weeping. But when they heard that he was alive and had been seen by her, they would not believe it. After this he appeared in another form to two of them, as they were walking into the country. And they went back and told the rest, but they did not believe them. Later he appeared to the eleven themselves as they were sitting at the table; and he upbraided them for their lack of faith and stubbornness, because they had not believed those who saw him after he had risen.

And he said to them, "Go into all the world and proclaim the good news to the whole creation."

- The light dawned gradually for the disciples: the message of Easter was not received immediately or wholeheartedly by all. Sometimes outwardly confident yet harboring doubts, at other times hesitant to proclaim what seems certain to me, I am like the disciples. Jesus invites me to a fullness of faith. He sees and understands my stubbornness and reluctance yet trusts me. Calmly and gently he sends me to "the whole world."

- The disciples' lack of faith showed itself not only in their resistance to believe he had been raised but also perhaps in their forgetting that Jesus had told them all along he would rise again. Perhaps that's why Jesus was so angry with them. We can also fail to see the signs of the risen Lord around us. Where are they in your life today?

April 3—April 9

Something to think and pray about each day this week:

Touching the Flesh of Christ

The ecclesial community is a place to grow our faith. Pope Francis often urges Christians not to lose confidence in the church, despite its obvious failings. It makes mistakes and clearly needs institutional reform, and this is a major task for the Holy Spirit. But the church will be chiefly reformed by dedicating itself to its central mission. This means that it must move "to the periphery" and proclaim the Good News to all people from the standpoint of solidarity with the poor.

Only in self-giving do we find ourselves. Only by opening ourselves to a partner, to children, and to family needs—which may be painful—do we discover the breadth of our humanity. But while family is the birthplace of our ability to give of ourselves, it does not represent the limit of where we express this love. We must open ourselves to the ecclesial community, and to the world. We cannot turn our backs on our struggling sisters and brothers. In the words of Pope Francis, we are to "touch the flesh of Christ" by caring for the needy.

The church is meant to be a servant of all in need. This is a humble role. According to the Second Vatican Council, whatever promotes human dignity among the people of the world becomes the agenda of the church. Injustice anywhere must stir the Christian heart to an appropriate response.

The Presence of God

As I sit here, the beating of my heart, the ebb and flow of my breathing, and the movements of my mind are all signs of God's ongoing creation of me. I pause for a moment, and become aware of this presence of God within me.

Freedom

Saint Ignatius of Loyola thought that a thick and shapeless tree trunk would never believe that it could become a statue, admired as a miracle of sculpture, and would never submit itself to the chisel of the sculptor, who sees by her genius what she can make of it. I ask for the grace to let myself be shaped by my loving Creator.

Consciousness

In God's loving presence I unwind the past day, starting from now and looking back, moment by moment. I gather in all the goodness and light, in gratitude. I attend to the shadows and what they say to me, seeking healing, courage, forgiveness.

The Word

I read the Word of God slowly, a few times over, and I listen to what God is saying to me. (Please turn to the Scripture on the following pages. Inspiration points are provided should you need them. When you are ready, return here to continue.)

Conversation

Begin to talk to Jesus about the piece of Scripture you have just read. What part of it strikes a chord in you? Perhaps the words of a friend— or some story you have heard recently—will slowly rise to the surface of your consciousness. If so, does the story throw light on what the Scripture passage may be trying to say to you?

Conclusion

Glory be to the Father, and to the Son, and to the Holy Spirit, as it was in the beginning, is now and ever shall be, world without end. Amen.

Sunday 3rd April
Second Sunday of Easter
John 20:19–31

When it was evening on that day, the first day of the week, and the doors of the house where the disciples had met were locked for fear of the Jews, Jesus came and stood among them and said, "Peace be with you." After he said this, he showed them his hands and his side. Then the disciples rejoiced when they saw the Lord. Jesus said to them again, "Peace be with you. As the Father has sent me, so I send you." When he had said this, he breathed on them and said to them, "Receive the Holy Spirit. If you forgive the sins of any, they are forgiven them; if you retain the sins of any, they are retained." But Thomas (who was called the Twin), one of the twelve, was not with them when Jesus came. So the other disciples told him, "We have seen the Lord." But he said to them, "Unless I see the mark of the nails in his hands, and put my finger in the mark of the nails and my hand in his side, I will not believe." A week later his disciples were again in the house, and Thomas was with them. Although the doors were shut, Jesus came and stood among them and said, "Peace be with you." Then he said to Thomas, "Put your finger here and see my hands. Reach out your hand and put it in my side. Do not doubt but believe." Thomas answered him, "My Lord and my God!" Jesus said to him, "Have you believed because you have seen me? Blessed are those who have not seen and yet have come to believe." Now Jesus did many other signs in the presence of his disciples, which are not written in this book. But these are written so that you may come to believe that Jesus is the Messiah, the Son of God, and that through believing you may have life in his name.

- Unbelief colors many of the resurrection encounters. Fear and shame fill the disciples. They cling to one another behind locked doors. The risen Lord comes bearing his wounds, in his side, in his hands and feet. He does not blame or chide. Instead he speaks words of peace and gives them his best gift, his Holy Spirit.

- Jesus, you invite me also to touch your wounds. Then I can find you in my own wounds and allow you to touch me. Touch my hurts and my hardened heart with your healing hand. Then may I be a gift to others.

Monday 4th April
The Annunciation of the Lord
Luke 1:26–38

In the sixth month the angel Gabriel was sent by God to a town in Galilee called Nazareth, to a virgin engaged to a man whose name was Joseph, of the house of David. The virgin's name was Mary. And he came to her and said, "Greetings, favored one! The Lord is with you." But she was much perplexed by his words and pondered what sort of greeting this might be. The angel said to her, "Do not be afraid, Mary, for you have found favor with God. And now, you will conceive in your womb and bear a son, and you will name him Jesus. He will be great, and will be called the Son of the Most High, and the Lord God will give to him the throne of his ancestor David. He will reign over the house of Jacob forever, and of his kingdom there will be no end." Mary said to the angel, "How can this be, since I am a virgin?" The angel said to her, "The Holy Spirit will come upon you, and the power of the Most High will overshadow you; therefore the child to be born will be holy; he will be called Son of God. And now, your relative Elizabeth in her old age has also conceived a son; and this is the sixth month for her who was said to be barren. For nothing will be impossible with God." Then Mary said, "Here am I, the servant of the Lord; let it be with me according to your word." Then the angel departed from her.

- Hail Mary, full of grace; *Ave Maria, gratia plena*. As Mary heard that greeting, she grew shy and confused. I can never plumb the meaning of God made into man. But that mantra, "Hail Mary, full of grace," engages my tongue while my mind tries to follow Mary in her joy and astonishment.

- The angel's message troubled Mary. It was leading her into uncharted waters, into a life of unimaginable risk. She is willing to take the risk and to trust God's invitation. Lord, you ask me, too, to be your presence in the world. Your will be done.

Tuesday 5th April

John 3:7b–15

Jesus said, "Do not be astonished that I said to you, 'You must be born from above.' The wind blows where it chooses, and you hear the sound of it, but you do not know where it comes from or where it goes. So it is with everyone who is born of the Spirit." Nicodemus said to him, "How can these things be?" Jesus answered him, "Are you a teacher of Israel, and yet you do not understand these things? Very truly, I tell you, we speak of what we know and testify to what we have seen; yet you do not receive our testimony. If I have told you about earthly things and you do not believe, how can you believe if I tell you about heavenly things? No one has ascended into heaven except the one who descended from heaven, the Son of Man. And just as Moses lifted up the serpent in the wilderness, so must the Son of Man be lifted up, that whoever believes in him may have eternal life."

- Nicodemus was a clever teacher but lacked a certain wisdom. Used to citing authorities, he was unable to recognize the authority of Jesus, who spoke of what he knew. Before God I recognize my habits, my preferences, and my inclinations; I ask God to give me the freedom I need to be touched by Jesus' words, to awaken to his imagination, and to want for myself the freedom that he desires for me.

- There is a divine dimension to each person. There is a depth in our hearts where God dwells. It is our most sacred space. God works there. Our DNA is divine.

Wednesday 6th April

John 3:16–21

Jesus said to Nicodemus, "For God so loved the world that he gave his only Son, so that everyone who believes in him may not perish but may have eternal life. Indeed, God did not send the Son into the world to condemn the world, but in order that the world might be saved through him. Those who believe in him are not condemned; but those who do not believe are condemned already, because they have not believed in the name of the only Son of God. And this is the judgment, that the light has come into the world, and people loved darkness rather than light because their deeds were evil. For all who do evil hate the light and do not come to the light, so that their deeds may not be exposed. But those who do what is true come to the light, so that it may be clearly seen that their deeds have been done in God."

- I take some time in my prayer to recognize what God is doing, even if it is difficult for me to lay aside my own needs and preoccupations. The Word of God seeks a home in my heart and calls me to life—eternal life. This is how God loves the world, sending Jesus so that I might truly live.

- Considering how God so loves the world, I pray for God's creation, for all God's people; listening to Jesus, may we be brought to life.

Thursday 7th April
John 3:31–36

The one who comes from above is above all; the one who is of the earth belongs to the earth and speaks about earthly things. The one who comes from heaven is above all. He testifies to what he has seen and heard, yet no one accepts his testimony. Whoever has accepted his testimony has certified this, that God is true. He whom God has sent speaks the words of God, for he gives the Spirit without measure. The Father loves the Son and has placed all things in his hands. Whoever believes in the Son has eternal life; whoever disobeys the Son will not see life, but must endure God's wrath.

- Call some words to mind: "flight," "light," "air"—things that come "from above"; then consider "gravity," "weighty," "plodding," and what it is to be earthbound. Jesus models for us a way of being in balance: he knows that his identity is from above even as he moves on the earth. Our daily prayer helps us to search out where there is inspiration, promise, and hope in our lives. We acknowledge light where we find it, recognizing that it is from God and is a call to us to really receive the good news in our hearts.

- We easily become preoccupied with what we see, touch, own, or want to own. John the Baptist reminds his followers of another truth, drawing their attention to what is above. I consider what I should hold on to and what I should let go.

Friday 8th April

John 6:1–15

After this Jesus went to the other side of the Sea of Galilee, which is the Sea of Tiberias. And a multitude followed him, because they saw the signs which he did on those who were diseased. Jesus went up on the mountain, and there sat down with his disciples. Now the Passover, the feast of the Jews, was at hand. Lifting up his eyes, then, and seeing that a multitude was coming to him, Jesus said to Philip, "How are we to buy bread, so that these people may eat?" This he said to test him, for he himself knew what he would do. Philip answered him, "Two hundred denarii would not buy enough bread for each of them to get a little." One of his disciples, Andrew, Simon Peter's brother, said to him, "There is a lad here who has five barley loaves and two fish; but what are they among so many?" Jesus said, "Make the people sit down." Now there was much grass in the place; so the men sat down, in number about five thousand. Jesus then took the loaves, and when he had given thanks, he distributed them to those who were seated; so also the fish, as much as they wanted. And when they had eaten their fill, he told his disciples, "Gather up the fragments left over, that nothing may be lost." So they gathered them up and filled twelve baskets with fragments from the five barley loaves, left by those who had eaten. When the people saw the sign which he had done, they said, "This is indeed the prophet who is to come into the world!" When Jesus realized that they were about to come and take him by force to make him king, he withdrew again to the mountain by himself.

- The disciples saw overwhelming need and focused on their meager resources; Jesus saw the hungry crowd and looked at the needs of the people. Help me, Lord, not to be deterred by the many needs I notice but to do what I can in your name, assisted by your grace.

• Jesus was able to live in a community of ritual and tradition; he accepted it but called people to see more deeply. As Passover approaches he moves the people he meets on the hillside to appreciate its meaning in a profoundly new way, one that would connect them, not just with the past, but with their neighbors and with a broader community. For some the miracle was for that moment, and they demanded that Jesus be made king. For Jesus it was a threshold to prayer, an invitation to spend time with God.

Saturday 9th April

John 6:16–21

When evening came, his disciples went down to the sea, got into a boat, and started across the sea to Capernaum. It was now dark, and Jesus had not yet come to them. The sea became rough because a strong wind was blowing. When they had rowed about three or four miles, they saw Jesus walking on the sea and coming near the boat, and they were terrified. But he said to them, "It is I; do not be afraid." Then they wanted to take him into the boat, and immediately the boat reached the land toward which they were going.

• The disciples knew they were in a difficult situation and had work to do. They would have been keenly aware of Jesus' absence. Now, seeing him approach them, they had to ask what they meant to him. I consider how I sometimes struggle "against the wind" and am slow to recognize the help Jesus offers to me.

• I pray for all people who are in trouble or in need, that they might recognize the approach of Jesus in experiencing some care from others. May they not be afraid but be embraced by the one who approaches those who know their need.

The Third Week of Easter
April 10—April 16

Something to think and pray about each day this week:

No Sacred Space?

A recent report claims that in today's world we have no sacred space due to the overuse of digital technology. Online dependency is growing, even among young children. A parent describes how she took away her child's iPad one night, and the child had "an absolute meltdown." First thing in the morning, the child searched for it and used it all day. But the child may be only imitating the parents, who feel "left out" if they are not responding to the endless calls made to them.

To free ourselves from IOD (internet-overuse disorder), we need discipline. Its positive purpose would be to safeguard sacred space in our lives. Saint Paul insists that God is generous (2 Corinthians 9:8) so we will never regret quality time given to prayer and reflection on the things of God. To stay alive and grow deep down, we need to preserve a silent, empty, open space that only the Word of God can fill. Jesus was very aware of this. As he says, "We do not live by bread alone, but by every word that comes from the mouth of God" (Matthew 4:4, from Deuteronomy 8:3). In the cave of our hearts the Lord waits—for what? God waits "to be gracious to us" (Isaiah 30:18). It is thus that divine love is kindled in us that enriches us and radiates to others.

The Presence of God

I remind myself that, as I sit here now, God is gazing on me with love and holding me in being. I pause for a moment and think of this.

Freedom

Lord, you created me to live in freedom. Mostly I take this gift for granted. Inspire me to live in the freedom you intended, with a heart untroubled and with complete trust in you.

Consciousness

In the presence of my loving Creator, I look honestly at my feelings over the past day—the highs, the lows, and the level ground. Can I see where the Lord has been present?

The Word

God speaks to each one of us individually. I listen attentively to hear what he is saying to me. Read the text a few times, then listen. (Please turn to the Scripture on the following pages. Inspiration points are provided should you need them. When you are ready, return here to continue.)

Conversation

I know with certainty there were times when you carried me, Lord. When it was through your strength I got through the dark times in my life.

Conclusion

I thank God for these few moments we have spent alone together and for any insights I may have been given concerning the text.

Sunday 10th April
Third Sunday of Easter

John 21:1–14

After these things Jesus showed himself again to the disciples by the Sea of Tiberias; and he showed himself in this way. Gathered there together were Simon Peter, Thomas called the Twin, Nathanael of Cana in Galilee, the sons of Zebedee, and two others of his disciples. Simon Peter said to them, "I am going fishing." They said to him, "We will go with you." They went out and got into the boat, but that night they caught nothing. Just after daybreak, Jesus stood on the beach; but the disciples did not know that it was Jesus. Jesus said to them, "Children, you have no fish, have you?" They answered him, "No." He said to them, "Cast the net to the right side of the boat, and you will find some." So they cast it, and now they were not able to haul it in because there were so many fish. That disciple whom Jesus loved said to Peter, "It is the Lord!" When Simon Peter heard that it was the Lord, he put on some clothes, for he was naked, and jumped into the sea. But the other disciples came in the boat, dragging the net full of fish, for they were not far from the land, only about a hundred yards off. When they had gone ashore, they saw a charcoal fire there, with fish on it, and bread. Jesus said to them, "Bring some of the fish that you have just caught." So Simon Peter went aboard and hauled the net ashore, full of large fish, a hundred fifty-three of them; and though there were so many, the net was not torn. Jesus said to them, "Come and have breakfast." Now none of the disciples dared to ask him, "Who are you?" because they knew it was the Lord. Jesus came and took the bread and gave it to them, and did the same with the fish. This was now the third time that Jesus appeared to the disciples after he was raised from the dead.

- Peter was not one for sitting around moping; he knew where Jesus had found him before and was confident that his busyness would not hide him from the Lord. We see him now, directing the activity of the others yet remaining open to the direction of the stranger. What does this say to me about my own life? Where do I need to take control? How is it that I need to be open to a voice that calls me beyond myself?

- Jesus, you meet me at the water's edge of my ordinary life. You accept me lovingly, you encourage me, you invite me to abundance. Nourished by the food of your word, warmed by the fire of your unfailing love, may I in turn nourish, heal, and love those I meet today.

Monday 11th April
John 6:22–29

The next day the crowd that had stayed on the other side of the lake saw that there had been only one boat there. They also saw that Jesus had not got into the boat with his disciples, but that his disciples had gone away alone. Then some boats from Tiberias came near the place where they had eaten the bread after the Lord had given thanks. So when the crowd saw that neither Jesus nor his disciples were there, they themselves got into the boats and went to Capernaum looking for Jesus. When they found him on the other side of the lake, they said to him, "Rabbi, when did you come here?" Jesus answered them, "Very truly, I tell you, you are looking for me, not because you saw signs, but because you ate your fill of the loaves. Do not work for the food that perishes, but for the food that endures for eternal life, which the Son of Man will give you. For it is on him that God the Father has set his seal." Then they said to him, "What must we do to perform the works of God?" Jesus answered them, "This is the work of God, that you believe in him whom he has sent."

- There is a lot of activity on the lake: boats come and go, the people watch for Jesus, wonder where he might be, and set off to find him. But somehow, even when found, Jesus eludes them. He doesn't allow them much satisfaction or relief in catching up with him but calls them to question what is in their hearts. Our prayer teaches us something like this: we will never capture Jesus or pin him down; engaging with Jesus helps us to see what is really in our hearts; our first call is not to do but to believe.

- The story of Holy Week and Easter tells us how Jesus resists being imprisoned or walled in; he wants only to point us to life, to reveal truth. Help us, Lord, to approach you with reverence and to allow you to meet us where we are. Purify our searching for you; let us not seek you for our own sakes but so that you may find life in us.

Tuesday 12th April

John 6:30–35

The crowd said to Jesus, "What sign are you going to give us then, so that we may see it and believe you? What work are you performing? Our ancestors ate the manna in the wilderness; as it is written, 'He gave them bread from heaven to eat.'" Then Jesus said to them, "Very truly, I tell you, it was not Moses who gave you the bread from heaven, but it is my Father who gives you the true bread from heaven. For the bread of God is that which comes down from heaven and gives life to the world." They said to him, "Sir, give us this bread always." Jesus said to them, "I am the bread of life. Whoever comes to me will never be hungry, and whoever believes in me will never be thirsty."

- The people were sure about what they wanted and clear about how God had worked in the past; they had a template and they wanted to see whether Jesus fit it. We sometimes approach Jesus in the same way, asking for what we need, expecting a particular answer. Jesus wants to open our hearts to receive what God is offering; we need to open our eyes to recognize it.

- Jesus, be for me the bread of life. I ask each day for my "daily bread," for what sustains me. Help me, God, to notice where nourishment is to be found, to savor it because it comes from you, and to share it generously with those in need.

Wednesday 13th April

John 6:35–40

Jesus said to them, "I am the bread of life. Whoever comes to me will never be hungry, and whoever believes in me will never be thirsty. But

I said to you that you have seen me and yet do not believe. Everything that the Father gives me will come to me, and anyone who comes to me I will never drive away; for I have come down from heaven, not to do my own will, but the will of him who sent me. And this is the will of him who sent me, that I should lose nothing of all that he has given me, but raise it up on the last day. This is indeed the will of my Father, that all who see the Son and believe in him may have eternal life; and I will raise them up on the last day."

- It is not unusual nowadays for bread to be presented as "artisan," "craft," or "specialty" or for people to make lifestyle choices to avoid it; it ceases to be a humble food when given such attention. When Jesus speaks about bread, he is not speaking about selection and preference; he is asking us to identify our essential nourishment and to recognize that it lies in him. Our prayer helps us to know what we really need and to recognize God as its source. We look beyond our preferences and selections, our comforts and wants, and, learning what we really need, trust in God to feed us and lead us into life.

- Many people today are searching for God. They need signs to know where God is. Am I such a sign in any way? We need not look in the sky for signs: Jesus himself is the sign we need, and he is close. He feeds me with his own life. Do I nourish others?

Thursday 14th April

John 6:44–51

Jesus said, "No one can come to me unless drawn by the Father who sent me; and I will raise that person up on the last day. It is written in the prophets, 'And they shall all be taught by God.' Everyone who has heard and learned from the Father comes to me. Not that anyone has seen the Father except the one who is from God; he has seen the Father. Very truly, I tell you, whoever believes has eternal life. I am the bread of life. Your ancestors ate the manna in the wilderness, and they died. This is the bread that comes down from heaven, so that one may eat of it and not die. I am the living bread that came down from heaven.

Whoever eats of this bread will live forever; and the bread that I will give for the life of the world is my flesh."

- When Jesus talks about "living water" and, now, "living bread," he encourages us to think about lasting sources of life and nourishment. Recall the question of the prophet Isaiah (55:2) when he reminds us not to spend our money or efforts on what is of passing value. Help me, Lord, to look with honesty at how I spend my resources and energies.

- Our prayer is not our own initiative but is itself a response to God, who draws us. We're invited to leave home so that we might learn and be drawn more fully into life.

Friday 15th April
John 6:52–59

The Jews then disputed among themselves, saying, "How can this man give us his flesh to eat?" So Jesus said to them, "Very truly, I tell you, unless you eat the flesh of the Son of Man and drink his blood, you have no life in you. Those who eat my flesh and drink my blood have eternal life, and I will raise them up on the last day; for my flesh is true food and my blood is true drink. Those who eat my flesh and drink my blood abide in me, and I in them. Just as the living Father sent me, and I live because of the Father, so whoever eats me will live because of me. This is the bread that came down from heaven, not like that which your ancestors ate, and they died. But the one who eats this bread will live forever." He said these things while he was teaching in the synagogue at Capernaum.

- Jesus did not want the people simply to agree with him, to assent to his ideas. He wanted them to be drawn fully into the life of God, just as he was. He invites us to be consumed by God, to let go of our reservations and hesitations and trust in the one who gives life.

- John tells us that Jesus' words created acrimony, setting the people against each other. But Jesus was resolute: sharing in the life of God is not a part-time or trivial thing; God wants nothing less than to give us eternal life.

Saturday 16th April
John 6:60–69

When many of his disciples heard it, they said, "This teaching is difficult; who can accept it?" But Jesus, being aware that his disciples were complaining about it, said to them, "Does this offend you? Then what if you were to see the Son of Man ascending to where he was before? It is the spirit that gives life; the flesh is useless. The words that I have spoken to you are spirit and life. But among you there are some who do not believe." For Jesus knew from the first who were the ones that did not believe, and who was the one that would betray him. And he said, "For this reason I have told you that no one can come to me unless it is granted by the Father." Because of this many of his disciples turned back and no longer went about with him. So Jesus asked the twelve, "Do you also wish to go away?" Simon Peter answered him, "Lord, to whom can we go? You have the words of eternal life. We have come to believe and know that you are the Holy One of God."

- Jesus seems ready to let the disciples go: he respects their freedom and lets them choose. I am here, praying not only through my own choice but through the grace of God, who desires to open my mind and heart. My discipleship is God's doing; it's not for me to arrange just as I want.

- Peter finds that Jesus' words are "words of eternal life." What does this mean? A new and better world is opening up for him, the world of God. He is beginning to see things as Jesus sees them. He is learning to love people as Jesus loves them. His dull, predictable life is becoming fresh, surprising, and hopeful because of Jesus. And my life—what is happening for me?

April 17—April 23

Something to think and pray about each day this week:

Meeting God Within

When people succeed in coming home to themselves and glimpsing their own inner beauty, something amazing happens: they are blessed with a real compassion for who they themselves are, in all their vulnerability.

This compassion in turn carves out a space where they can welcome God into their hearts. It is as if they must first become aware of the marvel of themselves, and only then are they ready to get in touch with the wonder of God. Their new relationship with themselves ushers in a nourishing friendship with the One who has always been calling them.

This journey inward does not take place overnight. Although the heart is only fifteen inches from the head, it can take us years to arrive at our emotional core. I used to imagine that God didn't particularly like the world because it wasn't spiritual enough. Only later did it dawn on me that God had created the world in love and had passionately left clues to this fact everywhere. The persons and events of my daily life were already signs of God. Had I paid compassionate attention to my longings and my joys, I would have heard in them the symphony of God's own infinite joy. To find God I did not have to leave the world but to come home to it—and to myself—and God would be there, waiting for me.

The Presence of God
I stand at the door and knock, says the Lord. What a wonderful privilege that the Lord of all creation desires to come to me. I welcome his presence.

Freedom
Lord, grant me the grace to be free from the excesses of this life. Let me not get caught up with the desire for wealth. Keep my heart and mind free to love and serve you.

Consciousness
To be conscious about something is to be aware of it. Dear Lord, help me to remember that you gave me life. Thank you for the gift of life. Teach me to slow down, to be still, and to enjoy the pleasures created for me. To be aware of the beauty that surrounds me. The marvel of mountains, the calmness of lakes, the fragility of a flower petal. I need to remember that all these things come from you.

The Word
I take my time to read the Word of God slowly, a few times, allowing myself to dwell on anything that strikes me. (Please turn to the Scripture on the following pages. Inspiration points are provided should you need them. When you are ready, return here to continue.)

Conversation
How has God's Word moved me? Has it left me cold? Has it consoled me or moved me to act in a new way? I imagine Jesus standing or sitting beside me. I turn and share my feelings with him.

Conclusion
Glory be to the Father, and to the Son, and to the Holy Spirit, as it was in the beginning, is now and ever shall be, world without end. Amen.

Sunday 17th April
Fourth Sunday of Easter
John 10:27–30

Jesus said, "My sheep hear my voice. I know them, and they follow me. I give them eternal life, and they will never perish. No one will snatch them out of my hand. What my Father has given me is greater than all else, and no one can snatch it out of the Father's hand. The Father and I are one."

• Those who identify with Jesus hear his voice and come to know and trust in him. They follow in love, wanting only to be in relationship with him.

• Lord, thank you that you always know me. I am forever held in your hands in a deep and intimate relationship. I pray for those sick folk who no longer recognize the ones they loved, and for those who care for them. Be their Good Shepherd in their valley of darkness.

Monday 18th April
John 10:1–10

Jesus said, "Very truly, I tell you, anyone who does not enter the sheepfold by the gate but climbs in by another way is a thief and a bandit. The one who enters by the gate is the shepherd of the sheep. The gatekeeper opens the gate for him, and the sheep hear his voice. He calls his own sheep by name and leads them out. When he has brought out all his own, he goes ahead of them, and the sheep follow him because they know his voice. They will not follow a stranger, but they will run from him because they do not know the voice of strangers." Jesus used this figure of speech with them, but they did not understand what he was saying to them. So again Jesus said to them, "Very truly, I tell you, I am the gate for the sheep. All who came before me are thieves and bandits; but the sheep did not listen to them. I am the gate. Whoever enters by me will be saved, and will come in and go out and find pasture. The thief comes only to steal and kill and destroy. I came that they may have life, and have it abundantly."

- Our prayer trains us to recognize the voice of our Good Shepherd. We learn to distinguish the voice of the Lord from the other voices that appeal to us. Our cultures speak to us in authoritative ways: advertisers do everything they can to make their message compelling, and national identities flatter and appeal to us. It is easy for us to be lured away to another flock.

- Tone of voice makes all the difference. Truth can be offered in a way that invites, or it can be heard as being harsh and unwelcome. I consider how Jesus speaks to me, calling me to growth and life. Is this how I speak to others? To myself?

Tuesday 19th April

John 10:22–30

It was the Feast of the Dedication at Jerusalem; it was winter, and Jesus was walking in the temple, in the portico of Solomon. So the Jews gathered round him and said to him, "How long will you keep us in suspense? If you are the Christ, tell us plainly." Jesus answered them, "I told you, and you do not believe. The works that I do in my Father's name, they bear witness to me; but you do not believe, because you do not belong to my sheep. My sheep hear my voice, and I know them, and they follow me; and I give them eternal life, and they shall never perish, and no one shall snatch them out of my hand. My Father, who has given them to me, is greater than all, and no one is able to snatch them out of the Father's hand. I and the Father are one."

- "If only we had more evidence!"—the cry of the people of Jesus' time is still heard today; perhaps we can hear it in ourselves. Our habits often prompt us to look for more, making it difficult to accept that we have enough. Coming before God in this time of prayer, I thank God for what I have been given and ask only that I recognize where God seeks to be present in my life.

- The more I claim and the more I search for, the less I can realize how much I have. If I am able to say that what I have is enough, I may be better able to recognize the voice of Jesus; if I find myself saying that I have nothing, I pray that I am better able to allow God to give me what I need.

Wednesday 20th April

John 12:44–50

Jesus cried aloud, "Whoever believes in me believes not in me but in him who sent me. And whoever sees me sees him who sent me. I have come as light into the world, so that everyone who believes in me should not remain in the darkness. I do not judge anyone who hears my words and does not keep them, for I came not to judge the world, but to save the world. The one who rejects me and does not receive my word has a judge; on the last day the word that I have spoken will serve as judge, for I have not spoken on my own, but the Father who sent me has himself given me a commandment about what to say and what to speak. And I know that his commandment is eternal life. What I speak, therefore, I speak just as the Father has told me."

- The struggle between the powers of light and darkness dominates John's Gospel. Jesus' mission is clear. He has come from the Father, bearing the light of his love, revealed by word and deed. Those who receive him walk in this light. Those who reject him stumble around in the darkness and experience lostness.

- Lord, your one desire is that I make my home in you and live in the Light. Shine in the dark recesses of my heart and bring me and all others to the fullness of life that you offer us.

Thursday 21st April

John 13:16–20

"Very truly, I tell you, servants[a] are not greater than their master, nor are messengers greater than the one who sent them. If you know these things, you are blessed if you do them. I am not speaking of all of you; I know whom I have chosen. But it is to fulfil the scripture, 'The one who ate my bread[b] has lifted his heel against me.' I tell you this now, before it occurs, so that when it does occur, you may believe that I am he. Very truly, I tell you, whoever receives one whom I send receives me; and whoever receives me receives him who sent me."

- This is the light of God shining through the serving love of Jesus. When we allow ourselves be served by God, we are bathed in humble and bright light. The light which Jesus shone through his life is now ours to share. Without his disciples now, the light of God will be dim if not extinguished. Light of Christ, enlighten me, enlighten the world.

- When Jesus asks me to remember who I am, it is not to scold or reproach me but to help me not to be overburdened. I pray for the humility I need to remember that, though I am Jesus' servant and messenger, he also calls me friend and counts me among his beloved.

Friday 22nd April
John 14:1–6

Jesus said to the disciples, "Do not let your hearts be troubled. Believe in God, believe also in me. In my Father's house there are many dwelling places. If it were not so, would I have told you that I go to prepare a place for you? And if I go and prepare a place for you, I will come again and will take you to myself, so that where I am, there you may be also. And you know the way to the place where I am going." Thomas said to him, "Lord, we do not know where you are going. How can we know the way?" Jesus said to him, "I am the way, and the truth, and the life. No one comes to the Father except through me."

- Perhaps I am sometimes like Thomas: asking my question of Jesus while thinking that I am to be left on my own to work things out. Lord, help me to listen to your promises, to receive your assurances, to let you remove troubles from my heart. May I bear in mind that you are with me.

- That matters a lot to me, Lord. So many of my friends would not feel at ease in heaven's guest bedroom. They just hope they can fit in somewhere. The suicidal, the thieves, the sexually deviant, the pilloried—all count on your mercy to find a place for them, no matter how dirty they feel. Any room will do as long as it is heaven and you are there.

Saturday 23rd April

John 14:7–14

Jesus said to Thomas, "If you know me, you will know my Father also. From now on you do know him and have seen him." Philip said to him, "Lord, show us the Father, and we will be satisfied." Jesus said to him, "Have I been with you all this time, Philip, and you still do not know me? Whoever has seen me has seen the Father. How can you say, 'Show us the Father'? Do you not believe that I am in the Father and the Father is in me? The words that I say to you I do not speak on my own; but the Father who dwells in me does his works. Believe me that I am in the Father and the Father is in me; but if you do not, then believe me because of the works themselves. Very truly, I tell you, the one who believes in me will also do the works that I do and, in fact, will do greater works than these, because I am going to the Father. I will do whatever you ask in my name, so that the Father may be glorified in the Son. If in my name you ask me for anything, I will do it."

- It is consoling to think that even Jesus' closest friends failed to understand him. He is endlessly patient. He explains again and again until we catch on. He is always ready to speak to us in prayer.

- The gentle voice of God can speak to us in many ways: through friends and strangers and through the voice of conscience within ourselves. Am I open to these channels?

April 24—April 30

Something to think and pray about each day this week:

What Makes God Love Us?

It is good to be law-abiding and dependable—but it is bad to think that this makes God love us! Why so? Because Jesus shows us something totally different, and we need again and again to be shocked by God's upside-down ways of viewing things. Jesus reveals God's strange point of view by associating with the rejects and the despised of his society. The poor, the sick, the possessed, and the displaced are his table companions. So, too, are women, tax collectors, and prostitutes. Add in for good measure the "accursed crowd" who don't know the law (John 7:49), and you have a thoroughly disreputable bunch!

But these are in fact the associates of the Son of God. God's heart is drawn first to those at the bottom of the human pyramid, so Jesus has his eye out for them first. This means that God seems to love people just as they are, in all their inadequacy and brokenness. We don't earn God's love, because we don't have to! We are already totally loved. This leaves the law-abiding and dependable at a loss until they see that divine love is never merited. They are then challenged to abandon their self-sufficiency and to respond gratefully to this gratuitous love. They must then love their unlovable neighbor in the same way as God loves them. This, says God, is my best plan for the transformation of human society!

The Presence of God
The more we call on God, the more we can feel God's presence. Day by day we are drawn closer to the loving heart of God.

Freedom
Many countries are at this moment suffering the agonies of war. I bow my head in thanksgiving for my freedom. I pray for all prisoners and captives.

Consciousness
Help me, Lord, to be more conscious of your presence. Teach me to recognize your presence in others. Fill my heart with gratitude for the times your love has been shown to me through the care of others.

The Word
The Word of God comes down to us through the Scriptures. May the Holy Spirit enlighten my mind and my heart to respond to the gospel teachings. (Please turn to the Scripture on the following pages. Inspiration points are provided should you need them. When you are ready, return here to continue.)

Conversation
Sometimes I wonder what I might say if I were to meet you in person, Lord. I think I might say, "Thank you, Lord" for always being there for me.

Conclusion
I thank God for these few moments we have spent alone together and for any insights I may have been given concerning the text.

Sunday 24th April
Fifth Sunday of Easter

John 13:31–33a, 34–35

When Judas had gone out, Jesus said, "Now the Son of Man has been glorified, and God has been glorified in him. If God has been glorified in him, God will also glorify him in himself and will glorify him at once. Little children, I am with you only a little longer. I give you a new commandment, that you love one another. Just as I have loved you, you also should love one another. By this everyone will know that you are my disciples, if you have love for one another."

- Right through his final meal, Jesus has been revealing the depth of his love for his disciples. Judas's heart, however, is coarsened by greed: he moves from light into shadow-land, into the night. Hate replaces love, and betrayal replaces committed friendship.

- Lord, like Judas, I can turn from you, lured by my own autonomous ways. In this place of prayer let me recline on your heart, as the beloved disciple did. May I thus be attuned to the very heartbeat of God and grow steadily in living in a loving mode.

Monday 25th April

Mark 16:15–20

Jesus said to the apostles, "Go into all the world and proclaim the good news to the whole creation. The one who believes and is baptized will be saved; but the one who does not believe will be condemned. And these signs will accompany those who believe: by using my name they will cast out demons; they will speak in new tongues; they will pick up snakes in their hands, and if they drink any deadly thing, it will not hurt them; they will lay their hands on the sick, and they will recover." So then the Lord Jesus, after he had spoken to them, was taken up into heaven and sat down at the right hand of God. And they went out and proclaimed the good news everywhere, while the Lord worked with them and confirmed the message by the signs that accompanied it.

- Believing is not a matter of the mind, nor is it something private and self-contained. The disciple is not asked to be self-confident but to be humble, remain in relationship, and be able to act in the name of Jesus.

- The marks of the disciples are many: they resist any diminishing spirit; are not confined by language; may be unafraid of what others prefer to avoid; and refuse to take in what poisons. If I hear myself intimidated, I am listening to the world; if I sense an invitation, I am listening for what Jesus asks of me.

Tuesday 26th April
John 14:27–31a

Jesus said to his disciples, "Peace I leave with you; my peace I give to you. I do not give to you as the world gives. Do not let your hearts be troubled, and do not let them be afraid. You heard me say to you, 'I am going away, and I am coming to you.' If you loved me, you would rejoice that I am going to the Father, because the Father is greater than I. And now I have told you this before it occurs, so that when it does occur, you may believe. I will no longer talk much with you, for the ruler of this world is coming. He has no power over me; but I do as the Father has commanded me, so that the world may know that I love the Father."

- The peace that Jesus gives is available to me; I have to do nothing to receive it. But maybe that's the problem—I want to do something to earn what Jesus offers as a free gift. Lord, help me to do nothing in this time of prayer but to be ready to receive what you offer.

- Jesus' farewell wish is "Peace!" His gift of peace is not a state, but a relationship. It is the fruit of deeply abiding in him. This relationship will never fail. It will enable the disciples to endure suffering and rejection. Lord, may my prayer shape me to be an instrument of your peace in a divided world. As I emerge from prayer each day, may I be more peace-filled than when I began.

Wednesday 27th April

John 15:1–8

Jesus said, "I am the true vine, and my Father is the vine-grower. He removes every branch in me that bears no fruit. Every branch that bears fruit he prunes to make it bear more fruit. You have already been cleansed by the word that I have spoken to you. Abide in me as I abide in you. Just as the branch cannot bear fruit by itself unless it abides in the vine, neither can you unless you abide in me. I am the vine, you are the branches. Those who abide in me and I in them bear much fruit, because apart from me you can do nothing. Whoever does not abide in me is thrown away like a branch and withers; such branches are gathered, thrown into the fire, and burned. If you abide in me, and my words abide in you, ask for whatever you wish, and it will be done for you. My Father is glorified by this, that you bear much fruit and become my disciples."

- Jesus invites me to "abide," to rest, to stay, to remain. Perhaps it is a challenge to me, as I would like to be active and doing. I take some time to realize how it is that I need to be connected with the very life of Jesus, to know the beating of his heart, to receive life from him just as a branch from the vine.

- Teach me, Lord Jesus, what it is to live in you and for you to live in me. It means being in love with you, being at ease with you, finding my strength in you, and being ready, when questioned, to explain to others what you are in my life.

Thursday 28th April

John 15:9–11

Jesus said to his disciples, "As the Father has loved me, so I have loved you; abide in my love. If you keep my commandments, you will abide in my love, just as I have kept my Father's commandments and abide in his love. I have said these things to you so that my joy may be in you, and that your joy may be complete."

- I take some time to think of Jesus' generosity: he loves me in the same way as the Father loves him. He is confident that I can be at home in his love. Can I doubt him?

- There are times when I seem to understand what this love means. Sometimes we can experience this love going through us, giving us joy in loving others. There is an energy in us that is not of our making. I think of one or two friends who radiate contentment; I think they are abiding in God's love and feeling joy from it. Lord, maybe you will one day surprise me with this joy.

Friday 29th April

John 15:12–17

Jesus said to his disciples, "This is my commandment, that you love one another as I have loved you. No one has greater love than this, to lay down one's life for one's friends. You are my friends if you do what I command you. I do not call you servants any longer, because the servant does not know what the master is doing; but I have called you friends, because I have made known to you everything that I have heard from my Father. You did not choose me but I chose you. And I appointed you to go and bear fruit, fruit that will last, so that the Father will give you whatever you ask him in my name. I am giving you these commands so that you may love one another."

- My focus now is not on my faith, on what I think or believe. Jesus invites me to accept what he believes about me, how he sees me to be. I am sent to bear fruit. I am trusted. I am loved.

- Jesus, my friend, in your company I can relax, be silent or talk, grumble or boast, complain or feel thankful and lighthearted. You know my heart and make allowances. I do not have to pretend.

Saturday 30th April

John 15:18–21

Jesus said to his disciples, "If the world hates you, be aware that it hated me before it hated you. If you belonged to the world, the world would love you as its own. Because you do not belong to the world, but I have chosen you out of the world—therefore the world hates you. Remember the word that I said to you, 'Servants are not greater than their master.' If they persecuted me, they will persecute you; if they kept my word, they will keep yours also. But they will do all these things to you on account of my name, because they do not know him who sent me."

- "Hate" may seem to be a strong word—to be overstating it a little. If everyone in my world is comfortable with me, could it be that my light has dimmed a little, that my salt has become less salty? I pray that I may know when any resistance I cause in others is from my being a disciple and when it is purely my own.

- When those in my world love me, I need to look hard at myself and remember that you, the most lovable of human beings, suffered hatred and execution. When people are giving me a hard time, it may well be that I am blessed.

May 1—May 7

Something to think and pray about each day this week:

A Vote of Confidence

The Jesus of the gospels was always surprising people. He constantly cut across expectations. He was never dull or bland. Someone recently expressed this well by saying that Jesus was "funny." She wasn't referring to his sense of humor but to the ways he disconcerted her and made her revise her own ways of looking at things. It is good for us to ask the Holy Spirit to help us to overcome our familiarity with the words and story of Jesus and to open us up daily to this surprising, disturbing, and captivating person. The gospel is like fresh bread for each day. Its freshness is a gift.

At the heart of the mystery of Jesus we find his unique relationship with God. He calls God "Father" or, even more intimately, "Abba." This relationship dominates his life. It is this experience of being totally loved by God that gives him the courage to set out on his public ministry. In preaching the kingdom of God, Jesus is inviting us to share in his special relationship with the Father. We are offered the extravagant gift of being children of God, just as we are.

Jesus fully accepted God's lavish love. It gave divine meaning to his life. It transformed everything he did and all that happened to him. When we live out of God's unconditional vote of confidence in us, everything changes, and our capacity for greatness is liberated.

The Presence of God

Lord, help me to be fully alive to your holy presence. Enfold me in your love. Let my heart become one with yours.

Freedom

Lord, you created me to live in freedom. Mostly I take this gift for granted. Inspire me to live in the freedom you intended, with a heart untroubled and with complete trust in you.

Consciousness

I ask how I am within myself today. Am I particularly tired, stressed, or off-form? If any of these characteristics apply, can I try to let go of the concerns that disturb me?

The Word

I read the Word of God slowly, a few times over, and I listen to what God is saying to me. (Please turn to the Scripture on the following pages. Inspiration points are provided should you need them. When you are ready, return here to continue.)

Conversation

What is stirring in me as I pray? Am I consoled, troubled, left cold? I imagine Jesus himself standing or sitting at my side, and I share my feelings with him.

Conclusion

Glory be to the Father, and to the Son, and to the Holy Spirit, as it was in the beginning, is now and ever shall be, world without end. Amen.

Sunday 1st May
Sixth Sunday of Easter
John 14:23–29

Jesus answered Judas (not Iscariot), "Those who love me will keep my word, and my Father will love them, and we will come to them and make our home with them. Whoever does not love me does not keep my words; and the word that you hear is not mine, but is from the Father who sent me. I have said these things to you while I am still with you. But the Advocate, the Holy Spirit, whom the Father will send in my name, will teach you everything, and remind you of all that I have said to you. Peace I leave with you; my peace I give to you. I do not give to you as the world gives. Do not let your hearts be troubled, and do not let them be afraid. You heard me say to you, 'I am going away, and I am coming to you.' If you loved me, you would rejoice that I am going to the Father, because the Father is greater than I. And now I have told you this before it occurs, so that when it does occur, you may believe."

- Jesus gently tries to prepare the disciples for the day when he will no longer be present to them in bodily form. Unlike us, who know the story, they did not know what was coming next, so they are confused. God helps us to grow even in times of confusion.

- Jesus is inviting his followers not to cling to his physical presence but to be open to a deeper way of being in relationship with him. Often we find it hard to let go and embrace the new. But in clinging to the past we are in danger of letting the present become dead to us.

Monday 2nd May
John 15:26—16:4a

Jesus said to the disciples, "When the Advocate comes, whom I will send to you from the Father, the Spirit of truth who comes from the Father, he will testify on my behalf. You also are to testify because you have been with me from the beginning. I have said these things to you to keep you from stumbling. They will put you out of the synagogues. Indeed, an hour is coming when those who kill you will think that by doing so they are offering worship to God. And they will do this because they have not known the Father or me. But I have said these things to you so that when their hour comes you may remember that I told you about them."

- The work of the Holy Spirit affirms the life and love of Jesus, giving witness to what is true. We, too, can give witness to how we see the Spirit of Jesus to be alive in our lives. What evidence do you see of the Spirit working in your life? Speak to God about it. Perhaps you can speak to people you trust, too.

- The Holy Spirit, the Counselor, does not operate as an alien intruder whispering surprising news into my ear. Rather he helps me to be myself and to learn from my experience. When Peter, James, and Paul, at the first council of Jerusalem, disagreed on whether to circumcise pagan converts, they resolved their arguments by reflecting on their experience; then they were able to conclude: it seems good to the Holy Spirit and to us.

Tuesday 3rd May
John 14:6–14

Jesus said to Thomas, "I am the way, and the truth, and the life. No one comes to the Father except through me. If you know me, you will know my Father also. From now on you do know him and have seen him." Philip said to him, "Lord, show us the Father, and we will be satisfied." Jesus said to him, "Have I been with you all this time, Philip, and you still do not know me? Whoever has seen me has seen the Father. How can you say, 'Show us the Father'? Do you not believe that I am in the Father and the Father is in me? The words that I say to you I do not speak on my own; but the Father who dwells in me does his works. Believe me that I am in the Father and the Father is in me; but if you do not, then believe me because of the works themselves. Very truly, I tell you, the one who believes in me will also do the works that I do and, in fact, will do greater works than these, because I am going to the Father. I will do whatever you ask in my name, so that the Father may be glorified in the Son. If in my name you ask me for anything, I will do it."

- How can we do greater works than Jesus did? Over the centuries, filled with the desire to heal and make the world a better place, we have mastered diseases, combated famine, tamed the flooding of rivers, and built alliances like the United Nations to make peace more possible. Lord, let me continue your work, filled with your Spirit.

- Can I see myself in Philip? One more thing and I will be satisfied. Jesus reminds him and me that we have enough already. Jesus and the Father are so united that I am drawn into the knowledge and love of God as I come to know and love Jesus. Jesus desires nothing less for me; he wishes to draw me deeply into the very life of God.

Wednesday 4th May

John 16:12–15

Jesus said, "I still have many things to say to you, but you cannot bear them now. When the Spirit of truth comes, he will guide you into all the truth; for he will not speak on his own, but will speak whatever he hears, and he will declare to you the things that are to come. He will glorify me, because he will take what is mine and declare it to you. All that the Father has is mine. For this reason I said that he will take what is mine and declare it to you."

- Jesus still speaks to us: prayer helps us to grow in love, in friendship, in understanding of the ways of God. The Spirit assists us, mediating God's message, helping us to recognize how our way of living conforms to what God asks of us, and revealing how it does not. Lord, strengthen my ability to receive and listen to your Spirit, to remember that your Spirit speaks your word to me.

- "You cannot bear them now," you said. Lord, you time your interventions for my readiness. They that wait upon you shall renew their strength, says the prophet Isaiah. May I learn how to wait upon you.

Thursday 5th May
The Ascension of the Lord
Luke 24:46–53

Jesus said to his disciples, "Thus it is written, that the Messiah is to suffer and to rise from the dead on the third day, and that repentance and forgiveness of sins is to be proclaimed in his name to all nations, beginning from Jerusalem. You are witnesses of these things. And see, I am sending upon you what my Father promised; so stay here in the city until you have been clothed with power from on high." Then he led them out as far as Bethany, and, lifting up his hands, he blessed them. While he was blessing them, he withdrew from them and was carried up into heaven. And they worshipped him, and returned to Jerusalem with great joy; and they were continually in the temple blessing God.

- Jesus connects what has happened to him to the Old Testament prophecies. Thus, hundreds of years on, God's promise is fulfilled. God's time is not always our time.

- The disciples experienced "great joy" when Jesus blessed them and moved fully into the divine dimension of reality—heaven. Such moments of insight and pure joy are rare but precious for us. While they eventually become dim, their memory can carry us through difficult times. Can I identify one such moment of "great joy"?

Friday 6th May
John 16:20–23

Jesus said to his disciples, "Very truly, I tell you, you will weep and mourn, but the world will rejoice; you will have pain, but your pain will turn into joy. When a woman is in labor, she has pain, because her hour has come. But when her child is born, she no longer remembers the anguish because of the joy of having brought a human being into the world. So you have pain now; but I will see you again, and your hearts will rejoice, and no one will take your joy from you. On that day you will ask nothing of me. Very truly, I tell you, if you ask anything of the Father in my name, he will give it to you."

- Jesus speaks of pain that turned to joy and invites the disciples to be patient, as he was. He is not talking about an empty waiting but sees an opportunity to grow in trust, to deepen our relationship with our loving God.

- "When a woman is in labor she has pain." Jesus reminds us today of the price that mothers pay for their children. There was a time when I was a helpless embryo in my mother's womb. For those heavy months my mother was not merely carrying my growing weight but concerned about how her life and behavior would affect my health. Then she faced the acute pain, which males can hardly imagine, of bringing me into the world; and she continued to feed me and stay on 24-hour duty to watch my breathing and well-being. Let me never take for granted the price that has been paid for my existence.

Saturday 7th May

John 16:23b–28

Jesus said to his disciples, "Very truly, I tell you, if you ask anything of the Father in my name, he will give it to you. Until now you have not asked for anything in my name. Ask and you will receive, so that your joy may be complete. I have said these things to you in figures of speech. The hour is coming when I will no longer speak to you in figures, but will tell you plainly of the Father. On that day you will ask in my name. I do not say to you that I will ask the Father on your behalf; for the Father himself loves you, because you have loved me and have believed that I came from God. I came from the Father and have come into the world; again, I am leaving the world and am going to the Father."

- Asking God for something in Jesus' name is different from asking in our own name. We are to include him in our decision-making and try to see things the way he does. When we do this we transcend ourselves; we are open to the will of God. God may not give us exactly what we ask, but he will never fail to give us what we need.

- Jesus speaks easily of coming from the Father and into the world and of leaving the world again to go to the Father. Do I have some sense of the Father being lovingly with me throughout my life, as he will be in the world to come?

The Seventh Week of Easter
May 8—May 14

Something to think and pray about each day this week:

Available to God

How do you feel about the time you dedicate to prayer? Do you feel that you are doing all the work but getting nowhere? Here your image of prayer can help or hinder you. If you have an unbalanced image, you may decide that the time "wasted in prayer" could be better used in reading a holy book or doing good somewhere. Thus you give up on prayer. Since God has his own image of what prayer is about, it helps if you can catch on to it. This will help you to cooperate better with the Holy Spirit, who is at work in you.

There is an old Latin tag for an extended time of prayer such as a retreat: *vacatio Deo*. It means idleness for God, emptiness before God, a vacation or holiday with God. The time you spend in prayer is time not spent doing something useful for yourself.

Prayer is not useful; it is of a different order. To set aside time for personal prayer, you come away from your usual preoccupations so as to be in some respect empty, idle, available to God. What you bring to prayer is yourself, your time, and your desire to be with God. You come with your openness to be slowly transformed by the Spirit.

The Presence of God

Dear Jesus, I come to you today longing for your presence. I desire to love you as you love me. May nothing ever separate me from you.

Freedom

I am free. When I look at these words in writing they seem to create in me a feeling of awe. Yes, a wonderful feeling of freedom. Thank you, God.

Consciousness

At this moment, Lord, I turn my thoughts to you. I will set aside my chores and preoccupations. I will take rest and refreshment in your presence, Lord.

The Word

God speaks to each one of us individually. I listen attentively to hear what he is saying to me. Read the text a few times, then listen. (Please turn to the Scripture on the following pages. Inspiration points are provided should you need them. When you are ready, return here to continue.)

Conversation

What feelings are rising in me as I pray and reflect on God's Word? I imagine Jesus himself sitting or standing near me, and I open my heart to him.

Conclusion

I thank God for these few moments we have spent alone together and for any insights I may have been given concerning the text.

Sunday 8th May
Seventh Sunday of Easter
John 17:20–26

Jesus prayed, "I ask not only on behalf of these, but also on behalf of those who will believe in me through their word, that they may all be one. As you, Father, are in me and I am in you, may they also be in us, so that the world may believe that you have sent me. The glory that you have given me I have given them, so that they may be one, as we are one, I in them and you in me, that they may become completely one, so that the world may know that you have sent me and have loved them even as you have loved me. Father, I desire that those also, whom you have given me, may be with me where I am, to see my glory, which you have given me because you loved me before the foundation of the world. Righteous Father, the world does not know you, but I know you; and these know that you have sent me. I made your name known to them, and I will make it known, so that the love with which you have loved me may be in them, and I in them."

- Jesus is praying for me! I am one of those who believe through the word handed on over the years, person to person in an unbroken chain. I take my place in that honorable line and ask that I may pass on the word in all its truth, remembering that it comes from Jesus.

- That Jesus was and is the Son of God is the underlying theme in the Gospel of St. John. In turn, Jesus calls us to oneness with each other and with God.

Monday 9th May
John 16:29–33

Jesus' disciples said, "Yes, now you are speaking plainly, not in any figure of speech! Now we know that you know all things, and do not need to have anyone question you; by this we believe that you came from God." Jesus answered them, "Do you now believe? The hour is coming, indeed it has come, when you will be scattered, each one to his home, and you will leave me alone. Yet I am not alone because the

Father is with me. I have said this to you, so that in me you may have peace. In the world you face persecution. But take courage; I have conquered the world!"

- Despite the many ways in which we are digitally connected with one another, it is easy for people to feel alone. Jesus knew that he was in relationship with his Father and drew strength from this. He invites us into the same relationship!

- Peace and courage are two gifts that Jesus wants to leave with us. Peace comes from knowing that he will be with us always. Courage comes from knowing that when we try to live in the light of the gospel, God's strength will shine out through our human weakness (2 Corinthians 12:9). In what areas of my life do I need peace and courage at the present time?

Tuesday 10th May

John 17:1–11a

After Jesus had spoken these words, he looked up to heaven and said, "Father, the hour has come; glorify your Son so that the Son may glorify you, since you have given him authority over all people, to give eternal life to all whom you have given him. And this is eternal life, that they may know you, the only true God, and Jesus Christ whom you have sent. I glorified you on earth by finishing the work that you gave me to do. So now, Father, glorify me in your own presence with the glory that I had in your presence before the world existed. I have made your name known to those whom you gave me from the world. They were yours, and you gave them to me, and they have kept your word. Now they know that everything you have given me is from you; for the words that you gave to me I have given to them, and they have received them and know in truth that I came from you; and they have believed that you sent me. I am asking on their behalf; I am not asking on behalf of the world, but on behalf of those whom you gave me, because they are yours. All mine are yours, and yours are mine; and I have been glorified in them. And now I am no longer in the world, but they are in the world, and I am coming to you."

- This is eternal life, to know the one true God and Jesus Christ whom God has sent. Islam, too, knows Allah as the one true God and recognizes Jesus as sent by God. All our life we struggle to know him through words and parables and through the world that he has entrusted to us. At no stage can we say that we understand God. Saint Augustine wrote: "God is not what you imagine or think you understand. If you understand him, you have failed." My human mission is to seek him through every means and to remain a God-seeker until the day when he reveals himself to me face to face.

- Lord, I relax my body, quiet my mind, and focus on my breathing. Then I seek you there, in the silence.

Wednesday 11th May

John 17:11b–19

Jesus prayed, "Holy Father, protect them in your name that you have given me, so that they may be one, as we are one. While I was with them, I protected them in your name that you have given me. I guarded them, and not one of them was lost except the one destined to be lost, so that the Scripture might be fulfilled. But now I am coming to you, and I speak these things in the world so that they may have my joy made complete in themselves. I have given them your word, and the world has hated them because they do not belong to the world, just as I do not belong to the world. I am not asking you to take them out of the world, but I ask you to protect them from the evil one. They do not belong to the world, just as I do not belong to the world. Sanctify them in the truth; your word is truth. As you have sent me into the world, so I have sent them into the world. And for their sakes I sanctify myself, so that they also may be sanctified in truth."

- Jesus' love for his disciples does not fade. It endures eternally. He asks the Father to protect and guide them. He entrusts us, his friends and companions, to the loving care of his Father.

- Parents and guardians spend their best years guiding children in life and in faith. Then there is a gradual letting go as they grow into adulthood. Like Jesus we should pray for those who move beyond our active care. The Father's arms are a safe place for them.

Thursday 12th May

John 17:20–26

Jesus prayed, "I ask not only on behalf of these, but also on behalf of those who will believe in me through their word, that they may all be one. As you, Father, are in me and I am in you, may they also be in us, so that the world may believe that you have sent me. The glory that you have given me I have given them, so that they may be one, as we are one, I in them and you in me, that they may become completely one, so that the world may know that you have sent me and have loved them even as you have loved me. Father, I desire that those also, whom you have given me, may be with me where I am, to see my glory, which you have given me because you loved me before the foundation of the world. Righteous Father, the world does not know you, but I know you; and these know that you have sent me. I made your name known to them, and I will make it known, so that the love with which you have loved me may be in them, and I in them."

- Lord, I treasure all the chances of fellowship with others who do not believe in you. When I work or talk with them, or love them, or serve or pray with them, your grace is at work in us. These occasions may not be labeled "ecumenical events," but they carry your blessing.

- Jesus' second prayer at the Last Supper is for future generations of believers, including ourselves. His prayer is that all of us will be united with God our Father and with him. He is to share with all of us what is deepest in his heart—the glory he had from the beginning of time. Love wants to share all that is best with the beloved.

Friday 13th May

John 21:15–19

When they had finished breakfast, Jesus said to Simon Peter, "Simon son of John, do you love me more than these?" He said to him, "Yes, Lord; you know that I love you." Jesus said to him, "Feed my lambs." A second time he said to him, "Simon son of John, do you love me?" He said to him, "Yes, Lord; you know that I love you." Jesus said to him, "Tend my sheep." He said to him the third time, "Simon son of John, do you love me?" Peter felt hurt because he said to him the third time, "Do you love me?" And he said to him, "Lord, you know everything; you know that I love you." Jesus said to him, "Feed my sheep. Very truly, I tell you, when you were younger, you used to fasten your own belt and to go wherever you wished. But when you grow old, you will stretch out your hands, and someone else will fasten a belt around you and take you where you do not wish to go." (He said this to indicate the kind of death by which he would glorify God.) After this he said to him, "Follow me."

- Peter, despite his failings, is chosen to continue the ministry of Jesus by humble service to others. Jesus gives me a ministry of service also. Am I aware of it? Do I carry it out even if it means pain?

- What answer do I give when, like Peter, I am questioned regarding the extent of my love for Jesus? Can I at least say, "You know that I try to love you."

Saturday 14th May

John 15:9–17

Jesus said to his disciples, "As the Father has loved me, so I have loved you; abide in my love. If you keep my commandments, you will abide in my love, just as I have kept my Father's commandments and abide in his love. I have said these things to you so that my joy may be in you, and that your joy may be complete. This is my commandment, that you love one another as I have loved you. No one has greater love than this, to lay down one's life for one's friends. You are my friends if you do what I command you. I do not call you servants any longer, because the servant does not know what the master is doing; but I have called you friends, because I have made known to you everything that I have heard from my Father. You did not choose me but I chose you. And I appointed you to go and bear fruit, fruit that will last, so that the Father will give you whatever you ask him in my name. I am giving you these commands so that you may love one another."

- "You did not choose me but I chose you." Jesus' choosing of me gives me a sense of my place in the world, a sense of purpose. What fruit am I called on to bear?

- To love one another as Jesus has loved us, we need first to allow ourselves to experience Jesus' love. I can love myself because I am the beloved of God (Romans 1:7)!

May 15—May 21

Something to think and pray about each day this week:

Babylon
In the Christian Scriptures, Babylon is a godless construction that tries to reach to the skies and displace God. Today the term can stand for a widespread culture that is seductive and glamorous but unreal and unsatisfying. It is superficial and one-dimensional. Instead of fostering healthy imagination, it limits and prepackages it. Thus advertisements tell us what to eat and drink, what to do, and what to wear. Babylon impoverishes us. It cuts us off from many enriching dimensions of human life. It imprisons the spark that is within us, the soul that is invisible, intelligent, free, and immortal.

The churches are not safe from this culture. In the United States today, there are 22 million ex-Catholics. Their overriding reason for leaving their church is that their spiritual needs were not being met. The task of the churches is to rediscover the riches of faith, for God has bigger hopes for us than Babylon could ever entertain. God offers us an undreamt-of gift, conveyed to us by his Son. We live in an open-ended world where we can risk becoming who we really are: persons who can love without limits. We need then to cultivate our Christian imagination carefully.

The Presence of God

I pause for a moment and reflect on God's life-giving presence in every part of my body, in everything around me, in the whole of my life. I remind myself that I am in your presence, O Lord. I will take refuge in your loving heart. You are my strength in times of weakness. You are my comforter in times of sorrow.

Freedom

Lord, you gave me life and the gift of freedom. Through your love I exist in this world. May I never take the gift of life for granted. May I always respect the right to life of others.

Consciousness

How do I find myself today? Where am I with God? With others? Do I have something to be grateful for? Then I give thanks. Is there something I am sorry for? Then I ask forgiveness.

The Word

I take my time to read the Word of God slowly, a few times, allowing myself to dwell on anything that strikes me. (Please turn to the Scripture on the following pages. Inspiration points are provided should you need them. When you are ready, return here to continue.)

Conversation

Conversation requires talking and listening. As I talk to Jesus may I also learn to be still and listen. I picture the gentleness in his eyes and the smile full of love as he gazes on me. I can be totally honest with Jesus as I tell him of my worries and my cares. I will open up my heart to him as I tell him of my fears and my doubts. I will ask him to help me to place myself fully in his care, to abandon myself to him, knowing that he always wants what is best for me.

Conclusion

Glory be to the Father, and to the Son, and to the Holy Spirit, as it was in the beginning, is now and ever shall be, world without end. Amen.

Sunday 15th May
Pentecost Sunday
John 20:19–23

When it was evening on that day, the first day of the week, and the doors of the house where the disciples had met were locked for fear of the Jews, Jesus came and stood among them and said, "Peace be with you." After he said this, he showed them his hands and his side. Then the disciples rejoiced when they saw the Lord. Jesus said to them again, "Peace be with you. As the Father has sent me, so I send you." When he had said this, he breathed on them and said to them, "Receive the Holy Spirit. If you forgive the sins of any, they are forgiven them; if you retain the sins of any, they are retained."

• Let me take time to be still, to wait on the Lord, to realize that Jesus approaches me as he did the disciples, wishing me peace. I hear him say, "Peace be with you." I notice my reactions, my protests. I see, too, where I am able to receive his gift of God's Spirit and pray that I may pass these gifts freely to others.

• The risen Jesus penetrates the disciples' defenses, overcomes their fears, and brings them joy. I ask him to pass through all my security systems and liberate me from whatever prevents me from "having life and having it in all its fullness."

Monday 16th May
Mark 9:14–29

When they came to the disciples, they saw a great crowd around them, and some scribes arguing with them. When the crowd saw Jesus, they were immediately overcome with awe, and they ran forward to greet him. He asked them, "What are you arguing about with them?" Someone from the crowd answered him, "Teacher, I brought you my son; he has a spirit that makes him unable to speak; and whenever it seizes him, it dashes him down; and he foams and grinds his teeth and becomes rigid; and I asked your disciples to cast it out, but they could not do so." He answered them, "You faithless generation, how much longer must I be among you? How much longer must I put up with you? Bring him to me." And they brought the boy to him. When the spirit saw him, immediately it threw the boy into convulsions, and he fell on the ground and rolled about, foaming at the mouth. Jesus asked the father, "How long has this been happening to him?" And he said, "From childhood. It has often cast him into the fire and into the water, to destroy him; but if you are able to do anything, have pity on us and help us." Jesus said to him, "If you are able!—All things can be done for the one who believes." Immediately the father of the child cried out, "I believe; help my unbelief!" When Jesus saw that a crowd came running together, he rebuked the unclean spirit, saying to it, "You spirit that keeps this boy from speaking and hearing, I command you, come out of him, and never enter him again!" After crying out and convulsing him terribly, it came out, and the boy was like a corpse, so that most of them said, "He is dead." But Jesus took him by the hand and lifted him up, and he was able to stand. When he had entered the house, his disciples asked him privately, "Why could we not cast it out?" He said to them, "This kind can come out only through prayer."

- Imagine this scene; notice the hubbub and commotion of the crowd. There seems to be much argument, dispute, and exclamation—but little wisdom. What Jesus says needs to be taken into each heart, one by one. I take this time of prayer to stand apart from "the crowd," to listen to Jesus, who speaks to my heart.

- The last words of the father in this story have been a common prayer for so many people. We are a mixture of faith and unbelief. We pray from a combination of faith and doubt, on days when faith is dry and prayer seems useless. We can ask for help; we know we cannot exist on unbelief. In prayer we come as we are, with different levels of faith, and pray for help. When we pray we are heard. Cardinal John Henry Newman prayed, "The night is dark and I am far from home, lead thou me on."

Tuesday 17th May
Mark 9:30–37

Jesus and the disciples went on from there and passed through Galilee. He did not want anyone to know it; for he was teaching his disciples, saying to them, "The Son of Man is to be betrayed into human hands, and they will kill him, and three days after being killed, he will rise again." But they did not understand what he was saying and were afraid to ask him. Then they came to Capernaum; and when he was in the house he asked them, "What were you arguing about on the way?" But they were silent, for on the way they had argued with one another who was the greatest. He sat down, called the twelve, and said to them, "Whoever wants to be first must be last of all and servant of all." Then he took a little child and put it among them; and taking it in his arms, he said to them, "Whoever welcomes one such child in my name welcomes me, and whoever welcomes me welcomes not me but the one who sent me."

- In welcoming Jesus Christ into our lives, we welcome the Father and the Spirit. We welcome the Divine. With him we are part of a total world, spanning heaven and earth, reaching out to all of humanity. Prayer is part of that mystery. Prayer connects us to the links of heaven and earth. It links us also to all of humanity. When we pray we join the whole human race in their prayer to God, and we join Jesus in his prayer for us.

- God has chosen to be mysteriously close to the lowly—children, the poor, the outcast—and so to welcome them is to welcome God, and to be able to welcome the lowly means becoming humble yourself.

Wednesday 18th May
Mark 9:38–40

John said to Jesus, "Teacher, we saw someone casting out demons in your name, and we tried to stop him, because he was not following us." But Jesus said, "Do not stop him; for no one who does a deed of power in my name will be able soon afterward to speak evil of me. Whoever is not against us is for us."

- Jesus seems to be saying to the apostles, "It's not about you!" He points them to the good that is being done. Help me, Lord, not to think that those who agree with me are more favored in your sight.

- Gathering and belonging are important human needs, but Jesus shows us how we can lead ourselves astray. The reign of God is advanced wherever good is done, where truth is spoken, when love wins out. Lord, help me not to be narrow-minded or judgmental but to give thanks to you for all that is good.

Thursday 19th May
Mark 9:41–50

Jesus said to his disciples, "For truly I tell you, whoever gives you a cup of water to drink because you bear the name of Christ will by no means lose the reward. If any of you put a stumbling block before one of these little ones who believe in me, it would be better for you if a great millstone were hung around your neck and you were thrown into the sea. If your hand causes you to stumble, cut it off; it is better for you to enter life maimed than to have two hands and to go to hell, to the unquenchable fire. And if your foot causes you to stumble, cut it off; it is better for you to enter life lame than to have two feet and to be thrown into hell. And if your eye causes you to stumble, tear it out; it is better for you to enter the kingdom of God with one eye than to have two eyes and to be thrown into hell, where their worm never dies, and the fire is never quenched. For everyone will be salted with fire. Salt is good; but if salt has lost its saltiness, how can you season it? Have salt in yourselves, and be at peace with one another."

- "A cup of water . . ." Even in small actions, we contribute to shaping the society and civilization we live in.

- Have I ever placed a stumbling block before "one of these little ones" whom Jesus fiercely defends? I, too, am one of the "little ones," and he defends me as well.

Friday 20th May

Mark 10:1–12

Jesus left that place and went to the region of Judea and beyond the Jordan. And crowds again gathered around him; and, as was his custom, he again taught them. Some Pharisees came, and to test him they asked, "Is it lawful for a man to divorce his wife?" He answered them, "What did Moses command you?" They said, "Moses allowed a man to write a certificate of dismissal and to divorce her." But Jesus said to them, "Because of your hardness of heart he wrote this commandment for you. But from the beginning of creation, 'God made them male and female. For this reason a man shall leave his father and mother and be joined to his wife, and the two shall become one flesh.' So they are no longer two, but one flesh. Therefore what God has joined together, let no one separate." Then in the house the disciples asked him again about this matter. He said to them, "Whoever divorces his wife and marries another commits adultery against her; and if she divorces her husband and marries another, she commits adultery."

- Jesus sets out the ideal for marriage. He reminds us of what it is meant to be, even though, perhaps through no fault of our own, we may fail to live up to it. God is always lovingly present to the partners, even if through human weakness they have to part.

- Jesus denounces any hardness of heart that can bring about divorce. Spouses must not treat each other as worthless property to be discarded. They are called instead to a life of mutual respect and interdependence.

Saturday 21st May

Mark 10:13–16

People were bringing little children to Jesus in order that he might touch them; and the disciples spoke sternly to them. But when Jesus saw this, he was indignant and said to them, "Let the little children come to me; do not stop them; for it is to such as these that the kingdom of God belongs. Truly I tell you, whoever does not receive the kingdom of God as a little child will never enter it." And he took them up in his arms, laid his hands on them, and blessed them.

- The disciples were protective of Jesus, believing that they should decide who was worthy of his attention. In this time of prayer I let all my concerns come before God, being careful not to let through only the ones that I think presentable.

- Do I take the time to nourish and connect with my childlike qualities? This will help me retain a sense of wonder, awe, gratitude, and excitement in the small things of creation.

May 22—May 28

Something to think and pray about each day this week:

Searching for God

Imagine two little children looking up at the stars on a dark, clear night. One child says: "I bet you those stars are five miles away. . . ." The other says: "No, they're not—they're ten miles away." The first child says: "Don't be stupid. If they were ten miles away you wouldn't be able to see them."

We can laugh at the children. But we adults also disagree and fight and trash one another—over our contradictory understandings of God! These children are trying to express a truth on which they both agree, namely that the stars are a very, very long way away. Five miles or ten are hopelessly inadequate concepts to express how far away the stars really are. But they are the only concepts the children have, and they are doing their best to express a truth.

Likewise, God is beyond our understanding. But like the children, we, too, make the mistake of trying to "capture" God with our small minds. We claim that we know God while we think that everyone who disagrees with us is wrong. In fact we can never know God: we must only search for God. To search for God is to acknowledge that we have not found him yet. Were we to stop searching, we might start claiming that we have found him and that we now understand him fairly well. And then of course we would miss God, who is too big to understand.

The Presence of God

Dear Lord, as I come to you today, fill my heart and my whole being with the wonder of your presence. Help me to be open to you for this time as I put aside the cares of this world. Fill my mind with your peace, your love.

Freedom

I will ask God's help to be free from my own preoccupations, to be open to God in this time of prayer, and to come to know, love, and serve God more.

Consciousness

Where do I sense hope, encouragement, and growth areas in my life? By looking back over the last few months, I may be able to see which activities and occasions have produced rich fruit. If I do notice such areas, I will determine to give those areas both time and space in the future.

The Word

The Word of God comes down to us through the Scriptures. May the Holy Spirit enlighten my mind and my heart to respond to the gospel teachings. (Please turn to the Scripture on the following pages. Inspiration points are provided should you need them. When you are ready, return here to continue.)

Conversation

Jesus, you always welcomed little children when you walked on this earth. Teach me to have a childlike trust in you, to live in the knowledge that you will never abandon me.

Conclusion

I thank God for these few moments we have spent alone together and for any insights I may have been given concerning the text.

Sunday 22nd May
The Most Holy Trinity
John 16:12–15

Jesus said to his disciples, "I still have many things to say to you, but you cannot bear them now. When the Spirit of truth comes, he will guide you into all the truth; for he will not speak on his own, but will speak whatever he hears, and he will declare to you the things that are to come. He will glorify me, because he will take what is mine and declare it to you. All that the Father has is mine. For this reason I said that he will take what is mine and declare it to you."

• Jesus still speaks to us: prayer helps us to grow in love, in friendship, in understanding of the ways of God. The Spirit assists us, mediating God's message, helping us to recognize how our way of living conforms to what God asks of us and revealing how it does not. Lord, strengthen my ability to receive and listen to your Spirit, to remember that your Spirit speaks your word to me.

• It is in the nature of God to be giving and generous; Jesus shows us how to relate to his Father with humility, joy, and generosity. Following Jesus calls me to life, to accept my true identity and dignity.

Monday 23rd May
Mark 10:17–27

As Jesus was setting out on a journey, a man ran up and knelt before him, and asked him, "Good Teacher, what must I do to inherit eternal life?" Jesus said to him, "Why do you call me good? No one is good but God alone. You know the commandments: 'You shall not murder; You shall not commit adultery; You shall not steal; You shall not bear false witness; You shall not defraud; Honor your father and mother.'" He said to him, "Teacher, I have kept all these since my youth." Jesus, looking at him, loved him and said, "You lack one thing; go, sell what you own, and give the money to the poor, and you will have treasure in heaven; then come, follow me." When he heard this, he was shocked and went away grieving, for he had many possessions. Then Jesus looked around and said to his disciples, "How hard it will be for those who have wealth to enter the kingdom of God!" And the disciples were perplexed at these words. But Jesus said to them again, "Children, how hard it is to enter the kingdom of God! It is easier for a camel to go through the eye of a needle than for someone who is rich to enter the kingdom of God." They were greatly astounded and said to one another, "Then who can be saved?" Jesus looked at them and said, "For mortals it is impossible, but not for God; for God all things are possible."

- Have you ever been sad because you didn't do something good that you could have done? The visit to a sick or lonely person postponed, the help not given to someone in great financial need, the prayertime not made, the failure to listen to your children or people close to you—the many ways in which you could, without too much difficulty, have said a "yes" to love. This is something like the rich man's feeling when he walked away with his wealth and his sadness. Let that be part of your prayer today.

- The rich man had kept the commandments but was unable to sacrifice his wealth for the kingdom of God. Jesus asks us to give until it hurts. Yet this is sometimes the hardest thing to do. Remember, however, that Jesus looks at those in this situation with love. When you need the strength to give until you feel it, call in prayer on God, for whom all things are possible.

Tuesday 24th May

Mark 10:28–31

Peter began to say to Jesus, "Look, we have left everything and followed you." Jesus said, "Truly I tell you, there is no one who has left house or brothers or sisters or mother or father or children or fields, for my sake and for the sake of the good news, who will not receive a hundredfold now in this age—houses, brothers and sisters, mothers and children, and fields with persecutions—and in the age to come eternal life. But many who are first will be last, and the last will be first."

- Let us make space in our prayer today for all who have heard the gospel call, for people who have "left everything"; may they be a sign and encouragement to all who seek to follow Jesus.

- Lord, grant that I may see you more clearly in the outcasts of this world, love you more dearly in the poor and the rejected, and follow you more nearly by responding to the needs of your deprived sisters and brothers.

Wednesday 25th May
Mark 10:32–45

The disciples were on the road, going up to Jerusalem, and Jesus was walking ahead of them; they were amazed, and those who followed were afraid. He took the twelve aside again and began to tell them what was to happen to him, saying, "See, we are going up to Jerusalem, and the Son of Man will be handed over to the chief priests and the scribes, and they will condemn him to death; then they will hand him over to the Gentiles; they will mock him, and spit upon him, and flog him, and kill him; and after three days he will rise again." James and John, the sons of Zebedee, came forward to him and said to him, "Teacher, we want you to do for us whatever we ask of you." And he said to them, "What is it you want me to do for you?" And they said to him, "Grant us to sit, one at your right hand and one at your left, in your glory." But Jesus said to them, "You do not know what you are asking. Are you able to drink the cup that I drink, or be baptized with the baptism that I am baptized with?" They replied, "We are able." Then Jesus said to them, "The cup that I drink you will drink; and with the baptism with which I am baptized, you will be baptized; but to sit at my right hand or at my left is not mine to grant, but it is for those for whom it has been prepared." When the ten heard this, they began to be angry with James and John. So Jesus called them and said to them, "You know that among the Gentiles those whom they recognize as their rulers lord it over them, and their great ones are tyrants over them. But it is not so among you; but whoever wishes to become great among you must be your servant, and whoever wishes to be first among you must be slave of all. For the Son of Man came not to be served but to serve, and to give his life a ransom for many."

- The apostles heard what Jesus told them with their heads but not their hearts. We become able to hear with the heart only when we enter into the experience of another. But this means making ourselves vulnerable to their pain.

- We can sometimes feel that friends and family do not really understand and support us. They may be preoccupied with their own cares. This is what Jesus experiences here. But he understands and supports me in my struggles, and I in turn can learn to support others.

Thursday 26th May
Mark 10:46–52

They came to Jericho. As Jesus and his disciples and a large crowd were leaving Jericho, Bartimaeus son of Timaeus, a blind beggar, was sitting by the roadside. When he heard that it was Jesus of Nazareth, he began to shout out and say, "Jesus, Son of David, have mercy on me!" Many sternly ordered him to be quiet, but he cried out even more loudly, "Son of David, have mercy on me!" Jesus stood still and said, "Call him here." And they called the blind man, saying to him, "Take heart; get up, he is calling you." So throwing off his cloak, he sprang up and came to Jesus. Then Jesus said to him, "What do you want me to do for you?" The blind man said to him, "My teacher, let me see again." Jesus said to him, "Go; your faith has made you well." Immediately he regained his sight and followed him on the way.

- It can be hard to stand up and be counted in society. We are conditioned not to make spectacles of ourselves. But unless we stand up for truth and justice, we fail others and condemn ourselves to mediocrity.

- What do you say to Jesus when he turns to you and says, "What do you want me to do for you?"

Friday 27th May
Mark 11:11–26

Jesus entered Jerusalem and went into the temple; and when he had looked around at everything, as it was already late, he went out to Bethany with the twelve. On the following day, when they came from Bethany, he was hungry. Seeing in the distance a fig tree in leaf, he went to see whether perhaps he would find anything on it. When he came to it, he found nothing but leaves, for it was not the season for figs. He said to it, "May no one ever eat fruit from you again." And his disciples heard it. Then they came to Jerusalem. And he entered the temple and began to drive out those who were selling and those who were buying in the temple, and he overturned the tables of the money changers and the seats of those who sold doves; and he would not allow anyone to carry anything through the temple. He was teaching and saying, "Is it not written, 'My house shall be called a house of prayer for all the nations'? But you have made it a den of robbers." And when the chief priests and the scribes heard it, they kept looking for a way to kill him; for they were afraid of him, because the whole crowd was spellbound by his teaching. And when evening came, Jesus and his disciples went out of the city. In the morning as they passed by, they saw the fig tree withered away to its roots. Then Peter remembered and said to him, "Rabbi, look! The fig tree that you cursed has withered." Jesus answered them, "Have faith in God. Truly I tell you, if you say to this mountain, 'Be taken up and thrown into the sea,' and if you do not doubt in your heart, but believe that what you say will come to pass, it will be done for you. So I tell you, whatever you ask for in prayer, believe that you have received it, and it will be yours. Whenever you stand praying, forgive, if you have anything against anyone; so that your Father in heaven may also forgive you your trespasses."

- What aroused anger in Jesus was that commerce and caste had ousted reverence. The money changers and sellers of doves used their privilege and license to extort high prices from poor pilgrims. Men had created barriers and divisions between the courts, to exclude Gentiles and women from some areas.

- Do I always respect what a church should be? A house of prayer, not of commerce; for all nations, without compartments; and a place where all can seek God.

Saturday 28th May
Mark 11:27–33

Again they came to Jerusalem. As he was walking in the temple, the chief priests, the scribes, and the elders came to him and said, "By what authority are you doing these things? Who gave you this authority to do them?" Jesus said to them, "I will ask you one question; answer me, and I will tell you by what authority I do these things. Did the baptism of John come from heaven, or was it of human origin? Answer me." They argued with one another, "If we say, 'From heaven,' he will say, 'Why then did you not believe him?' But shall we say, 'Of human origin'?"—they were afraid of the crowd, for all regarded John as truly a prophet. So they answered Jesus, "We do not know." And Jesus said to them, "Neither will I tell you by what authority I am doing these things."

- The opponents of Jesus question the source of his authority. They fear it may undermine their own power. Jesus preferred the company of sinners and tax collectors, who made no claim to any authority of their own.

- True authority is not a personal possession. It comes from God and is to be used always with an eye on God. Whatever authority we have—as parents, teachers, priests, and others—we must use sensitively, so that God would be pleased.

May 29—June 4

Something to think and pray about each day this week:

A Here and Now Kingdom

What does Jesus mean when he states that his kingdom "is not of this world" (John 18:36)? Does he mean that his kingdom belongs to another world, so that we can ignore it for now? No! He means rather that his project for our world comes from God, not from human beings. And when Matthew uses the term "kingdom of heaven" is he referring to a kingdom distant from ours? No! He is respecting Jewish sensitivity about God's holy name, but he tells us clearly that the kingdom is at hand.

Jesus ushers in a new world order in which divine values prevail right now. He tells us to pray that God's will be done here on earth, in the present time. This is our task. God will look after the heaven of the future.

We think of Mary as mild. But her Magnificat is an impassioned comment about what God is doing right before our eyes. "He has scattered the proud. He has brought down the powerful, and lifted up the lowly; he has filled the hungry, and sent the rich away empty" (Luke 1:46–55). She sees the kingdom already being made visible in human history. Mary focuses on serving those around us in justice and love. Her concern is to be in tune with the divine project in the here and now. This concern is to be ours also.

The Presence of God

Be still and know that I am God. Lord, may your spirit guide me to seek your loving presence more and more. For it is there I find rest and refreshment from this busy world.

Freedom

Everything has the potential to draw forth from me a fuller love and life. Yet my desires are often fixed, caught on illusions of fulfillment. I ask that God through my freedom may orchestrate my desires in a vibrant, loving melody rich in harmony.

Consciousness

I exist in a web of relationships—links to nature, people, God. I trace out these links, giving thanks for the life that flows through them. Some links are twisted or broken: I may feel regret, anger, disappointment. I pray for the gift of acceptance and forgiveness.

The Word

I read the Word of God slowly, a few times over, and I listen to what God is saying to me. (Please turn to the Scripture on the following pages. Inspiration points are provided should you need them. When you are ready, return here to continue.)

Conversation

Remembering that I am still in God's presence, I imagine Jesus himself standing or sitting beside me, and I say whatever is on my mind, whatever is in my heart, speaking as one friend to another.

Conclusion

Glory be to the Father, and to the Son, and to the Holy Spirit, as it was in the beginning, is now and ever shall be, world without end. Amen.

Sunday 29th May
The Most Holy Body and Blood of Christ
Luke 9:11b–17

Jesus welcomed the crowds, and spoke to them about the kingdom of God, and healed those who needed to be cured. The day was drawing to a close, and the twelve came to him and said, "Send the crowd away, so that they may go into the surrounding villages and countryside, to lodge and get provisions; for we are here in a deserted place." But he said to them, "You give them something to eat." They said, "We have no more than five loaves and two fish—unless we are to go and buy food for all these people." For there were about five thousand men. And he said to his disciples, "Make them sit down in groups of about fifty each." They did so and made them all sit down. And taking the five loaves and the two fish, he looked up to heaven, and blessed and broke them, and gave them to the disciples to set before the crowd. And all ate and were filled. What was left over was gathered up, twelve baskets of broken pieces.

- This miracle reveals the heart of God, who cares about our every need. God also expects us to come to the aid of one another and to share what little we have.

- Lord, the hunger of the world screams for my attention. But what can I do? Give me a willingness to go beyond myself, to share my little resources toward building a community where people love and care for one another.

Monday 30th May
Mark 12:1–12

Jesus began to speak to them in parables. "A man planted a vine-yard, put a fence around it, dug a pit for the wine press, and built a watch-tower; then he leased it to tenants and went to another country. When the season came, he sent a slave to the tenants to collect from them his share of the produce of the vineyard. But they seized him, and beat him, and sent him away empty-handed. And again he sent another slave to them; this one they beat over the head and insulted. Then he sent another, and that one they killed. And so it was with many others; some they beat, and others they killed. He had still one other, a beloved son. Finally he sent him to them, saying, 'They will respect my son.' But those tenants said to one another, 'This is the heir; come, let us kill him, and the inheritance will be ours.' So they seized him, killed him, and threw him out of the vineyard. What then will the owner of the vineyard do? He will come and destroy the tenants and give the vineyard to others. Have you not read this Scripture: 'The stone that the builders rejected has become the cornerstone; this was the Lord's doing, and it is amazing in our eyes'?" When they realized that he had told this parable against them, they wanted to arrest him, but they feared the crowd. So they left him and went away.

- Overcome by greed and lust for power, the tenants mistreat messenger after messenger. The prophets got the same treatment as they warned against arrogance, greed, and corruption. Yet God loves us so much as to finally send his Son to win us over. And when he is murdered, God is still on our side!

- Do I support today's prophets who speak out against domination, exclusion, and injustice in the church and in the world?

Tuesday 31st May
The Visitation of the Blessed Virgin Mary
Luke 1:39–56

In those days Mary set out and went with haste to a Judean town in the hill country, where she entered the house of Zechariah and greeted Elizabeth. When Elizabeth heard Mary's greeting, the child leapt in her womb. And Elizabeth was filled with the Holy Spirit and exclaimed with a loud cry, "Blessed are you among women, and blessed is the fruit of your womb. And why has this happened to me, that the mother of my Lord comes to me? For as soon as I heard the sound of your greeting, the child in my womb leapt for joy. And blessed is she who believed that there would be a fulfillment of what was spoken to her by the Lord." And Mary said, "My soul magnifies the Lord, and my spirit rejoices in God my Savior, for he has looked with favor on the lowliness of his servant. Surely, from now on all generations will call me blessed; for the Mighty One has done great things for me, and holy is his name. His mercy is for those who fear him from generation to generation. He has shown strength with his arm; he has scattered the proud in the thoughts of their hearts. He has brought down the powerful from their thrones, and lifted up the lowly; he has filled the hungry with good things, and sent the rich away empty. He has helped his servant Israel, in remembrance of his mercy, according to the promise he made to our ancestors, to Abraham and to his descendants forever." And Mary remained with her for about three months and then returned to her home.

- Mary and Elizabeth are kindred spirits, sharing a bond and relationship that goes beyond words. Such friendship is a real gift from God and, as with every blessing, awaits the appreciation of prayer. I bring to mind my best experiences of friendship and let them speak to me about who God is to me and who God calls me to be.

- Consider Elizabeth: no longer young, yet pregnant, she seems to have little concern for herself. She preserved a clarity of vision, able to recognize Mary and appreciate her blessedness. I ask for something of her character—to be able to see what is happening around me, to recognize blessing, to rejoice in the good in others.

Wednesday 1st June
Mark 12:18–27

Some Sadducees, who say there is no resurrection, came to Jesus and asked him a question, saying, "Teacher, Moses wrote for us that 'if a man's brother dies, leaving a wife but no child, the man shall marry the widow and raise up children for his brother.' There were seven brothers; the first married and, when he died, left no children; and the second married her and died, leaving no children; and the third likewise; none of the seven left children. Last of all the woman herself died. In the resurrection whose wife will she be? For the seven had married her." Jesus said to them, "Is not this the reason you are wrong, that you know neither the Scriptures nor the power of God? For when they rise from the dead, they neither marry nor are given in marriage, but are like angels in heaven. And as for the dead being raised, have you not read in the book of Moses, in the story about the bush, how God said to him, 'I am the God of Abraham, the God of Isaac, and the God of Jacob'? He is God not of the dead, but of the living; you are quite wrong."

- The mystery of the dead being raised lies beyond the belief of the Sadducees. Am I a bit like them? Can I trust God to bring me safely home, or do I think I am abandoned at my death?

- What inhibits me from plunging fully into the embrace of the living and loving God?

Thursday 2nd June
Mark 12:28–34

One of the scribes came near and heard them disputing with one another, and seeing that he answered them well, he asked him, "Which commandment is the first of all?" Jesus answered, "The first is, 'Hear, O Israel: the Lord our God, the Lord is one; you shall love the Lord your God with all your heart, and with all your soul, and with all your mind, and with all your strength.' The second is this, 'You shall love your neighbor as yourself.' There is no other commandment greater than these." Then the scribe said to him, "You are right, Teacher; you have truly said that 'he is one, and besides him there is no other'; and 'to love him with all the heart, and with all the understanding, and with all the strength,' and 'to love one's neighbor as oneself'—this is much more important than all whole burnt offerings and sacrifices." When Jesus saw that he answered wisely, he said to him, "You are not far from the kingdom of God." After that no one dared to ask him any question.

- Real prayer brings us into the kingdom of God; in prayer the kingdom or reign of God grows within us. Prayer that does not reach the heart can leave us dry, unenthusiastic about the things of God, and dissatisfied.

- "Love your neighbor as yourself"—just how do I love myself? I am not just aware of present pleasure or pain. I think ahead, protect my routines, and give energy to ensuring my comfort. Lord, if you are asking me to do all that for my neighbor, I will need to try much harder than I am now.

Friday 3rd June
The Most Sacred Heart of Jesus
Luke 15:3–7

Jesus told them this parable: "Which one of you, having a hundred sheep and losing one of them, does not leave the ninety-nine in the wilderness and go after the one that is lost until he finds it? When he has found it, he lays it on his shoulders and rejoices. And when he comes home, he calls together his friends and neighbors, saying to them, 'Rejoice with me, for I have found my sheep that was lost.' Just so, I tell you, there will be more joy in heaven over one sinner who repents than over ninety-nine righteous persons who need no repentance."

- I know what it feels like to be lost in the wilderness but then found! Do I believe that my return is truly an important ingredient in divine happiness?
- What paths have led me toward the wilderness, and how did God rescue me? I ponder and then give thanks to my rescuer.

Saturday 4th June
The Immaculate Heart of the Blessed Virgin Mary
Luke 2:41–51

Now every year Jesus' parents went to Jerusalem for the festival of the Passover. And when he was twelve years old, they went up as usual for the festival. When the festival was ended and they started to return, the boy Jesus stayed behind in Jerusalem, but his parents did not know it. Assuming that he was in the group of travelers, they went a day's journey. Then they started to look for him among their relatives and friends. When they did not find him, they returned to Jerusalem to search for him. After three days they found him in the temple, sitting among the teachers, listening to them and asking them questions. And all who heard him were amazed at his understanding and his answers. When his parents saw him they were astonished; and his mother said to him, "Child, why have you treated us like this? Look, your father and I have been searching for you in great anxiety." He said to them, "Why were you searching for me? Did you not know that I must be in my Father's house?" But they did not understand what he said to them. Then he went down with them and came to Nazareth, and was obedient to them. His mother treasured all these things in her heart.

- Mary treasured the events around the finding of Jesus in the temple in her heart. The gospel says she did the same after hearing Simeon's words that her child was "destined for the rising and falling of many." Both these occasions were prophecies about a future she was only beginning to grasp. The course of our own lives is not always clear and is sometimes marked by signs we don't at first understand. But if we trust in God and seek to do God's will for us, we know we will be going in the right direction.

- Jesus would make a number of trips to Jerusalem and the temple— including the final journey of his earthly life. Where are the holy places in your life to which you return again and again to feel the closeness and to find God's guidance?

June 5—June 11

Something to think and pray about each day this week:

How to Love

Imagine Joe, a 22-year-old who is out robbing to feed his drug habit. He is breaking into people's homes and taking their valuables. An old woman, lying in bed at night, hears the downstairs window breaking and is frightened to death. She feels so insecure now that she wants to leave her home, but she can't. I ask myself: "How does a God of compassion see Joe?" I imagine that God must want justice for the old woman and the hundred others whom Joe has frightened. But as for Joe? I don't know.

A mother once came to me and said: "Father, I don't know what to do. My son is a drug user. He has often come into the house demanding money, and if I didn't have it to give him, he'd smash all the windows in the room. Sometimes he has even beaten me because I didn't have the money for his drugs. I don't know what to do." "Where is he now?" I asked. "Declan's in jail, Father, and now I have my first bit of peace in five years." "And do you ever go to visit him?" I asked. "Ah, Father, I go up to see him every Saturday afternoon without fail. Sure, isn't he still my son?" I learned a lot from her about love, and about God, and about how I should love.

The Presence of God
At any time of the day or night we can call on Jesus. He is always waiting, listening for our call. What a wonderful blessing. No phone needed, no e-mails, just a whisper.

Freedom
If God were trying to tell me something, would I know? If God were reassuring me or challenging me, would I notice? I ask for the grace to be free of my own preoccupations and open to what God may be saying to me.

Consciousness
In the presence of my loving Creator, I look honestly at my feelings over the past day—the highs, the lows, and the level ground. Can I see where the Lord has been present?

The Word
God speaks to each one of us individually. I listen attentively to hear what he is saying to me. Read the text a few times, then listen. (Please turn to the Scripture on the following pages. Inspiration points are provided should you need them. When you are ready, return here to continue.)

Conversation
Do I notice myself reacting as I pray with the Word of God? Do I feel challenged, comforted, angry? Imagining Jesus sitting or standing by me, I speak out my feelings, as one trusted friend to another.

Conclusion
I thank God for these few moments we have spent alone together and for any insights I may have been given concerning the text.

Sunday 5th June
Tenth Sunday in Ordinary Time

Luke 7:11–17

Soon afterwards Jesus went to a town called Nain, and his disciples and a large crowd went with him. As he approached the gate of the town, a man who had died was being carried out. He was his mother's only son, and she was a widow; and with her was a large crowd from the town. When the Lord saw her, he had compassion for her and said to her, "Do not weep." Then he came forward and touched the bier, and the bearers stood still. And he said, "Young man, I say to you, rise!" The dead man sat up and began to speak, and Jesus gave him to his mother. Fear seized all of them; and they glorified God, saying, "A great prophet has risen among us!" and "God has looked favorably on his people!" This word about him spread throughout Judea and all the surrounding country.

• Funeral processions rely on custom and tradition, yet, even here, Jesus is prepared to act in a new way. He recognizes life in the hope and love of the distressed mother and sympathetic crowd. He shows them that their hopes are not dashed, that love is not over. Help me, Lord, to see how you are at work, bringing life even in seemingly impossible circumstances.

• Death, as Jesus speaks of it and lives it, is that moment in which total defeat is transformed by total victory. The world bids us farewell, but God welcomes us home. We are already children of the Father, whose love is stronger than death. Life is eternal because his love is everlasting.

Monday 6th June

Matthew 5:1–12

When Jesus saw the crowds, he went up the mountain; and after he sat down, his disciples came to him. Then he began to speak, and taught them, saying: "Blessed are the poor in spirit, for theirs is the kingdom of heaven. Blessed are those who mourn, for they will be comforted.

Blessed are the meek, for they will inherit the earth. Blessed are those who hunger and thirst for righteousness, for they will be filled. Blessed are the merciful, for they will receive mercy. Blessed are the pure in heart, for they will see God. Blessed are the peacemakers, for they will be called children of God. Blessed are those who are persecuted for righteousness sake, for theirs is the kingdom of heaven. Blessed are you when people revile you and persecute you and utter all kinds of evil against you falsely on my account. Rejoice and be glad, for your reward is great in heaven, for in the same way they persecuted the prophets who were before you."

- Can I sit before Jesus and listen to him, as if I had never heard these Beatitudes before? What effect do they have on my heart? Joy, tears, confusion, longing? Where do I fit in the Beatitudes? Perhaps there is something especially difficult going on in my life right now, such as sickness, or the challenge to be a good caregiver, or the loss of faith and hope. I ask Jesus to make my difficulty into a blessing.

- The Beatitudes reveal to me what Jesus values in a life of discipleship; they show me what Jesus looks for and praises. With Jesus I review my own life and attitudes. I see where I am blessed already—even if what Jesus sees is not what I might look for. I might choose two of these Beatitudes to be a backdrop to my prayer and reflection today: one that affirms me and one that calls me further.

Tuesday 7th June
Matthew 5:13–16

Jesus said to the crowds, "You are the salt of the earth; but if salt has lost its taste, how can its saltiness be restored? It is no longer good for anything, but is thrown out and trampled under foot. You are the light of the world. A city built on a hill cannot be hid. No one after lighting a lamp puts it under the bushel basket, but on the lampstand, and it gives light to all in the house. In the same way, let your light shine before others, so that they may see your good works and give glory to your Father in heaven."

- Salt and light add to human experience. When in proper balance, they do not draw attention to themselves but enhance what is already there. Living as a person of faith does not require me always to speak, proclaim, and announce; I can also bring flavor and enlightenment by my attitude and disposition.

- People do not usually praise a meal for its saltiness, but many will miss the salt if it is absent. How do I contribute something vital to the world—something that does not draw attention to me but that is needed?

Wednesday 8th June
Matthew 5:17–19

Jesus said to the crowds, "Do not think that I have come to abolish the law or the prophets; I have come not to abolish but to fulfill. For truly I tell you, until heaven and earth pass away, not one letter, not one stroke of a letter, will pass from the law until all is accomplished. Therefore, whoever breaks one of the least of these commandments, and teaches others to do the same, will be called least in the kingdom of heaven; but whoever does them and teaches them will be called great in the kingdom of heaven."

- Lord, you summed up the law and the prophets in the love of God and our neighbor. You were not turning your back on the past, but deepening our sense of where we stand before God: not as scrupulous rule keepers, but as loving children.

- The primary role of a prophet was to teach, reminding people of God's message and calling them back when they strayed. Foretelling the future was not their main function. Jesus is the great prophet, bringing meaning and direction to life. When I pray with the gospels, Jesus is present, helping me to see my best way forward.

Thursday 9th June
Matthew 5:20–26

Jesus said to the crowds, "For I tell you, unless your righteousness exceeds that of the scribes and Pharisees, you will never enter the kingdom of heaven. You have heard that it was said to those of ancient times, 'You shall not murder'; and 'whoever murders shall be liable to judgment.' But I say to you that if you are angry with a brother or sister, you will be liable to judgment; and if you insult a brother or sister, you will be liable to the council; and if you say, 'You fool,' you will be liable to the hell of fire. So when you are offering your gift at the altar, if you remember that your brother or sister has something against you, leave your gift there before the altar and go; first be reconciled to your brother or sister, and then come and offer your gift. Come to terms quickly with your accuser while you are on the way to court with him, or your accuser may hand you over to the judge, and the judge to the guard, and you will be thrown into prison. Truly I tell you, you will never get out until you have paid the last penny."

• Our modern media outlets often tell stories about performance, looking at what people do and presuming to judge what is in their hearts. Jesus reminds us that our proper task is for each of us to look into our own hearts and ask for the grace we need to be able to forgive.

• Jesus' true disciples are ambassadors of reconciliation in every age. Whom do I need to be reconciled with? Am I a source of unity or division for others? Do others encounter the power of his resurrection through me?

Friday 10th June
Matthew 5:27–32

Jesus said to the crowds, "You have heard that it was said, 'You shall not commit adultery.' But I say to you that everyone who looks at a woman with lust has already committed adultery with her in his heart. If your right eye causes you to sin, tear it out and throw it away; it is better for you to lose one of your members than for your whole body to be thrown into hell. And if your right hand causes you to sin, cut it off and throw it away; it is better for you to lose one of your members than for your whole body to go into hell. It was also said, 'Whoever divorces his wife, let him give her a certificate of divorce.' But I say to you that anyone who divorces his wife, except on the ground of unchastity, causes her to commit adultery; and whoever marries a divorced woman commits adultery."

- Society in Jesus' time had a strong focus on law. But he says that mutual fidelity, reverence, and respect are to characterize all our relationships.

- Sin lies in spoiling relationships. Ideally the relationship of marriage would mirror God's unbroken relationship of fidelity and love for us. Can I help in any way to strengthen even one marriage—my own or another's?

Saturday 11th June
Matthew 5:33–37

Jesus said to the crowds, "Again, you have heard that it was said to those of ancient times, 'You shall not swear falsely, but carry out the vows you have made to the Lord.' But I say to you, Do not swear at all, either by heaven, for it is the throne of God, or by the earth, for it is his footstool, or by Jerusalem, for it is the city of the great King. And do not swear by your head, for you cannot make one hair white or black. Let your word be 'Yes, Yes' or 'No, No'; anything more than this comes from the evil one."

- How easy it is for us to fall into patterns of speech that do not really mean what they say. As I try to pay attention to how I communicate, I realize how I need to ask God to work on what is in my heart. Avoiding language that is offensive or hurtful is one thing; being sincere and seeing what is in my heart is another!

- Jesus asks us to be simple and straightforward. Yes or no will suffice once the truth is being spoken. Can people trust me to be truthful? Lord, let a simple faith inform all I say today. You were never complex and devious. You simply loved your Father and your people straight from the heart.

June 12—June 18

Something to think and pray about each day this week:

Conquering Love

In this Sunday's gospel story of a woman who anointed Jesus when he ate at the house of a Pharisee, the host, wrapped in the cloak of social respectability, watches with a critical gaze, a closed mind, and a judgmental heart. His image is of a God who doesn't mix with sinners. He despises this woman, who has no name but "sinner." Yet she recognizes her need for Jesus and encounters his compassionate gaze, his total forgiveness, and his peace. Tears of gratitude flow from her converted heart. The Pharisee, however, who feels no need of forgiveness, misses the point completely.

This is a story of extravagance and generosity. The ointment was expensive—and so was the alabaster jar it came in. The woman whom nobody wanted near the table or the feast was extravagant in love. Somehow Jesus' forgiving love had got through to her, and she responded as best she knew—giving something really expensive—her way of giving all. Jesus saw beyond the sin and behind the oil to the love. That would conquer all in the end. Somehow the compassion and forgiveness of Jesus hit her so deeply that she poured out love for him as a response to her relationship with him. In prayer we can sometimes think of God's care, protection, and forgiveness in our lives and be grateful, with words or in silence.

The Presence of God
Be still and know that I am God. Lord, your words lead us to the calmness and greatness of your presence.

Freedom
I am free. When I look at these words in writing they seem to create in me a feeling of awe. Yes, a wonderful feeling of freedom. Thank you, God.

Consciousness
At this moment, Lord, I turn my thoughts to you. I will set aside my chores and preoccupations. I will take rest and refreshment in your presence, Lord.

The Word
The Word of God comes down to us through the Scriptures. May the Holy Spirit enlighten my mind and my heart to respond to the gospel teachings. (Please turn to the Scripture on the following pages. Inspiration points are provided should you need them. When you are ready, return here to continue.)

Conversation
Begin to talk to Jesus about the piece of Scripture you have just read. What part of it strikes a chord in you? Perhaps the words of a friend— or some story you have heard recently—will slowly rise to the surface of your consciousness. If so, does the story throw light on what the Scripture passage may be trying to say to you?

Conclusion
Glory be to the Father, and to the Son, and to the Holy Spirit, as it was in the beginning, is now and ever shall be, world without end. Amen.

Sunday 12th June
Eleventh Sunday in Ordinary Time
Luke 7:36–50

One of the Pharisees asked Jesus to eat with him, and he went into the Pharisee's house and took his place at the table. And a woman in the city, who was a sinner, having learned that he was eating in the Pharisee's house, brought an alabaster jar of ointment. She stood behind him at his feet, weeping, and began to bathe his feet with her tears and to dry them with her hair. Then she continued kissing his feet and anointing them with the ointment. Now when the Pharisee who had invited him saw it, he said to himself, "If this man were a prophet, he would have known who and what kind of woman this is who is touching him—that she is a sinner." Jesus spoke up and said to him, "Simon, I have something to say to you." "Teacher," he replied, "speak." "A certain creditor had two debtors; one owed five hundred denarii, and the other fifty. When they could not pay, he cancelled the debts for both of them. Now which of them will love him more?" Simon answered, "I suppose the one for whom he cancelled the greater debt." And Jesus said to him, "You have judged rightly." Then turning towards the woman, he said to Simon, "Do you see this woman? I entered your house; you gave me no water for my feet, but she has bathed my feet with her tears and dried them with her hair. You gave me no kiss, but from the time I came in she has not stopped kissing my feet. You did not anoint my head with oil, but she has anointed my feet with ointment. Therefore, I tell you, her sins, which were many, have been forgiven; hence she has shown great love. But the one to whom little is forgiven, loves little." Then he said to her, "Your sins are forgiven." But those who were at the table with him began to say among themselves, "Who is this who even forgives sins?" And he said to the woman, "Your faith has saved you; go in peace."

- Simon had life mapped out: he had decided who deserved his attention and how they might be honored. He invited Jesus as a guest but withheld courtesy; he was prepared to listen to the words of Jesus but not ready to receive them in his heart. I ask God to help me, as I review my life, to recognize and remove any ways in which I resist God's Word.

- The Pharisee is surprised and shocked when Jesus allows a sinner to touch him. He has yet to understand that Jesus welcomes and heals sinners. But he does not think of himself as in need of healing. Did he perhaps reflect later over this incident and learn something? All sinners have a future—Lord, let me never despair of myself, since you do not do so. Forgiveness is for all, and the greater the need the more generous is God's response.

Monday 13th June
Matthew 5:38–42

Jesus said, "You have heard that it was said, 'An eye for an eye and a tooth for a tooth.' But I say to you, Do not resist an evildoer. But if anyone strikes you on the right cheek, turn the other also; and if anyone wants to sue you and take your coat, give your cloak as well; and if anyone forces you to go one mile, go also the second mile. Give to everyone who begs from you, and do not refuse anyone who wants to borrow from you."

- Think about the world as you experience it: Where do you notice attitudes that are defensive, reactive, and self-protecting? Where do you meet surprising generosity, graciousness, and hope? To which of these ways of interpreting do you give most attention? Talk to God about how you listen for, hear, receive, and express good news.

- Jesus seems to call for great courage, asking us to draw deeply on our reserves. He is really asking us to depend on him, to let his spirit come to life. What Jesus suggests would upset the balance of the world; it contradicts the neat arrangements of tidy minds. Help me, Lord, to receive courage and strength to act in unexpected and life-giving ways.

Tuesday 14th June
Matthew 5:43–48

Jesus said, "You have heard that it was said, 'You shall love your neighbor and hate your enemy.' But I say to you, Love your enemies and pray for those who persecute you, so that you may be children of your Father in heaven; for he makes his sun rise on the evil and on the good, and sends rain on the righteous and on the unrighteous. For if you love those who love you, what reward do you have? Do not even the tax collectors do the same? And if you greet only your brothers and sisters, what more are you doing than others? Do not even the Gentiles do the same? Be perfect, therefore, as your heavenly Father is perfect."

• Again Jesus shows how high the standards are in the new community he is establishing. This new community is no mere human one: at the heart of it is God. So all its relationships will have a divine quality. If we want to be "children of our Father in heaven" our hearts must embrace our enemies in genuine love.

• Before Jesus came, God was portrayed as destroying the wicked. But Jesus portrays God as pouring out good things on wicked people as well as good people. This seems like extravagant madness. But when we come to the Passion we find Jesus doing what he talks about here. He pours out divine love on everyone, bad and good. He prays for his enemies. On the world scene today, we have plenty of people to love and pray for!

Wednesday 15th June
Matthew 6:1–6, 16–18

Jesus said, "Beware of practicing your piety before others in order to be seen by them; for then you have no reward from your Father in heaven. So whenever you give alms, do not sound a trumpet before you, as the hypocrites do in the synagogues and in the streets, so that they may be praised by others. Truly I tell you, they have received their reward. But when you give alms, do not let your left hand know what your right hand is doing, so that your alms may be done in secret; and your Father who sees in secret will reward you. And whenever you pray, do not be like the hypocrites; for they love to stand and pray in the synagogues and at the street corners, so that they may be seen by others. Truly I tell you, they have received their reward. But whenever you pray, go into your room and shut the door and pray to your Father who is in secret; and your Father who sees in secret will reward you. And whenever you fast, do not look dismal, like the hypocrites, for they disfigure their faces so as to show others that they are fasting. Truly I tell you, they have received their reward. But when you fast, put oil on your head and wash your face, so that your fasting may be seen not by others but by your Father who is in secret; and your Father who sees in secret will reward you."

- What motivates me, deepest down? Do I act solely to please God? "Hypocrites" get a hard time from Jesus. They are people who pretend to be what they are not; they perform behind their masks. Is there any pretense about me? Do I ever catch myself telling small lies to give others a better impression of myself?

- I must be content to be who I am. My deepest identity is not the one I create for myself but the identity given to me by God. I am the beloved of God and always will be. That is enough. The important person in my life must not be myself, or others, but only God "who sees in secret." God also knows my secret: that when everything is said and done, I am infinitely loved!

Thursday 16th June
Matthew 6:7–15

Jesus said, "When you are praying, do not heap up empty phrases as the Gentiles do; for they think that they will be heard because of their many words. Do not be like them, for your Father knows what you need before you ask him. Pray then in this way: Our Father in heaven, hallowed be your name. Your kingdom come. Your will be done, on earth as it is in heaven. Give us this day our daily bread. And forgive us our debts, as we also have forgiven our debtors. And do not bring us to the time of trial, but rescue us from the evil one. For if you forgive others their trespasses, your heavenly Father will also forgive you; but if you do not forgive others, neither will your Father forgive your trespasses."

- As you pray now, is God a distant figure with little interest in your affairs? And what about your day: is God around you or are you alone? The good news is that God is indescribably close to us as we go about our affairs. "Your Father knows what you need before you ask him." We might say that God is infinite awareness, and that his focus is on us. "God is closer to me than I am to myself," says Saint Augustine.

- Try to imagine that God is with you every moment of this day. He is with you as someone who loves you and knows all you need. God is always helping you, especially as you try to bring his values into your everyday life.

Friday 17th June
Matthew 6:19–23

Jesus said, "Do not store up for yourselves treasures on earth, where moth and rust consume and where thieves break in and steal; but store up for yourselves treasures in heaven, where neither moth nor rust consumes and where thieves do not break in and steal. For where your treasure is, there your heart will be also. The eye is the lamp of the body. So, if your eye is healthy, your whole body will be full of light; but if your eye is unhealthy, your whole body will be full of darkness. If then the light in you is darkness, how great is the darkness!"

- The Mosaic laws were very precise, covering all situations and eventualities. Jesus invites his hearers to a deeper level of understanding by contrasting earthly treasures versus heavenly ones, and darkness versus light. Have I something to learn here?

- Do I greet the light or do I allow darkness to blur my vision? Lord, help me to focus on positive options in all situations.

Saturday 18th June

Matthew 6:24–34

Jesus said, "No one can serve two masters; for a slave will either hate the one and love the other, or be devoted to the one and despise the other. You cannot serve both God and wealth. Therefore I tell you, do not worry about your life, what you will eat or what you will drink, or about your body, what you will wear. Is not life more than food, and the body more than clothing? Look at the birds of the air; they neither sow nor reap nor gather into barns, and yet your heavenly Father feeds them. Are you not of more value than they? And can any of you by worrying add a single hour to your span of life? And why do you worry about clothing? Consider the lilies of the field, how they grow; they neither toil nor spin, yet I tell you, even Solomon in all his glory was not clothed like one of these. But if God so clothes the grass of the field, which is alive today and tomorrow is thrown into the oven, will he not much more clothe you—you of little faith? Therefore do not worry, saying, 'What will we eat?' or 'What will we drink?' or 'What will we wear?' For it is the Gentiles who strive for all these things; and indeed your heavenly Father knows that you need all these things. But strive first for the kingdom of God and his righteousness, and all these things will be given to you as well. So do not worry about tomorrow, for tomorrow will bring worries of its own. Today's trouble is enough for today."

• That seems easy for Jesus to say! I think of how I might receive this insight in trust, believing that Jesus seeks only my good.

• There are so many messages all around me telling me about what I should wear, what I should eat. Jesus reminds me that I am more than a consumer. My identity lies in my relationship with God, who loves me and leads me to trust.

June 19—June 25

Something to think and pray about each day this week:

Who Do You Say That He Is?

Lord, I hear the same question you asked the first disciples: Who do you say that I am? Your life and your words are not just for chatting about but for letting you change my life. People often prayed with Jesus, prayed near him at his prayer. Something of his prayer and relationship with his Father must have rubbed off on them. People can be helped by praying together, even in silence. Praying together gives courage to face difficulties together. When we believe in Jesus, we believe in death and resurrection. We believe that bad things can happen in life, often the result of others' actions. We believe also that nothing bad is ever final, but that the love and power of the risen Lord will be with us. I answer the question that Jesus asks in many ways. I show who Jesus is to me by attending church, by professing my faith, by acting as Jesus did. I ask God to help me to make it evident that I am a follower of Jesus. Every time I deny myself, I have an opportunity to express my faith in something greater than what I might enjoy here and now. I ask God's help to take up the crosses that I find, realizing that to follow Jesus is to live as he lived.

The Presence of God

Come to me all you who are burdened, and I will give you rest. Here I am, Lord. I come to seek your presence. I long for your healing power.

Freedom

"In these days, God taught me as a schoolteacher teaches a pupil" (Saint Ignatius of Loyola). I remind myself that there are things God has to teach me yet, and ask for the grace to hear them and let them change me.

Consciousness

Help me, Lord, to be more conscious of your presence. Teach me to recognize your presence in others. Fill my heart with gratitude for the times your love has been shown to me through the care of others.

The Word

I read the Word of God slowly, a few times over, and I listen to what God is saying to me. (Please turn to the Scripture on the following pages. Inspiration points are provided should you need them. When you are ready, return here to continue.)

Conversation

Conversation requires talking and listening. As I talk to Jesus, may I also learn to be still and listen. I picture the gentleness in his eyes and the smile full of love as he gazes on me. I can be totally honest with Jesus as I tell him of my worries and my cares. I will open up my heart to him as I tell him of my fears and my doubts. I will ask him to help me to place myself fully in his care, to abandon myself to him, knowing that he always wants what is best for me.

Conclusion

I thank God for these few moments we have spent alone together and for any insights I may have been given concerning the text.

Sunday 19th June
Twelfth Sunday in Ordinary Time
Luke 9:18–24

Once when Jesus was praying alone, with only the disciples near him, he asked them, "Who do the crowds say that I am?" They answered, "John the Baptist; but others, Elijah; and still others, that one of the ancient prophets has arisen." He said to them, "But who do you say that I am?" Peter answered, "The Messiah of God." He sternly ordered and commanded them not to tell anyone, saying, "The Son of Man must undergo great suffering, and be rejected by the elders, chief priests, and scribes, and be killed, and on the third day be raised." Then he said to them all, "If any want to become my followers, let them deny themselves and take up their cross daily and follow me. For those who want to save their life will lose it, and those who lose their life for my sake will save it."

- When questioned, Peter gives the right answer: "You are the Messiah of God." But this is mainly head knowledge as yet. He will later deny that he even knows Jesus. But at the lake he shows that his heart is at last fully engaged: "You know I love you!"

- Note that this event emerges from Jesus' prayer. Luke thus gives us a hint that what Jesus says is of critical importance. Do I pray before important events, asking that I may be in tune with what God would wish?

Monday 20th June
Matthew 7:1–5

Jesus said, "Do not judge, so that you may not be judged. For with the judgment you make you will be judged, and the measure you give will be the measure you get. Why do you see the speck in your neighbor's eye, but do not notice the log in your own eye? Or how can you say to your neighbor, 'Let me take the speck out of your eye,' while the log is in your own eye? You hypocrite, first take the log out of your own eye, and then you will see clearly to take the speck out of your neighbor's eye."

- His time at the woodworker's bench had taught Jesus all about splinters! His time at prayer helped him to receive insight and truth. I take this time of prayer to stand back from my everyday concerns, to realize my need of forgiveness, to ask God's help, and to pray for God's blessing on those around me.

- We can be quite blind to our own faults but very alert to those of others. Human bias tends to favor ourselves and be prejudiced regarding others. It is easier to propose that the problem is not in me but out there. The truth is more often that the other person is a challenge to me; otherwise why would I need to be critical? It can be challenging to admit the truth about myself.

Tuesday 21st June
Matthew 7:6, 12–14

Jesus said, "Do not give what is holy to dogs; and do not throw your pearls before swine, or they will trample them under foot and turn and maul you. In everything do to others as you would have them do to you; for this is the law and the prophets. Enter through the narrow gate; for the gate is wide and the road is easy that leads to destruction, and there are many who take it. For the gate is narrow and the road is hard that leads to life, and there are few who find it."

- The easy option is to avoid personal responsibilities and go with the crowd. The choice between right and wrong can often be lonely and narrow. Lord, please show me the road that leads to you. May I follow it with joy, whether it is hard or easy.

- The gifts God gives to each of us must not be wasted or ignored but used in the service of others.

Wednesday 22nd June
Matthew 7:15–20

Jesus told the crowds, "Beware of false prophets, who come to you in sheep's clothing but inwardly are ravenous wolves. You will know them by their fruits. Are grapes gathered from thorns, or figs from thistles?

In the same way, every good tree bears good fruit, but the bad tree bears bad fruit. A good tree cannot bear bad fruit, nor can a bad tree bear good fruit. Every tree that does not bear good fruit is cut down and thrown into the fire. Thus you will know them by their fruits."

• Saint Paul wrote of the "fruit of the Spirit" (Galatians 5:22–23) when he lists love, joy, peace, patience, kindness, generosity, faithfulness, gentleness, and self-control as evidence of God's work. With God I review these characteristics, giving thanks for where I find them present, asking for their strengthening, and seeing how I am invited to fill out the character of my discipleship.

• How can I deal with false prophets who show up in my day or week?

Thursday 23rd June
Matthew 7:21–29

Jesus said, "Not everyone who says to me, 'Lord, Lord,' will enter the kingdom of heaven, but only the one who does the will of my Father in heaven. On that day many will say to me, 'Lord, Lord, did we not prophesy in your name, and cast out demons in your name, and do many deeds of power in your name?' Then I will declare to them, 'I never knew you; go away from me, you evildoers.' Everyone then who hears these words of mine and acts on them will be like a wise man who built his house on rock. The rain fell, the floods came, and the winds blew and beat on that house, but it did not fall, because it had been founded on rock. And everyone who hears these words of mine and does not act on them will be like a foolish man who built his house on sand. The rain fell, and the floods came, and the winds blew and beat against that house, and it fell—and great was its fall!" Now when Jesus had finished saying these things, the crowds were astounded at his teaching, for he taught them as one having authority, and not as their scribes.

• Jesus hits hard at every form of pretense. He has no time for it. Does he see any traces of pretense in me? Do I tell small lies? I ask him to remove my deceptiveness.

- The humble people begin to discern the source of Jesus' authority, and see his teachings as a benchmark for their own beliefs and practices. Lord, may you be the rock that supports my faith and my actions, so that I fear neither wind nor flood.

Friday 24th June
The Nativity of Saint John the Baptist
Luke 1:57–66, 80

Now the time came for Elizabeth to give birth, and she bore a son. Her neighbors and relatives heard that the Lord had shown his great mercy to her, and they rejoiced with her. On the eighth day they came to circumcise the child, and they were going to name him Zechariah after his father. But his mother said, "No; he is to be called John." They said to her, "None of your relatives has this name." Then they began motioning to his father to find out what name he wanted to give him. He asked for a writing tablet and wrote, "His name is John." And all of them were amazed. Immediately his mouth was opened and his tongue freed, and he began to speak, praising God. Fear came over all their neighbors, and all these things were talked about throughout the entire hill country of Judea. All who heard them pondered them and said, "What then will this child become?" For, indeed, the hand of the Lord was with him. The child grew and became strong in spirit, and he was in the wilderness until the day he appeared publicly to Israel.

- No doubt Elizabeth had wanted this birth and prayed for it for many years; instead she had her son in God's time.

- I imagine I am one of Elizabeth's relatives who comes to celebrate John's birth. I too wonder, "What will this child become?" Then I ask myself: "What am I becoming?"

Saturday 25th June
Matthew 8:5–17

When Jesus entered Capernaum, a centurion came to him, appealing to him and saying, "Lord, my servant is lying at home paralyzed, in terrible distress." And he said to him, "I will come and cure him." The centurion answered, "Lord, I am not worthy to have you come under my roof; but only speak the word, and my servant will be healed. For I also am a man under authority, with soldiers under me; and I say to one, 'Go,' and he goes, and to another, 'Come,' and he comes, and to my slave, 'Do this,' and the slave does it." When Jesus heard him, he was amazed and said to those who followed him, "Truly I tell you, in no one in Israel have I found such faith. I tell you, many will come from east and west and will eat with Abraham and Isaac and Jacob in the kingdom of heaven, while the heirs of the kingdom will be thrown into the outer darkness, where there will be weeping and gnashing of teeth." And to the centurion Jesus said, "Go; let it be done for you according to your faith." And the servant was healed in that hour. When Jesus entered Peter's house, he saw his mother-in-law lying in bed with a fever; he touched her hand, and the fever left her, and she got up and began to serve him. That evening they brought to him many who were possessed with demons; and he cast out the spirits with a word, and cured all who were sick. This was to fulfill what had been spoken through the prophet Isaiah, "He took our infirmities and bore our diseases."

• The centurion was an officer of the imperial army, a man with power and status. He was begging a favor from a penniless itinerant teacher and declaring himself unworthy even to entertain Jesus in his house. Jesus was amazed, not merely at the trust of the man, but at the fact that his love for his servant led him to cut through all the barriers of rank and race.

• Lord, so much of my life is structured by social conventions and barriers. Give me the grace to listen to my heart and reach out to those I can help.

The Thirteenth Week of Ordinary Time
June 26—July 2

Something to think and pray about each day this week:

Desert Fathers
Our Lady still keeps watch outside an abandoned monastery in Algeria where seven Trappist monks, its occupants, were abducted and murdered. Their story was later made into the film *Of Gods and Men,* described as perhaps the best-ever movie about Christian commitment.

Today we need examples of humble courage and dedication such as these monks provide. Despite the death threats issued to foreigners, the monks remained, out of solidarity with their Muslim neighbors. Their choice was made with pain, soul-searching, and disagreement. "Perhaps it would be better to go home to France and serve God in a quieter way?" "What good would our deaths bring? In a wave of violent deaths, the murder of a few monks would be nothing special." But they decided as a group to remain, come what might. These men did not choose death—rather it came their way and they had to adjust to it or feel that they had betrayed a silent God who was the love of their lives.

In his last testament the abbot addresses his final sentence to his prospective killer: "Thank you, my friend of the last moment, who will not know what you are doing. . . . May we meet in heaven, like happy thieves, if it pleases God, our common Father." Our Lady surely approved of that prayer and welcomed the monks home after their final ordeal.

The Presence of God
Dear Jesus, as I call on you today I realize that I often come asking for favors. Today I'd like just to be in your presence. Let me respond to your love.

Freedom
Everything has the potential to draw forth from me a fuller love and life. Yet my desires are often fixed, caught on illusions of fulfillment. I ask that God through my freedom may orchestrate my desires in a vibrant, loving melody rich in harmony.

Consciousness
How am I really feeling? Lighthearted? Heavyhearted? I may be very much at peace, happy to be here. Equally, I may be frustrated, worried, or angry. I acknowledge how I really am. It is the real me that the Lord loves.

The Word
God speaks to each one of us individually. I listen attentively to hear what he is saying to me. Read the text a few times, then listen. (Please turn to the Scripture on the following pages. Inspiration points are provided should you need them. When you are ready, return here to continue.)

Conversation
Do I notice myself reacting as I pray with the Word of God? Do I feel challenged, comforted, angry? Imagining Jesus sitting or standing by me, I speak out my feelings, as one trusted friend to another.

Conclusion
Glory be to the Father, and to the Son, and to the Holy Spirit, as it was in the beginning, is now and ever shall be, world without end. Amen.

Sunday 26th June
Thirteenth Sunday in Ordinary Time
Luke 9:51–62

When the days drew near for him to be taken up, he set his face to go to Jerusalem. And he sent messengers ahead of him. On their way they entered a village of the Samaritans to make ready for him; but they did not receive him, because his face was set towards Jerusalem. When his disciples James and John saw it, they said, "Lord, do you want us to command fire to come down from heaven and consume them?" But he turned and rebuked them. Then they went on to another village. As they were going along the road, someone said to him, "I will follow you wherever you go." And Jesus said to him, "Foxes have holes, and birds of the air have nests; but the Son of Man has nowhere to lay his head." To another he said, "Follow me." But he said, "Lord, first let me go and bury my father." But Jesus said to him, "Let the dead bury their own dead; but as for you, go and proclaim the kingdom of God." Another said, "I will follow you, Lord; but let me first say farewell to those at my home." Jesus said to him, "No one who puts a hand to the plough and looks back is fit for the kingdom of God."

- Jesus asks for commitment—real commitment. The time for it is now. On our own road today we must proclaim the kingdom of God. If we keep waiting for the right moment, the sands of time will run quickly through our fingers.

- The poet Robert Browning wrote: "Earth is full of Heaven, / And every common bush is alive with God." Seeing the world from this perspective, I daily try to serve the Lord.

Monday 27th June
Matthew 8:18–22

Now when Jesus saw great crowds around him, he gave orders to go over to the other side. A scribe then approached and said, "Teacher, I will follow you wherever you go." And Jesus said to him, "Foxes have holes, and birds of the air have nests; but the Son of Man has nowhere to lay his head." Another of his disciples said to him, "Lord, first let me go and bury my father." But Jesus said to him, "Follow me, and let the dead bury their own dead."

- The scribes were largely educated and earnest people, but Jesus called them to something more. Here, he seems to offer a caution to an enthusiastic follower and, to the one who seems to be preoccupied by a matter of importance, Jesus poses a question, Why should I be surprised when my discipleship is not easy? True prayer will always call me beyond my own interests and lead me to light.

- Lord, you constantly challenge me. I will try to hear your voice in what unsettles me.

Tuesday 28th June
Matthew 8:23–27

And when Jesus got into the boat, his disciples followed him. A windstorm arose on the sea, so great that the boat was being swamped by the waves; but he was asleep. And they went and woke him up, saying, "Lord, save us! We are perishing!" And he said to them, "Why are you afraid, you of little faith?" Then he got up and rebuked the winds and the sea; and there was a dead calm. They were amazed, saying, "What sort of man is this, that even the winds and the sea obey him?"

- Note the contrasts here: There is the terror of the disciples and the composure of Jesus, who is asleep! The chaos of the storm and the "dead calm" that follows Jesus' intervention. He shows complete trust in the protection of God, whereas the disciples are seen to be "of little faith." What about me?

- Only God has power over the natural forces of the sea. But Jesus demonstrates that he has access to that same power, which hints at his divinity. Have there been occasions in my own life when I invoked the Lord's help and he restored peace and calm to my troubled waters?

Wednesday 29th June
Saints Peter and Paul, Apostles
Matthew 16:13–19

Now when Jesus came into the district of Caesarea Philippi, he asked his disciples, "Who do people say that the Son of Man is?" And they said, "Some say John the Baptist, but others Elijah, and still others Jeremiah or one of the prophets." He said to them, "But who do you say that I am?" Simon Peter answered, "You are the Messiah, the Son of the living God." And Jesus answered him, "Blessed are you, Simon son of Jonah! For flesh and blood has not revealed this to you, but my Father in heaven. And I tell you, you are Peter, and on this rock I will build my church, and the gates of Hades will not prevail against it. I will give you the keys of the kingdom of heaven, and whatever you bind on earth will be bound in heaven, and whatever you loose on earth will be loosed in heaven."

• The traditional setting for this memorable encounter in Caesarea Philippi is a lovely riverbank under a huge rocky cliff. Impetuous Peter confesses Jesus as the Messiah. It is an inspired confession. This uneducated fisherman, who was to prove so shaky when Jesus was arrested, is rewarded with a new name, suggested by the great solid rock above them, and also with a new role, leading the people of God. We are the people of God, with a leader and the support of the Holy Spirit. I am not alone.

• The motley band of the twelve would guide the future community of Jesus. Our community today is somewhat similar—a motley group who are saintly and sinful but who with firm faith believe that Jesus is the Son of God. Peter is praised today within the church for his belief and faith in Jesus as the Son of the living God. The first call in his following of Jesus was to grow in the faith that would sustain his life. May our faith do the same.

Thursday 30th June

Matthew 9:1–8

After getting into a boat Jesus crossed the sea and came to his own town. And just then some people were carrying a paralyzed man lying on a bed. When Jesus saw their faith, he said to the paralytic, "Take heart, son; your sins are forgiven." Then some of the scribes said to themselves, "This man is blaspheming." But Jesus, perceiving their thoughts, said, "Why do you think evil in your hearts? For which is easier, to say, 'Your sins are forgiven,' or to say, 'Stand up and walk'? But so that you may know that the Son of Man has authority on earth to forgive sins"—he then said to the paralytic—"Stand up, take your bed and go to your home." And he stood up and went to his home. When the crowds saw it, they were filled with awe, and they glorified God, who had given such authority to human beings.

- The paralytic could not have come to Jesus if he was not carried by others. These nameless others had faith in the power of Jesus to heal him. I too am carried by anonymous good people who have more faith than I do. But I in turn carry others also!

- As I insert myself now into this story, where do I find myself? In the person of the paralytic? Or among those who carry him to Jesus? Or perhaps among the disbelieving and dismissive scribes. Or among the crowds who see and believe and who give glory to God acting through Jesus? Where does Jesus want to place me?

Friday 1st July

Matthew 9:9–13

As Jesus was walking along, he saw a man called Matthew sitting at the tax booth; and he said to him, "Follow me." And he got up and followed him. And as he sat at dinner in the house, many tax collectors and sinners came and were sitting with him and his disciples. When the Pharisees saw this, they said to his disciples, "Why does your teacher eat with tax collectors and sinners?" But when he heard this, he said, "Those who are well have no need of a physician, but those who are sick. Go and learn what this means, 'I desire mercy, not sacrifice.' For I have come to call not the righteous but sinners."

- Jesus is inclusive—even "tax collectors and sinners" are welcomed. They represent those whose professions and social status are "not respectable." But Jesus shows that he has come for all people, without exception, and especially the weak and the vulnerable, the "sick" and the "sinners."

- How inclusive and compassionate Jesus is in his ministry! I ask myself if I am prejudiced against any individuals or groups. Lord, help me to become more like you in thought, word, and deed. Make me large-hearted.

Saturday 2nd July

Matthew 9:14–17

The disciples of John came to Jesus, saying, "Why do we and the Pharisees fast often, but your disciples do not fast?" And Jesus said to them, "The wedding guests cannot mourn as long as the bridegroom is with them, can they? The days will come when the bridegroom is taken away from them, and then they will fast. No one sews a piece of unshrunk cloth on an old cloak, for the patch pulls away from the cloak, and a worse tear is made. Neither is new wine put into old wineskins; otherwise, the skins burst, and the wine is spilled, and the skins are destroyed; but new wine is put into fresh wineskins, and so both are preserved."

- Jesus often refers to the kingdom of God as a wedding feast, with God as the bridegroom and believers as the wedding guests. During Jesus' own lifetime, God—embodied in Jesus—was always present among his people. Accordingly it was not a time for fasting or mourning.

- The Lord says, "See, I am making all things new" (Revelation 21:5). Lord, renew your Spirit within me so that I may always possess the new wine of your Good News and share it generously with others.

July 3—July 9

Something to think and pray about each day this week:

Lost and Gone Forever?

"Put my tears in your bottle. Are they not in your record?" (Psalm 56:8). What a splendid demand this is! While we weep for our losses, God is watching with compassion. God respects our tears and gathers them up because they are precious. The Bible is the Book of Tears. Jesus weeps over Jerusalem, and over Lazarus. Tears are the concern of God: at the end "he will wipe every tear from our eyes" (Revelation 21:4). So while death indeed brings tears, we believe that we do not weep before an uncaring universe. Saint Paul says to his early converts: Do not grieve "as others do who have no hope" (1 Thessalonians 4:13).

There is a lasting blessing attached to tears: "Blessed are you who weep now, for you will laugh" (Luke 6:21). Tears reveal our love for those who have died. But ours is not a lost love. Our tears are never wasted. Those who seem to be gone will be restored to us. Jesus says: "If I go and prepare a place for you, I will come again and take you to myself, so that where I am you may be also" (John 14:3). He promises this reunion to his disciples, not only as individuals, but as a community. The whole body of Christ will finally be gathered into one, and all of us will rejoice together.

The Presence of God
Be still and know that I am God. What a wonderful privilege that the Lord of all creation desires to come to me. I welcome his presence.

Freedom
God is not foreign to my freedom. Instead the Spirit breathes life into my most intimate desires, gently nudging me toward all that is good. I ask for the grace to let myself be enfolded by the Spirit.

Consciousness
How do I find myself today? Where am I with God? With others? Do I have something to be grateful for? Then I give thanks. Is there something I am sorry for? Then I ask forgiveness.

The Word
I take my time to read the Word of God slowly, a few times, allowing myself to dwell on anything that strikes me. (Please turn to the Scripture on the following pages. Inspiration points are provided should you need them. When you are ready, return here to continue.)

Conversation
How has God's Word moved me? Has it left me cold? Has it consoled me or moved me to act in a new way? I imagine Jesus standing or sitting beside me. I turn and share my feelings with him.

Conclusion
I thank God for these few moments we have spent alone together and for any insights I may have been given concerning the text.

Sunday 3rd July
Fourteenth Sunday in Ordinary Time
Luke 10:1–12, 17–20

The Lord appointed seventy others and sent them on ahead of him in pairs to every town and place where he himself intended to go. He said to them, "The harvest is plentiful, but the laborers are few; therefore ask the Lord of the harvest to send out laborers into his harvest. Go on your way. See, I am sending you out like lambs into the midst of wolves. Carry no purse, no bag, no sandals; and greet no one on the road. Whatever house you enter, first say, 'Peace to this house!' And if anyone is there who shares in peace, your peace will rest on that person; but if not, it will return to you. Remain in the same house, eating and drinking whatever they provide, for the laborer deserves to be paid. Do not move about from house to house. Whenever you enter a town and its people welcome you, eat what is set before you; cure the sick who are there, and say to them, 'The kingdom of God has come near to you.' But whenever you enter a town and they do not welcome you, go out into its streets and say, 'Even the dust of your town that clings to our feet, we wipe off in protest against you. Yet know this: the kingdom of God has come near.' I tell you, on that day it will be more tolerable for Sodom than for that town." The seventy returned with joy, saying, "Lord, in your name even the demons submit to us!" He said to them, "I watched Satan fall from heaven like a flash of lightning. See, I have given you authority to tread on snakes and scorpions, and over all the power of the enemy; and nothing will hurt you. Nevertheless, do not rejoice at this, that the spirits submit to you, but rejoice that your names are written in heaven."

• Our joy is in our identity with Jesus, not in what we do. Our names are written in heaven because we are his beloved sons and daughters. Our names are never erased or crossed out. Can I believe that my name delights God? Maybe in prayer repeat your own name for a while and sense the tone of God as God would say your name—with warmth and love.

- Jesus is preparing his disciples for mission. He leaves them in no doubt about the challenges, obstacles, and dangers that await them. They will succeed, however, because the power of God is working with them. Do I experience that joy when I do what the Lord wants? The message entrusted to the disciples by Jesus is peace and the nearness of the kingdom of God. This same message of peace and justice, forgiveness and healing, and the Good News of God's kingdom, has been entrusted to the church through the centuries. Now it is my turn to witness to it.

Monday 4th July

Matthew 9:18–26

While Jesus was saying these things to them, suddenly a leader of the synagogue came in and knelt before him, saying, "My daughter has just died; but come and lay your hand on her, and she will live." And Jesus got up and followed him, with his disciples. When Jesus came to the leader's house and saw the flute players and the crowd making a commotion, he said, "Go away; for the girl is not dead but sleeping." And they laughed at him. But when the crowd had been put outside, he went in and took her by the hand, and the girl got up. And the report of this spread throughout that district.

- The faith of the synagogue leader is striking. Jesus responds generously to it. This deep faith contrasts sharply with the flute players and the crowd, who laugh at Jesus' statement that the girl is not dead but sleeping.

- This event challenges the strength of my own faith in the power of Christ to work effectively in my life, too, if I but turn to him. Is my own faith weakened by the same skepticism and cynicism as expressed by the flute players and the crowd? Lord, "I believe, help my unbelief" (Mark 9:24).

Tuesday 5th July
Matthew 9:32–38

A demoniac who was mute was brought to Jesus. And when the demon had been cast out, the one who had been mute spoke; and the crowds were amazed and said, "Never has anything like this been seen in Israel." But the Pharisees said, "By the ruler of the demons he casts out the demons." Then Jesus went about all the cities and villages, teaching in their synagogues, and proclaiming the good news of the kingdom, and curing every disease and every sickness. When he saw the crowds, he had compassion for them, because they were harassed and helpless, like sheep without a shepherd. Then he said to his disciples, "The harvest is plentiful, but the laborers are few; therefore ask the Lord of the harvest to send out laborers into his harvest."

- I sometimes feel harassed and helpless as I become aware of the many needs around me: the media outlets that tell me of threats to security also offer me many solutions. I allow myself to be compassionate, as Jesus was. I think of how he looks on me with love, wanting to shepherd me, asking me to listen to his voice so that he can lead me to peace and happiness.

- "When he saw the crowds, he had compassion for them, because they were harassed and helpless." Surely compassion is the hallmark of Jesus? Such is his humanity that he feels deeply for the people who are lost, like sheep without a shepherd. To what extent am I like Jesus in my attitude toward others, especially the poor and the needy? Am I dismissive and judgmental toward others, as are the Pharisees in today's gospel? Lord, please give me something of your genuine humanity and compassion in all my relations with others.

Wednesday 6th July
Matthew 10:1–7

Jesus summoned his twelve disciples and gave them authority over unclean spirits, to cast them out, and to cure every disease and every sickness. These are the names of the twelve apostles: first, Simon, also known as Peter, and his brother Andrew; James son of Zebedee, and his brother John; Philip and Bartholomew; Thomas and Matthew the tax collector; James son of Alphaeus, and Thaddaeus; Simon the Cananaean, and Judas Iscariot, the one who betrayed him. These twelve Jesus sent out with the following instructions: "Go nowhere among the Gentiles, and enter no town of the Samaritans, but go rather to the lost sheep of the house of Israel. As you go, proclaim the good news, 'The kingdom of heaven has come near.'"

- Jesus did not first send the disciples to the ends of the earth: he asks them to open their eyes to the needs of those around them. There are people around me who are like lost sheep—I bring them to my prayer. I think of people who are fragile, deflated, or confused and pray that I might know what gesture, word, or way of being present might let them know that the reign of God is indeed very near.

- I take time to hear my name being called. Jesus chooses me because he knows me, trusts me, and loves me. Jesus called people by name, recognizing their dignity and worth. As I address those around me I pray that I remain aware of the gift that each person is to the world.

Thursday 7th July

Matthew 10:7–15

Jesus said to the twelve, "As you go, proclaim the good news, 'The kingdom of heaven has come near.' Cure the sick, raise the dead, cleanse the lepers, cast out demons. You received without payment; give without payment. Take no gold, or silver, or copper in your belts, no bag for your journey, or two tunics, or sandals, or a staff; for laborers deserve their food. Whatever town or village you enter, find out who in it is worthy, and stay there until you leave. As you enter the house, greet it. If the house is worthy, let your peace come upon it; but if it is not worthy, let your peace return to you. If anyone will not welcome you or listen to your words, shake off the dust from your feet as you leave that house or town. Truly I tell you, it will be more tolerable for the land of Sodom and Gomorrah on the day of judgement than for that town."

- Jesus instructs his disciples to travel lightly—how unlike the modern traveler they are! He is not concerned with baggage allowances but asks us to look at our hearts to see how free we are. Am I defined by my luggage? Can I relax into my true identity and let go of what does not matter? I picture my concerns on an airport carousel: here they come around again—what happens if I don't pick them up?

- "Keep it simple" could describe the apostles' mission. They are to announce the gospel in its most basic form, proclaiming that the kingdom is near and healing and restoring to life the sick and the dead, all the while depending only on God. It's also our call as disciples today: carried by faith and prayer, we help make God's kingdom visible and bring wholeness and life to the world.

Friday 8th July
Matthew 10:16–23

Jesus said to the twelve, "See, I am sending you out like sheep into the midst of wolves; so be wise as serpents and innocent as doves. Beware of them, for they will hand you over to councils and flog you in their synagogues; and you will be dragged before governors and kings because of me, as a testimony to them and the Gentiles. When they hand you over, do not worry about how you are to speak or what you are to say; for what you are to say will be given to you at that time; for it is not you who speak, but the Spirit of your Father speaking through you. Brother will betray brother to death, and a father his child, and children will rise against parents and have them put to death; and you will be hated by all because of my name. But the one who endures to the end will be saved. When they persecute you in one town, flee to the next; for truly I tell you, you will not have gone through all the towns of Israel before the Son of Man comes."

- Jesus teaches the twelve how to persevere in times of persecution. He warns them that they will be met with hostility and hatred because of him, but they are to continue to bear witness to his values. The ultimate reassurance and promise of the Lord is that the one who endures to the end will be saved.

• Just as Jesus was not abandoned by his Father in his hour of need, so, too, Christian believers are not abandoned in difficulty and persecution. Rather the Spirit of God will enlighten and strengthen them. Lord, grant me also the courage and strength of your Spirit to persevere and to witness, especially in difficult times.

Saturday 9th July
Matthew 10:24–33

Jesus said to the twelve, "A disciple is not above the teacher, nor a slave above the master; it is enough for the disciple to be like the teacher, and the slave like the master. If they have called the master of the house Beelzebul, how much more will they malign those of his household! So have no fear of them; for nothing is covered up that will not be uncovered, and nothing secret that will not become known. What I say to you in the dark, tell in the light; and what you hear whispered, proclaim from the housetops. Do not fear those who kill the body but cannot kill the soul; rather fear him who can destroy both soul and body in hell. Are not two sparrows sold for a penny? Yet not one of them will fall to the ground unperceived by your Father. And even the hairs of your head are all counted. So do not be afraid; you are of more value than many sparrows. Everyone therefore who acknowledges me before others, I also will acknowledge before my Father in heaven; but whoever denies me before others, I also will deny before my Father in heaven."

• Is Jesus really asking me to settle for being treated as he was treated? I can admire him and seek to follow him—but to be ready to be treated as he was seems too much to ask. Jesus, only if my heart is like yours can I live as you did. Speak now to my heart and help me to listen, to learn, and to love as you did.

• Without neglecting our basic equality, I can realize that I have much to learn from others. I ask for the humility I need to remain a learner and disciple. It is enough for me to be like Jesus. I am made in the image of God. I pray that I may bear in mind how deeply I am honored and blessed by God's love for me.

July 10—July 16

Something to think and pray about each day this week:

Humility and Compassion

Truly humble people have deep compassion. They may be saddened when others are unresponsive, but they do not lose their serenity through making harsh judgments. Instead, they step into the shoes of ungrateful people, trying to love in their place.

They plead that God's love may shine forth upon the bad as well as good, upon the indifferent as well as the committed. They do not rely upon their own resources, and their trust in God is so overwhelming that God cannot but respond to their prayers. They are kind enough to see that the badness of most people is due to the little love they may have received in their lives. They give their hearts and heads and hands to God so that God may work through them.

They are not burdened. They have responded to the gravitational pull of God, and so their yoke is easy and their burden is light. Love has given them wings. They have renounced their attempts to run their own lives, and in surrendering themselves to God they experience a joy that lifts them. They have become so attuned to God that they have also gratefully tuned in to the wavelength of service.

The Presence of God

As I sit here, the beating of my heart, the ebb and flow of my breathing, and the movements of my mind are all signs of God's ongoing creation of me. I pause for a moment, and become aware of this presence of God within me.

Freedom

I will ask God's help to be free from my own preoccupations, to be open to God in this time of prayer, and to come to know, love, and serve God more.

Consciousness

I ask how I am within myself today. Am I particularly tired, stressed, or off-form? If any of these characteristics apply, can I try to let go of the concerns that disturb me?

The Word

The Word of God comes down to us through the Scriptures. May the Holy Spirit enlighten my mind and my heart to respond to the gospel teachings. (Please turn to the Scripture on the following pages. Inspiration points are provided should you need them. When you are ready, return here to continue.)

Conversation

Jesus, you speak to me through the words of the gospels. May I respond to your call today. Teach me to recognize your hand at work in my daily living.

Conclusion

Glory be to the Father, and to the Son, and to the Holy Spirit, as it was in the beginning, is now and ever shall be, world without end. Amen.

Sunday 10th July
Fifteenth Sunday in Ordinary Time

Luke 10:25–37

Just then a lawyer stood up to test Jesus. "Teacher," he said, "what must I do to inherit eternal life?" He said to him, "What is written in the law? What do you read there?" He answered, "You shall love the Lord your God with all your heart, and with all your soul, and with all your strength, and with all your mind; and your neighbor as yourself." And he said to him, "You have given the right answer; do this, and you will live." But wanting to justify himself, he asked Jesus, "And who is my neighbor?" Jesus replied, "A man was going down from Jerusalem to Jericho, and fell into the hands of robbers, who stripped him, beat him, and went away, leaving him half dead. Now by chance a priest was going down that road; and when he saw him, he passed by on the other side. So likewise a Levite, when he came to the place and saw him, passed by on the other side. But a Samaritan while traveling came near him; and when he saw him, he was moved with pity. He went to him and bandaged his wounds, having poured oil and wine on them. Then he put him on his own animal, brought him to an inn, and took care of him. The next day he took out two denarii, gave them to the innkeeper, and said, 'Take care of him; and when I come back, I will repay you whatever more you spend.' Which of these three, do you think, was a neighbor to the man who fell into the hands of the robbers?" He said, "The one who showed him mercy." Jesus said to him, "Go and do likewise."

• Modern urban life trains us to walk on by, to be like the priest or Levite in the parable. I ask God to help me preserve the compassion to which Jesus calls us.

• To be a neighbor is to be one who shows mercy. I consider my attitude to those among whom I live and imagine how I might be merciful to them as God is to me.

Monday 11th July

Matthew 10:34—11:1

Jesus said, "Do not think that I have come to bring peace to the earth; I have not come to bring peace, but a sword. For I have come to set a man against his father, and a daughter against her mother, and a daughter-in-law against her mother-in-law; and one's foes will be members of one's own household. Whoever loves father or mother more than me is not worthy of me; and whoever loves son or daughter more than me is not worthy of me; and whoever does not take up the cross and follow me is not worthy of me. Those who find their life will lose it, and those who lose their life for my sake will find it. Whoever welcomes you welcomes me, and whoever welcomes me welcomes the one who sent me. Whoever welcomes a prophet in the name of a prophet will receive a prophet's reward; and whoever welcomes a righteous person in the name of a righteous person will receive the reward of the righteous; and whoever gives even a cup of cold water to one of these little ones in the name of a disciple—truly I tell you, none of these will lose their reward." Now when Jesus had finished instructing his twelve disciples, he went on from there to teach and proclaim his message in their cities.

- Being a follower of Jesus is not only about proclaiming and announcing the word: it is necessary also to receive the word graciously. I pray for the generosity I need to be able to both give freely and receive fully the Word of God. I ask God for the humility to listen, to notice, to hear, and to receive God's Word.

- This Gospel consists of a number of sayings by Jesus on discipleship. He does not directly intend these tensions and divisions in family life, but he wants us to put God first and accept the consequences. The different ways in which the gospel is welcomed or rejected brings its own pain. "A cup of cold water to one of these little ones" has eternal significance. This truth highlights the dignity of each and every human being, no matter how lowly or insignificant they are. Lord, help me to see your face in my neighbor, especially the poor and the needy, and to respond accordingly.

Tuesday 12th July
Matthew 11:20–24

Then Jesus began to reproach the cities in which most of his deeds of power had been done, because they did not repent. "Woe to you, Chorazin! Woe to you, Bethsaida! For if the deeds of power done in you had been done in Tyre and Sidon, they would have repented long ago in sackcloth and ashes. But I tell you, on the day of judgment it will be more tolerable for Tyre and Sidon than for you. And you, Capernaum, will you be exalted to heaven? No, you will be brought down to Hades. For if the deeds of power done in you had been done in Sodom, it would have remained until this day. But I tell you that on the day of judgment it will be more tolerable for the land of Sodom than for you."

• Jesus calls the townspeople to realize how fortunate they are: the message of life has been available to them, but they have not paid attention. I take some time in quiet, asking God to reveal to me what I may have neglected. I want to turn from nothing that is for my good, and so I ask God for the humility I need to listen again.

• In Matthew's Gospel people show great enthusiasm for Jesus on the level of getting him to cure their sick. But discipleship must go beyond only these motivations. I must ask: "Lord, what do you need me to do to further the kingdom of God in my part of the world?"

Wednesday 13th July
Matthew 11:25–27

At that time Jesus said, "I thank you, Father, Lord of heaven and earth, because you have hidden these things from the wise and the intelligent and have revealed them to infants; yes, Father, for such was your gracious will. All things have been handed over to me by my Father; and no one knows the Son except the Father, and no one knows the Father except the Son and anyone to whom the Son chooses to reveal him."

• There are so many clever and well-educated people around nowadays! But, just as in the time of Jesus, wisdom may sometimes elude them. I will never acquire the insight or perspective that Jesus values through my own efforts. As in his life, a habit of regular prayer, of communication with God, who loves me, will reveal to me the secrets of God's heart.

• When we ask about Jesus' knowledge of himself, this is a crucial passage. He calls on his father with the intimate "Abba." He claims to be the unique channel of the love and knowledge of God. Theologians have used long terms, like *hypostatic union,* to describe the joining of divine and human natures in Jesus. He insists that access to the Father is granted not so much to the intelligent as to those who come before him as his trusting children.

Thursday 14th July
Matthew 11:28–30

Jesus said, "Come to me, all you that are weary and are carrying heavy burdens, and I will give you rest. Take my yoke upon you, and learn from me; for I am gentle and humble in heart, and you will find rest for your souls. For my yoke is easy, and my burden is light."

• I am often weary, Lord, and my burden feels heavy. When I look at Christians, some of them indeed seem relaxed and easy in your company. Others appear uptight and driven, not restful people to be near.

• You are a gentle, humble presence. If I feel under pressure in prayer, something is wrong. It is a sign of your presence to me that my soul feels rested.

Friday 15th July
Matthew 12:1–8

At that time Jesus went through the grainfields on the sabbath; his disciples were hungry, and they began to pluck heads of grain and to eat. When the Pharisees saw it, they said to him, "Look, your disciples are doing what is not lawful to do on the sabbath." He said to them, "Have you not read what David did when he and his companions were hungry? He entered the house of God and ate the bread of the presence, which it was not lawful for him or his companions to eat, but only for the priests. Or have you not read in the law that on the sabbath the priests in the temple break the sabbath and yet are guiltless? I tell you, something greater than the temple is here. But if you had known what this means, 'I desire mercy and not sacrifice,' you would not have condemned the guiltless. For the Son of Man is lord of the sabbath."

- The Pharisees were stuck in their habit of finding fault—an easy trap for religious people to fall into. Jesus reminds them to really listen. The Word of God is not given to us as an instruction manual but calls us to form our hearts. Jesus' heart was not set on sacrifice but on making evident God's tender mercy.

- Jesus shows understanding and compassion for his disciples who are hungry on the sabbath. He says that a compassionate response to human need is certainly more important than slavish sabbath observance. For Jesus the practice of mercy and compassion, especially toward the "guiltless" and the needy, is far more important than temple sacrifice and empty ritual. Lord, release me from slavery to law and help me to experience "the freedom of the glory of the children of God" (Romans 8:21).

Saturday 16th July
Matthew 12:14–21

The Pharisees went out and conspired against Jesus, how to destroy him. When Jesus became aware of this, he departed. Many crowds followed him, and he cured all of them, and he ordered them not to make him known. This was to fulfill what had been spoken through the prophet Isaiah: "Here is my servant, whom I have chosen, my beloved, with whom my soul is well pleased. I will put my Spirit upon him, and he will proclaim justice to the Gentiles. He will not wrangle or cry aloud, nor will anyone hear his voice in the streets. He will not break a bruised reed or quench a smoldering wick until he brings justice to victory. And in his name the Gentiles will hope."

- The Pharisees used the Scriptures as a code of law, always looking outward to see how well it was observed. For Jesus, the Scripture was a communication with God, a heart-to-heart. I pray this text from Isaiah as Jesus did, reassured as I notice how God's promise calls me to hope and promises me life.

- Jesus values even what is fragile or bruised; I bring the hopes I cherish before him and ask for blessing and hope. I acknowledge my hopes for myself and my relationships, and I consider how I might work with God to bring them to life. The voice of Jesus is not shrill or contentious: the Spirit of God speaks to our hearts in a gentle and undramatic way. I pray that I may hear the voice of the Lord.

The Sixteenth Week of Ordinary Time
July 17—July 23

Something to think and pray about each day this week:

Seeing Things Differently

Good decisions emerge from deep prayer. In the story of Martha and Mary, Jesus highlights two dimensions that must be balanced in the life of a Christian. In my life, how well do I balance the Martha and the Mary? Do I ever feel called by God to give priority to the contemplative dimension of life? Am I quiet enough within to notice what God may be asking of me? Or do I never even imagine that I am sufficiently important for God to ask me anything? Do I rush into decisions and ignore "the still small voice" that Elijah heard on the mountain? Saint Ignatius of Loyola, although a busy administrator, advised against making any decision without first consulting God, "as a wise and loving Father."

"To live is to change, and to be perfect is to have changed often," says John Henry Newman. Am I truly alive and open to "new things" (Isaiah 48:6) that have the touch of God about them? And finally, am I strong enough to go against the expectations of those around me in responding to God's call?

The Presence of God

At any time of the day or night we can call on Jesus. He is always waiting, listening for our call. What a wonderful blessing. No phone needed, no e-mails, just a whisper.

Freedom

If God were trying to tell me something, would I know? If God were reassuring me or challenging me, would I notice? I ask for the grace to be free of my own preoccupations and open to what God may be saying to me.

Consciousness

I exist in a web of relationships—links to nature, people, God. I trace out these links, giving thanks for the life that flows through them. Some links are twisted or broken: I may feel regret, anger, disappointment. I pray for the gift of acceptance and forgiveness.

The Word

I read the Word of God slowly, a few times over, and I listen to what God is saying to me. (Please turn to the Scripture on the following pages. Inspiration points are provided should you need them. When you are ready, return here to continue.)

Conversation

Jesus, you always welcomed little children when you walked on this earth. Teach me to have a childlike trust in you, to live in the knowledge that you will never abandon me.

Conclusion

I thank God for these few moments we have spent alone together and for any insights I may have been given concerning the text.

Sunday 17th July
Sixteenth Sunday in Ordinary Time
Luke 10:38–42

Now as they went on their way, Jesus entered a certain village, where a woman named Martha welcomed him into her home. She had a sister named Mary, who sat at the Lord's feet and listened to what he was saying. But Martha was distracted by her many tasks; so she came to him and asked, "Lord, do you not care that my sister has left me to do all the work by myself? Tell her then to help me." But the Lord answered her, "Martha, Martha, you are worried and distracted by many things; there is need of only one thing. Mary has chosen the better part, which will not be taken away from her."

- It is easy to be distracted and fragmented when many things call for attention—even what is good can lose its luster if we forget what busyness is about. Martha seems to have been distracted by the many things she had to do; she forgot whom she was doing them for.

- I pray that I, like Mary, can be drawn to the presence of Jesus and, like Martha, can be honest with him about what distracts me.

Monday 18th July
Matthew 12:38–42

Some of the scribes and Pharisees said to Jesus, "Teacher, we wish to see a sign from you." But he answered them, "An evil and adulterous generation asks for a sign, but no sign will be given to it except the sign of the prophet Jonah. For just as Jonah was three days and three nights in the belly of the sea monster, so for three days and three nights the Son of Man will be in the heart of the earth. The people of Nineveh will rise up at the judgment with this generation and condemn it, because they repented at the proclamation of Jonah, and see, something greater than Jonah is here! The queen of the South will rise up at the judgment with this generation and condemn it, because she came from the ends of the earth to listen to the wisdom of Solomon, and see, something greater than Solomon is here!"

- Most of us are fascinated by spectacular events. This is why the scribes want "a sign" from Jesus to prove that he possessed exceptional powers. But Jesus is not interested in superficial curiosity about himself. He is not a magician! Rather, he is God-among-them, mysterious and blessed.

- How deep is my faith? Does it depend on dramatic things happening in answer to my prayer? Or do I simply and humbly place my faith and hope in the person of Jesus Christ and unite my prayer with his? Can I simply say: "Your will be done" (Matthew 6:10)?

Tuesday 19th July
Matthew 12:46–50

While Jesus was still speaking to the crowds, his mother and his brothers were standing outside, wanting to speak to him. Someone told him, "Look, your mother and your brothers are standing outside, wanting to speak to you." But to the one who had told him this, Jesus replied, "Who is my mother, and who are my brothers?" And pointing to his disciples, he said, "Here are my mother and my brothers! For whoever does the will of my Father in heaven is my brother and sister and mother."

- When was the last time I felt I was left "standing outside"? When I feel this way, do I try to speak to Jesus?

- Because I at least try to do the will of God, I am a member of Jesus' inner family circle! Let this make me happy today.

Wednesday 20th July
Matthew 13:1–9

Jesus went out of the house and sat beside the lake. Such great crowds gathered around him that he got into a boat and sat there, while the whole crowd stood on the beach. And he told them many things in parables, saying: "Listen! A sower went out to sow. And as he sowed, some seeds fell on the path, and the birds came and ate them up. Other seeds fell on rocky ground, where they did not have much soil, and they sprang up quickly, since they had no depth of soil. But when the sun rose, they were scorched; and since they had no root, they withered away. Other seeds fell among thorns, and the thorns grew up and choked them. Other seeds fell on good soil and brought forth grain, some a hundredfold, some sixty, some thirty. Let anyone with ears listen!"

- Jesus made the boat his pulpit, announcing the Word of God from this unlikely place. The Word of God has been scattered in my life—sometimes flourishing, sometimes seeming to fade away. I think of where I am strong and consider how I might give witness to God's goodness from that place, just as Jesus chose the best place from which to make his voice heard.

- As I think of myself as the field in which the Word of God is scattered, I may recognize the barren places, the dry patches, and the fertile parts. To which do I pay attention? I take some time to appreciate where God's Word has found a root in me, and I ask God's help to remain open to such seed as may be scattered again today.

Thursday 21st July
Matthew 13:10–17

The disciples came and asked him, "Why do you speak to them in parables?" He answered, "To you it has been given to know the secrets of the kingdom of heaven, but to them it has not been given. For to those who have, more will be given, and they will have an abundance; but from those who have nothing, even what they have will be taken away. The reason I speak to them in parables is that 'seeing they do not perceive, and hearing they do not listen, nor do they understand.' With them indeed is fulfilled the prophecy of Isaiah that says: 'You will indeed listen, but never understand, and you will indeed look, but never perceive. For this people's heart has grown dull, and their ears are hard of hearing, and they have shut their eyes; so that they might not look with their eyes, and listen with their ears, and understand with their heart and turn—and I would heal them.' But blessed are your eyes, for they see, and your ears, for they hear. Truly I tell you, many prophets and righteous people longed to see what you see, but did not see it, and to hear what you hear, but did not hear it."

- It may seem strange that Jesus was prepared to be misunderstood but, like every good teacher, he wanted his hearers to do some work themselves. He wanted them to receive the word in their hearts and to make the personal connections that would make his message meaningful. I take some time to appreciate the fact that Jesus trusts me to understand his message in my particular way.

- Jesus speaks in parables so that his meaning may take root in the soil of my life: only I can, in my prayer, receive the Word of God that is addressed to me. I quiet the voices of my habits and of usual interpretations, listening for the whisper that speaks to my heart. Even though he offers life in abundance, Jesus accepts that there are those who will learn nothing. I do not have to be anxious about them but pray with compassion for all who have not found the source of life. Jesus offers me more, strengthening my faith, building me up in love, nurturing my hope.

Friday 22nd July

John 20:1–2, 11–18

Early on the first day of the week, while it was still dark, Mary Magdalene came to the tomb and saw that the stone had been removed from the tomb. So she ran and went to Simon Peter and the other disciple, the one whom Jesus loved, and said to them, "They have taken the Lord out of the tomb, and we do not know where they have laid him." Mary stood weeping outside the tomb. As she wept, she bent over to look into the tomb; and she saw two angels in white, sitting where the body of Jesus had been lying, one at the head and the other at the feet. They said to her, "Woman, why are you weeping?" She said to them, "They have taken away my Lord, and I do not know where they have laid him." When she had said this, she turned around and saw Jesus standing there, but she did not know that it was Jesus. Jesus said to her, "Woman, why are you weeping? Whom are you looking for?" Supposing him to be the gardener, she said to him, "Sir, if you have carried him away, tell me where you have laid him, and I will take him away." Jesus said to her, "Mary!" She turned and said to him in Hebrew, "Rabbouni!" (which means Teacher). Jesus said to her, "Do not hold on to me, because I have not yet ascended to the Father. But go to my brothers and say to them, 'I am ascending to my Father and your Father, to my God and your God.'" Mary Magdalene went and announced to the disciples, "I have seen the Lord"; and she told them that he had said these things to her.

- Mary weeps for what she sees as missing, her tears making it difficult for her to recognize who is present. Easter rescues us not just from our sin but calls us beyond our dutiful habits, our worthy projects, and our personal values. Jesus asks us, "Whom are you looking for?" and invites us to let our hopes find true life. He wants to enrich us and to help us to recognize where his Spirit is moving in our lives.

- Do we sometimes think the Lord has been taken away? Prayer and Christian life can be drab, dry, and tiresome; institutional scandals drain energy. Jesus is always new, part of the prayer and Christian life of us all. We are not to hold on to an "old Jesus" but walk with him as he walks the new journey of life and prayer with us.

Saturday 23rd July

Matthew 13:24–30

Jesus put before them another parable: "The kingdom of heaven may be compared to someone who sowed good seed in his field; but while everybody was asleep, an enemy came and sowed weeds among the wheat, and then went away. So when the plants came up and bore grain, then the weeds appeared as well. And the slaves of the householder came and said to him, 'Master, did you not sow good seed in your field? Where, then, did these weeds come from?' He answered, 'An enemy has done this.' The slaves said to him, 'Then do you want us to go and gather them?' But he replied, 'No; for in gathering the weeds you would uproot the wheat along with them. Let both of them grow together until the harvest; and at harvest time I will tell the reapers. Collect the weeds first and bind them in bundles to be burned, but gather the wheat into my barn.'"

- The farmer discovers the malicious act but avoids a hasty response. He is prepared to wait until the proper time, knowing that, while the seedlings are indistinguishable, the plants will be evidently different from one another. As I lay my life before God, I remind myself that the task of judgment is not mine, nor is it for now.

- Good and evil coexist in human life and in the world. Nothing and no one is perfect. We are all in need of forgiveness and redemption. Lord Jesus, you know my strengths and my weaknesses. Help me to produce a rich harvest of good works to the greater glory of the Father.

The Seventeenth Week of Ordinary Time
July 24—July 30

Something to think and pray about each day this week:

The Play of Prayer

Wisdom, the first of all creation and God's endless delight, is described as follows:

"I was beside him, like a master worker,
And I was daily his delight,
rejoicing before him always,
rejoicing in his inhabited world and delighting in the human race" (Proverbs 8:30–31).

If we are indeed created in God's image, then our human play is rooted in divine play. Every creature plays, especially the young—from kittens and puppies to calves and tiger cubs. As children we play with joyful abandon, delighting our parents as Wisdom delighted God day after day. But in our prayer, the child in us is often stifled. Without a child's sense of wonder, our praise of God becomes sterile.

Yet it is the child in us who can most truly live in a state of becoming—untrammeled by the past, always open to growth and change. It is the child in us who can truly be open to God's constant invitation to be born again, to be part of the creation that is itself constantly being re-created. It is the child in us who can thrill to a sense of closeness to the source of all creation. I am God's delight: I can play spontaneously before my Creator and take joy in the human story, despite its disasters. I can also become a "master worker" collaborating with God in the shaping of the future.

The Presence of God

I stand at the door and knock, says the Lord. What a wonderful privilege that the Lord of all creation desires to come to me. I welcome his presence.

Freedom

Lord, grant me the grace to have freedom of the spirit. Cleanse my heart and soul so I may live joyously in your love.

Consciousness

I remind myself that I am in the presence of the Lord. I will take refuge in his loving heart. He is my strength in times of weakness. He is my comforter in times of sorrow.

The Word

God speaks to each one of us individually. I listen attentively to hear what he is saying to me. Read the text a few times, then listen. (Please turn to the Scripture on the following pages. Inspiration points are provided should you need them. When you are ready, return here to continue.)

Conversation

Remembering that I am still in God's presence, I imagine Jesus himself standing or sitting beside me, and I say whatever is on my mind, whatever is in my heart, speaking as one friend to another.

Conclusion

Glory be to the Father, and to the Son, and to the Holy Spirit, as it was in the beginning, is now and ever shall be, world without end. Amen.

Sunday 24th July
Seventeenth Sunday in Ordinary Time

Luke 11:1–13

Jesus was praying in a certain place, and after he had finished, one of his disciples said to him, "Lord, teach us to pray, as John taught his disciples." He said to them, "When you pray, say: Father, hallowed be your name. Your kingdom come. Give us each day our daily bread. And forgive us our sins, for we ourselves forgive everyone indebted to us. And do not bring us to the time of trial." And he said to them, "Suppose one of you has a friend, and you go to him at midnight and say to him, 'Friend, lend me three loaves of bread; for a friend of mine has arrived, and I have nothing to set before him.' And he answers from within, 'Do not bother me; the door has already been locked, and my children are with me in bed; I cannot get up and give you anything.' I tell you, even though he will not get up and give him anything because he is his friend, at least because of his persistence he will get up and give him whatever he needs. So I say to you, Ask, and it will be given to you; search, and you will find; knock, and the door will be opened for you. For everyone who asks receives, and everyone who searches finds, and for everyone who knocks, the door will be opened. Is there anyone among you who, if your child asks for a fish, will give a snake instead of a fish? Or if the child asks for an egg, will give a scorpion? If you then, who are evil, know how to give good gifts to your children, how much more will the heavenly Father give the Holy Spirit to those who ask him!"

- The disciples see how vitally important prayer is to Jesus. They want to be able to pray like him. What we call the Lord's Prayer is the model for all prayer because it contains all that Christians need for authentic prayer. I shall pray it slowly today, as if I were saying it for the first time.

- This passage is also a call to perseverance in prayer. It is based on the conviction that the caring, gracious, and generous Father of Jesus is always attentive to the needs of all who turn to him in prayer. Lord

Jesus, thank you for teaching us how to pray, just as you pray. Help us always to persevere in prayer and never to lose hope.

Monday 25th July
Matthew 20:20–28

The mother of the sons of Zebedee came to him with her sons, and kneeling before him, she asked a favor of him. And he said to her, "What do you want?" She said to him, "Declare that these two sons of mine will sit, one at your right hand and one at your left, in your kingdom." But Jesus answered, "You do not know what you are asking. Are you able to drink the cup that I am about to drink?" They said to him, "We are able." He said to them, "You will indeed drink my cup, but to sit at my right hand and at my left, this is not mine to grant, but it is for those for whom it has been prepared by my Father." When the ten heard it, they were angry with the two brothers. But Jesus called them to him and said, "You know that the rulers of the Gentiles lord it over them, and their great ones are tyrants over them. It will not be so among you; but whoever wishes to be great among you must be your servant, and whoever wishes to be first among you must be your slave; just as the Son of Man came not to be served but to serve, and to give his life a ransom for many."

• Jesus seems to ask, "Are you ready to endure hardship with the prospect of reward?" only to go on to say to the brothers that they should be ready to endure even without any promise of what they covet. They had to ask, "Are we in this for God or for ourselves?" True prayer will not allow us to shirk questions like these, which hook out the truth.

• Jesus came not only to serve but "to give his life as a ransom for many." The great saints were moved by the extremes to which Jesus went to demonstrate God's infinite love for humanity. May I be similarly moved so as to express always my profound love and gratitude to God for what Jesus has done.

Tuesday 26th July

Matthew 13:36–43

Then Jesus left the crowds and went into the house. And his disciples approached him, saying, "Explain to us the parable of the weeds of the field." He answered, "The one who sows the good seed is the Son of Man; the field is the world, and the good seed are the children of the kingdom; the weeds are the children of the evil one, and the enemy who sowed them is the devil; the harvest is the end of the age, and the reapers are angels. Just as the weeds are collected and burned up with fire, so will it be at the end of the age. The Son of Man will send his angels, and they will collect out of his kingdom all causes of sin and all evildoers, and they will throw them into the furnace of fire, where there will be weeping and gnashing of teeth. Then the righteous will shine like the sun in the kingdom of their Father. Let anyone with ears listen!"

- The parables Jesus tells are themselves like seeds: simple stories take root in our lives and, if allowed the light of our reflection and the nourishment of our prayer, grow to become meaningful landmarks. The kingdom of God proclaimed by Jesus may appear in subtle, undistinguished ways. Accepting the reality of the reign of God is not an immediate call to action: the first contact explores our wisdom, patience, and trust.

- Where there is life there is always hope of redemption and of the triumph of good over evil. The ultimate victory of goodness, love, truth, and justice will be accomplished by the Son of Man at "the harvest at the end of the age." Lord, take possession of my "field"— my heart and my life—so that "the evil one" may not have any power over me. Help my unique light to shine out in the world, just like "the righteous who shine like the sun in the kingdom of their Father."

Wednesday 27th July

Matthew 13:44–46

Jesus said, "The kingdom of heaven is like treasure hidden in a field, which someone found and hid; then in his joy he goes and sells all that he has and buys that field. Again, the kingdom of heaven is like a merchant in search of fine pearls; on finding one pearl of great value, he went and sold all that he had and bought it."

- Haven't I read this parable before? Jesus says, "Yes, of course you have. But have you really heard it?" I consider how I responded to the parable when I received it last and let my reaction then and my reaction now contrast with one another. The Word of God is alive and active (Hebrews 4:12). If I am awake to it, it will call me to life.

- In the Lord's Prayer we ask that the kingdom will come among us and within us. But that will not happen without our cooperation.

Thursday 28th July

Matthew 13:47–53

Jesus said, "Again, the kingdom of heaven is like a net that was thrown into the sea and caught fish of every kind; when it was full, they drew it ashore, sat down, and put the good into baskets but threw out the bad. So it will be at the end of the age. The angels will come out and separate the evil from the righteous and throw them into the furnace of fire, where there will be weeping and gnashing of teeth. "Have you understood all this?" They answered, "Yes." And he said to them, "Therefore every scribe who has been trained for the kingdom of heaven is like the master of a household who brings out of his treasure what is new and what is old." When Jesus had finished these parables, he left that place.

- A hoarder gathers junk and holds on to what has no further use; a wise householder, on the other hand, keeps what may be of value at hand. When your prayer calls things out of memory, consider how you turn over the past: are you seeing it as you saw it before, or are you discovering new evidence of God's abiding care?

- Father, as we weave our way through life, help us to discern what is pleasing to you and how we can reach for the heavens in our daily communion with our brothers and sisters. Help us to learn from our experience of life what helps us live lovingly.

Friday 29th July
Luke 10:38–42

Now as they went on their way, Jesus entered a certain village, where a woman named Martha welcomed him into her home. She had a sister named Mary, who sat at the Lord's feet and listened to what he was saying. But Martha was distracted by her many tasks; so she came to him and asked, "Lord, do you not care that my sister has left me to do all the work by myself? Tell her then to help me." But the Lord answered her, "Martha, Martha, you are worried and distracted by many things; there is need of only one thing. Mary has chosen the better part, which will not be taken away from her."

- It is easy to be distracted and fragmented when many things call for attention—even what is good can lose its luster if we forget what busyness is about. Martha seems to have been distracted by the many things she had to do; she forgot whom she was doing them for.
- I pray that I, like Mary, can be drawn to the presence of Jesus and, like Martha, can be honest with him about what distracts me.

Saturday 30th July
Matthew 14:1–12

At that time Herod the ruler heard reports about Jesus; and he said to his servants, "This is John the Baptist; he has been raised from the dead, and for this reason these powers are at work in him." For Herod had arrested John, bound him, and put him in prison on account of Herodias, his brother Philip's wife, because John had been telling him, "It is not lawful for you to have her." Though Herod wanted to put him to death, he feared the crowd, because they regarded him as a prophet. But when Herod's birthday came, the daughter of Herodias danced before the company, and she pleased Herod so much that he promised on oath to grant her whatever she might ask. Prompted by her mother, she said, "Give me the head of John the Baptist here on a platter." The king was grieved, yet out of regard for his oaths and for the guests, he commanded it to be given; he sent and had John beheaded in the prison. The head was brought on a platter and given to the girl, who brought it to her mother. His disciples came and took the body and buried it; then they went and told Jesus.

- Herod's generous promise was not balanced by wisdom and justice. I pray for people whose lives are out of balance and who have lost sight of their true good. I call to mind those who suffer injustice because of the pride of others, and I allow God to tell me what I might do, how I might pray.

- This is a story about negative emotions—fear, passion, hatred, lack of human respect. These can so overwhelm us that we ignore their consequences. Self-control isn't popular in our world. But it is a gift of the Spirit: perhaps I need to pray for it?

The Eighteenth Week of Ordinary Time
July 31—August 6

Something to think and pray about each day this week:

Contemplation in Action

Why should Christians struggle for justice, as Jesus did? After all, it can be difficult, self-sacrificing, and problematic.

Is it for fear of being punished, if we fail to show love? No. The unconditional love of God always forgives us our failings. Is it for the sake of reward? No, because there is no reward for all our hard, self-sacrificing efforts. Why not? Because the reward is already given! The moment we were created, we were given the gift of the infinite and unconditional love of God, and that gift is ours to keep forever.

For a Christian, the only motivation to do good is gratitude—gratitude for God's gifts and for the gift that comes with the gifts: God's infinite and unconditional love. The Eucharistic Prefaces say that it is right always and everywhere to give God thanks for all God's gifts. The deeper my awareness of these gifts, the deeper my gratitude, and this makes me more committed to reaching out to God's children on the margins. And the more I reach out to them, the closer they lead me to contemplation of the Giver of the Gifts. To work for social justice, I have to be contemplative.

The Presence of God
Dear Jesus, I call on you today longing for your presence. I desire to love you as you love me. May nothing ever separate me from you.

Freedom
Lord, you gave me life and the gift of freedom. Through your love I exist in this world. May I never take the gift of life for granted. May I always respect the right to life of others.

Consciousness
In God's loving presence I unwind the past day, starting from now and looking back, moment by moment. I gather in all the goodness and light, in gratitude. I attend to the shadows and what they say to me, seeking healing, courage, forgiveness.

The Word
I take my time to read the Word of God slowly, a few times, allowing myself to dwell on anything that strikes me. (Please turn to the Scripture on the following pages. Inspiration points are provided should you need them. When you are ready, return here to continue.)

Conversation
Sometimes I wonder what I might say if I were to meet you in person, Lord. I think I might say, "Thank you, Lord" for always being there for me.

Conclusion
I thank God for these few moments we have spent alone together and for any insights I may have been given concerning the text.

Sunday 31st July
Eighteenth Sunday in Ordinary Time
Luke 12:13–21

Someone in the crowd said to Jesus, "Teacher, tell my brother to divide the family inheritance with me." But he said to him, "Friend, who set me to be a judge or arbitrator over you?" And he said to them, "Take care! Be on your guard against all kinds of greed; for one's life does not consist in the abundance of possessions." Then he told them a parable: "The land of a rich man produced abundantly. And he thought to himself, 'What should I do, for I have no place to store my crops?' Then he said, 'I will do this: I will pull down my barns and build larger ones, and there I will store all my grain and my goods. And I will say to my soul, "Soul, you have ample goods laid up for many years; relax, eat, drink, be merry."' But God said to him, 'You fool! This very night your life is being demanded of you. And the things you have prepared, whose will they be?' So it is with those who store up treasures for themselves but are not rich toward God."

- Whenever Jesus meets the crowds, he meets many different needs. People present their sicknesses, tell him of the illnesses of others, seek out God's ways, and, here, speak of their ordinary concerns. It is often so for me as I pray: needs of different kinds come into my head, petitions surface, and arguments come to mind. As Jesus replied to the person in the crowd, he speaks to me to help me see what is of lasting importance. Help me, Jesus, not to be distracted by the waves on the surface but to be sensitive to the deeper current that draws me to you.

- Jesus is asked to settle an inheritance case. He cautions his listeners against any kind of greed. He tells them that their lives are not made secure by what they own. They must grow into a true sense of values and recognize that their real life cannot be measured in terms of material possessions. Jesus, how patient you are with us as we struggle with our earthly desires. We want more and yet more. We look with envy on what others seem to have—better homes, better jobs, better ways of living. Help us instead to be grateful for what we have, for your goodness to us, and for who we are as children of God.

Monday 1st August

Matthew 14:13–21

Now when Jesus heard of the death of John the Baptist, he withdrew from there in a boat to a deserted place by himself. But when the crowds heard it, they followed him on foot from the towns. When he went ashore, he saw a great crowd; and he had compassion for them and cured their sick. When it was evening, the disciples came to him and said, "This is a deserted place, and the hour is now late; send the crowds away so that they may go into the villages and buy food for themselves." Jesus said to them, "They need not go away; you give them something to eat." They replied, "We have nothing here but five loaves and two fish." And he said, "Bring them here to me." Then he ordered the crowds to sit down on the grass. Taking the five loaves and the two fish, he looked up to heaven, and blessed and broke the loaves, and gave them to the disciples, and the disciples gave them to the crowds. And all ate and were filled; and they took up what was left over of the broken pieces, twelve baskets full. And those who ate were about five thousand men, besides women and children.

- Here Jesus challenges the disciples to "feed" the people themselves. Is this a hint of how Jesus shares himself in the Eucharist? It hints that we in our own turn are to be given for others, like bread that he can take, bless, break, and share with those around us. To receive the Eucharist has this awesome dimension!

- Father, help us to share our giftedness with one another. Help us to share what we have with the poor. Free us from the desire to hold on to what we have. Every good thing is a gift from you, and gifts are to be generously shared.

Tuesday 2nd August

Matthew 14:22–36

Jesus made the disciples get into the boat and go on ahead to the other side, while he dismissed the crowds. And after he had dismissed the crowds, he went up the mountain by himself to pray. When evening came, he was there alone, but by this time the boat, battered by the waves, was far from the land, for the wind was against them. And early in the morning he came walking towards them on the lake. But when the disciples saw him walking on the lake, they were terrified, saying, "It is a ghost!" And they cried out in fear. But immediately Jesus spoke to them and said, "Take heart, it is I; do not be afraid." Peter answered him, "Lord, if it is you, command me to come to you on the water." He said, "Come." So Peter got out of the boat, started walking on the water, and came towards Jesus. But when he noticed the strong wind, he became frightened, and beginning to sink, he cried out, "Lord, save me!" Jesus immediately reached out his hand and caught him, saying to him, "You of little faith, why did you doubt?" When they got into the boat, the wind ceased. And those in the boat worshipped him, saying, "Truly you are the Son of God." When they had crossed over, they came to land at Gennesaret. After the people of that place recognized him, they sent word throughout the region and brought all who were sick to him, and begged him that they might touch even the fringe of his cloak; and all who touched it were healed.

- Having sent everybody away, Jesus went to pray. His prayer, however, did not distance himself from the needs of others but prompted him to go to the aid of his friends. Show me, Jesus, how you come to me when I am battered by the waves. Let me, like Peter, reach out to you in faith and seek to be close to you in times of trouble.

- Jesus did not come immediately to rescue the struggling disciples. He actually let them battle through most of the night. We experience this, too: our faith is sometimes stretched almost to the breaking point. The humanity of Peter is so reassuring. He jumps into the water without thinking. But once he takes his eyes off Jesus, he begins to sink. There's a lesson for us all here in these troubled times. We must keep our eye on Jesus, not on the waves in our lives.

Wednesday 3rd August
Matthew 15:21–28

Jesus left that place and went away to the district of Tyre and Sidon. Just then a Canaanite woman from that region came out and started shouting, "Have mercy on me, Lord, Son of David; my daughter is tormented by a demon." But he did not answer her at all. And his disciples came and urged him, saying, "Send her away, for she keeps shouting after us." He answered, "I was sent only to the lost sheep of the house of Israel." But she came and knelt before him, saying, "Lord, help me." He answered, "It is not fair to take the children's food and throw it to the dogs." She said, "Yes, Lord, yet even the dogs eat the crumbs that fall from their masters' table." Then Jesus answered her, "Woman, great is your faith! Let it be done for you as you wish." And her daughter was healed instantly.

- This woman was persistent in pursuing what she wanted as she announced her request. Jesus often meets such people and puts the question back to them: how important is it to you? Jesus, rescue me from any habit of prayer that focuses on my action or words instead of listening for your voice. Help me to enter into conversation with you now and to remain in relationship with you always.

- Even when the woman appeared to get no answer from Jesus, she persisted, showing the depth of her desire. I realize that my prayer often falters when I see no answer; I sometimes give up easily, not giving the energy, time, or attention that demonstrates my sincerity. The dialogue between Jesus and the woman seemed an embarrassment to the disciples; prayer, my conversation with Jesus, will always seem odd until I view it in faith.

Thursday 4th August

Matthew 16:13–23

Now when Jesus came into the district of Caesarea Philippi, he asked his disciples, "Who do people say that the Son of Man is?" And they said, "Some say John the Baptist, but others Elijah, and still others Jeremiah or one of the prophets." He said to them, "But who do you say that I am?" Simon Peter answered, "You are the Messiah, the Son of the living God." And Jesus answered him, "Blessed are you, Simon son of Jonah! For flesh and blood has not revealed this to you, but my Father in heaven. And I tell you, you are Peter, and on this rock I will build my church, and the gates of Hades will not prevail against it. I will give you the keys of the kingdom of heaven, and whatever you bind on earth will be bound in heaven, and whatever you loose on earth will be loosed in heaven." Then he sternly ordered the disciples not to tell anyone that he was the Messiah. From that time on, Jesus began to show his disciples that he must go to Jerusalem and undergo great suffering at the hands of the elders and chief priests and scribes, and be killed, and on the third day be raised. And Peter took him aside and began to rebuke him, saying, "God forbid it, Lord! This must never happen to you." But he turned and said to Peter, "Get behind me, Satan! You are a stumbling block to me; for you are setting your mind not on divine things but on human things."

• If Jesus' first disciple did not understand his message, how can I be quick to condemn myself or others who don't seem to get it? Jesus will not change his message to suit me but calls me to set my mind on what is important to him. Jesus, as you look at my life, show me what is really important.

• We do so much to make ourselves comfortable; protecting and looking after ourselves can become priorities when we think the world is a rough place. Perhaps we need to be careful not to cushion ourselves too much, to be careful not to forget that the cross is always within sight of the Christian. We may not want to make life difficult for ourselves, but our prayer acknowledges the pain that is experienced by others in which Jesus still suffers. I pray for the freedom I need to be able to let go, to realize that my life is not mine to save; it comes from God and its fullness lies in God.

Friday 5th August
Matthew 16:24–28

Then Jesus told his disciples, "If any want to become my followers, let them deny themselves and take up their cross and follow me. For those who want to save their life will lose it, and those who lose their life for my sake will find it. For what will it profit them if they gain the whole world but forfeit their life? Or what will they give in return for their life? For the Son of Man is to come with his angels in the glory of his Father, and then he will repay everyone for what has been done. Truly I tell you, there are some standing here who will not taste death before they see the Son of Man coming in his kingdom."

• It is impossible to follow Jesus without accepting the cross, without acknowledging and embracing all of life. Jesus does not allow me to close my eyes to what creates difficulty for me but wants me to be honest about what I think threatens my happiness. I think of what my happiness seems to rely on, consider where it comes from, and offer it back to God.

• When Ignatius of Loyola was guiding Francis Xavier in the early days of his discovery of God's love, he repeated, over and over, "Francis, what will it profit . . . ?" He obviously felt that Francis was stuck in some unfreedom and needed a bit of prodding. What about me? What holds me back from giving myself in trust and love to the Lord? What am I afraid of losing?

Saturday 6th August
Luke 9:28b–36

Now about eight days after these sayings Jesus took with him Peter and John and James, and went up on the mountain to pray. And while he was praying, the appearance of his face changed, and his clothes became dazzling white. Suddenly they saw two men, Moses and Elijah, talking to him. Now Peter and his companions were weighed down with sleep; but since they had stayed awake, they saw his glory and the two men who stood with him. Just as they were leaving him, Peter said to Jesus, "Master, it is good for us to be here; let us make three dwellings, one for you, one for Moses, and one for Elijah"—not knowing what he said. While he was saying this, a cloud came and overshadowed them; and they were terrified as they entered the cloud. Then from the cloud came a voice that said, "This is my Son, my Chosen; listen to him!" When the voice had spoken, Jesus was found alone. And they kept silent and in those days told no one any of the things they had seen.

- Peter, John, and James were heavy with sleep, but on waking they saw Jesus' glory! They slept again in Gethsemane. In the Bible such sleep signifies that the disciples do not understand Jesus and his relationship with his Father. Jesus is left to carry the work of salvation without their help.

- Jesus, how often have our eyes been closed in sleep as we walk with you through life? How often are our ears closed, too, to the word you speak to us through our daily conversations? May your word become awake, alive, and active in us each day as we travel the road with you.

August 7—August 13

Something to think and pray about each day this week:

God in a Slum

Father Pedro Arrupe, Superior General of the Jesuits after Vatican II, traveled extensively. In Latin America he was invited to celebrate Mass in a large slum located in a hollow that filled with mud when it rained. There was no church, just a canopy over the little altar. Animals wandered in and out. The guitarist played a hymn with the following words: "To love is to give yourself. It is to forget yourself, by seeking what can make others happy. How beautiful it is to live for love."

During the Mass the absolute silence of the consecration contrasted with the heartfelt shout of the Our Father. At communion he noticed tears on many faces. These people knew they were meeting Jesus, their only hope and consolation.

At the end, a big man said to him: "Come to my house. I have something to honor you with." The weather-beaten shack was on a hill. His host made him sit on a rickety chair, from which Pedro could see the setting sun, and said: "See, señor, how beautiful it is!" They sat silently, watching the sun disappear. The man added: "I did not know how to thank you for all that you have done for us. I have nothing to give you, but I thought you would like to see this sunset. It pleased you, didn't it? Good evening."

The Presence of God
Dear Lord, as I come to you today, fill my heart and my whole being with the wonder of your presence. Help me to be open to you for this time as I put aside the cares of this world. Fill my mind with your peace, your love.

Freedom
Lord, grant me the grace to be free from the excesses of this life. Let me not get caught up with the desire for wealth. Keep my heart and mind free to love and serve you.

Consciousness
In the presence of my loving Creator, I look honestly at my feelings over the past day—the highs, the lows, and the level ground. Can I see where the Lord has been present?

The Word
The Word of God comes down to us through the Scriptures. May the Holy Spirit enlighten my mind and my heart to respond to the gospel teachings. (Please turn to the Scripture on the following pages. Inspiration points are provided should you need them. When you are ready, return here to continue.)

Conversation
I know with certainty there were times when you carried me, Lord. When it was through your strength I got through the dark times in my life.

Conclusion
Glory be to the Father, and to the Son, and to the Holy Spirit, as it was in the beginning, is now and ever shall be, world without end. Amen.

Sunday 7th August
Nineteenth Sunday in Ordinary Time
Luke 12:35–40

Jesus said to his disciples, "Be dressed for action and have your lamps lit; be like those who are waiting for their master to return from the wedding banquet, so that they may open the door for him as soon as he comes and knocks. Blessed are those slaves whom the master finds alert when he comes; truly I tell you, he will fasten his belt and have them sit down to eat, and he will come and serve them. If he comes during the middle of the night, or near dawn, and finds them so, blessed are those slaves. But know this: if the owner of the house had known at what hour the thief was coming, he would not have let his house be broken into. You also must be ready, for the Son of Man is coming at an unexpected hour."

• The ordinary attitude of the Christian is to be awake, alert, and attentive, sensitive to the prompting of God's Spirit and aware of God's action in the world. I take some time in my prayer to be quiet so that I may hear the master's knock. In all the noise that surrounds me, where might it be that the Lord is close, ready to be with me more fully?

• The role reversal on the part of the master, who serves those slaves who were awake and alert, says much about God's gracious bounty and generosity. In discipleship there is no room for complacency or half-heartedness. The commitment required is total, and the reward is equally great. The lit lamps symbolize the alertness required of us. How is my lamp?

Monday 8th August
Matthew 17:22–27

As they were gathering in Galilee, Jesus said to them, "The Son of Man is going to be betrayed into human hands, and they will kill him, and on the third day he will be raised." And they were greatly distressed. When they reached Capernaum, the collectors of the temple tax came to Peter and said, "Does your teacher not pay the temple tax?" He said, "Yes, he does." And when he came home, Jesus spoke of it first, asking, "What do you think, Simon? From whom do kings of the earth take toll or tribute? From their children or from others?" When Peter said, "From others," Jesus said to him, "Then the children are free. However, so that we do not give offence to them, go to the lake and cast a hook; take the first fish that comes up; and when you open its mouth, you will find a coin; take that and give it to them for you and me."

- The disciples could not imagine how they might live without Jesus; they had become used to being with him, listening to him, observing him, and reflecting on his words. His talk about change threatened them. The future will threaten me, too, if I do not hear Jesus' words and receive the assurance of his abiding presence. I pray that I may receive again his words, "Peace be with you," "Take heart," and "Do not be afraid."

- This is a strange story about a coin in the mouth of a fish. We are not told that Peter actually found the coin. Michael Mullins writes, "It may well be another way of saying to those who were instructed to carry no gold, no silver, not even a few coppers in their purses, to trust in God who provides in unexpected ways."

Tuesday 9th August
Matthew 18:1–5, 10, 12–14

At that time the disciples came to Jesus and asked, "Who is the greatest in the kingdom of heaven?" He called a child, whom he put among them, and said, "Truly I tell you, unless you change and become like children, you will never enter the kingdom of heaven. Whoever becomes humble like this child is the greatest in the kingdom of heaven. Whoever welcomes one such child in my name welcomes me. Take care that you do not despise one of these little ones; for, I tell you, in heaven their angels continually see the face of my Father in heaven. What do you think? If a shepherd has a hundred sheep, and one of them has gone astray, does he not leave the ninety-nine on the mountains and go in search of the one that went astray? And if he finds it, truly I tell you, he rejoices over it more than over the ninety-nine that never went astray. So it is not the will of your Father in heaven that one of these little ones should be lost."

- Jesus turns popular values upside down. Who are the overlooked people around me? They are unlikely to be children—more probably it is those who offer humble service, the poor, people who are in some way different. Jesus asks what it would be like for me to be in their lowly state. How do I show welcome to the neglected? What do I learn from them?

- Jesus offers two strong images: the humble child and the dependent sheep. I might choose one of these and, in quiet prayer, let it unfold its meaning for me now. The disciples were used to the competitive and comparative habits of adults. Jesus showed them that there is another way of seeing the world. I pray for the humility that I need to walk more slowly and talk more simply.

Wednesday 10th August

John 12:24–26

Jesus said, "Very truly, I tell you, unless a grain of wheat falls into the earth and dies, it remains just a single grain; but if it dies, it bears much fruit. Those who love their life lose it, and those who hate their life in this world will keep it for eternal life. Whoever serves me must follow me, and where I am, there will my servant be also. Whoever serves me, the Father will honor."

- God can use us to affect the lives of many people for good. But for this we need to be following Jesus, not following our own whims and preferences. We are to surrender our lives and ask the question, "Lord, what do you want me to do with my life today?"

- Lord, grace me with the gift of letting go of all that I cling to. May I not block your Spirit moving in me. Work through me so that I may carry you to all those whose lives I touch.

Thursday 11th August

Matthew 18:21—19:1

Peter came and said to him, "Lord, if another member of the church sins against me, how often should I forgive? As many as seven times?" Jesus said to him, "Not seven times, but, I tell you, seventy-seven times. For this reason the kingdom of heaven may be compared to a king who wished to settle accounts with his slaves. When he began the reckoning, one who owed him ten thousand talents was brought to him; and, as he could not pay, his lord ordered him to be sold, together with his wife and children and all his possessions, and payment to be made. So the slave fell on his knees before him, saying, 'Have patience with me, and I will pay you everything.' And out of pity for him, the lord of that slave released him and forgave him the debt. But that same slave, as he went out, came upon one of his fellow slaves who owed him a hundred denarii; and seizing him by the throat, he said, 'Pay what you owe.' Then his fellow slave fell down and pleaded with him, 'Have patience with me, and I will pay you.' But he refused; then he went and threw him into prison until he should pay the debt. When his fellow slaves saw what had happened, they were greatly distressed, and they went and reported to their lord all that had taken place. Then his lord summoned him and said to him, 'You wicked slave! I forgave you all that debt because you pleaded with me. Should you not have had mercy on your fellow slave, as I had mercy on you?' And in anger his lord handed him over to be tortured until he should pay his entire debt. So my heavenly Father will also do to every one of you, if you do not forgive your brother or sister from your heart." When Jesus had finished saying these things, he left Galilee and went to the region of Judea beyond the Jordan.

- I realize that I can hoard nothing I receive in prayer but see that I receive every gift so that I might bless the world. God sends me to be a priestly person, bringing blessing to those around me. I take some time to grow in awareness of how God blesses me and to consider how my hands are open both to receive and to give generously.

- Forgiveness is tough. I ask Jesus now in my prayer: "Why should I forgive?" Let me listen to his reply: "Because you have been forgiven by God." We who have been forgiven so much by God do not have the right to withhold forgiveness from someone else, no matter how tough it may be.

Friday 12th August
Matthew 19:3–12

Some Pharisees came to him, and to test him they asked, "Is it lawful for a man to divorce his wife for any cause?" He answered, "Have you not read that the one who made them at the beginning 'made them male and female,' and said, 'For this reason a man shall leave his father and mother and be joined to his wife, and the two shall become one flesh'? So they are no longer two, but one flesh. Therefore what God has joined together, let no one separate." They said to him, "Why then did Moses command us to give a certificate of dismissal and to divorce her?" He said to them, "It was because you were so hard-hearted that Moses allowed you to divorce your wives, but at the beginning it was not so. And I say to you, whoever divorces his wife, except for unchastity, and marries another commits adultery." His disciples said to him, "If such is the case of a man with his wife, it is better not to marry." But he said to them, "Not everyone can accept this teaching, but only those to whom it is given. For there are eunuchs who have been so from birth, and there are eunuchs who have been made eunuchs by others, and there are eunuchs who have made themselves eunuchs for the sake of the kingdom of heaven. Let anyone accept this who can."

- It is a fact of life today that marriages do break up, and this leads to hardship and pain, particularly where children are concerned. Let us pray for all those who are going through tough times in their marriages. Let us intercede also for couples who are intending to enter this wonderful and blessed vocation.

- Lord, you were a guest at the marriage feast in Cana. You care about marriages. So we pray for all married couples. Turn the water of their anxiety and fear into the wine of trust in you. Enable them to call on the blessing of the sacrament they received when they were joined together as man and wife.

Saturday 13th August
Matthew 19:13–15

Little children were being brought to him in order that he might lay his hands on them and pray. The disciples spoke sternly to those who brought them; but Jesus said, "Let the little children come to me, and do not stop them; for it is to such as these that the kingdom of heaven belongs." And he laid his hands on them and went on his way.

- The disciples seem to have become like the security industry, inflating their own sense of importance and protecting their own ideas; their way of thinking and Jesus' way were at odds. Perhaps I need to be careful before I say what is important to Jesus, or I may overlook the very people Jesus cherishes.

- This tender incident comes after Jesus' teaching on marriage and divorce. The kingdom of God belongs to those who have the heart of a child. The disciples miss this point completely. Do I? Can I allow Jesus to lay his hands on me? Jesus, help us to understand that we are all your children. Teach us how to draw others to you. Do not let us turn them away through selfishness or insensitivity.

August 14—August 20

Something to think and pray about each day this week:

The Sounds of Silence

The monks of old fled from the noise and distraction of the world into the desert. If we did likewise today, our temptation would be to bring our mobile devices in our backpacks! But like the good monks, we, too, are meant to be seeking God. The movement called "The New Monasticism" tries to replant ancient values in our lives today. It proposes that our hearts can be our monasteries in the middle of busy lives. We can be still and quiet and can cultivate a place of silence in the cave of our hearts that we share only with God.

The experience of the prophet Elijah still raises an echo in us and tugs at our hearts. He was told to stand on the mountain, for the Lord was about to pass by. There came the roar of a mighty wind, but the Lord was not in the wind, nor in the earthquake that followed, nor again in the fire. Then we are told: "After the fire came a sound of sheer silence." Elijah heard this mysterious silence, and went out to meet God (1 Kings 19:11–13). They spoke together, and Elijah knew what he was to do.

Such experiences can be ours whenever we choose to leave the busy world behind and go down into the cave of our hearts, the secret place where, Jesus says, we "will meet our God who dwells there" (Matthew 6:6).

The Presence of God
God is with me, but more, God is within me. Let me dwell for a moment on God's life-giving presence in my body, in my mind, and in my heart, as I sit here, right now.

Freedom
Lord, you created me to live in freedom. May your Holy Spirit guide me to follow you freely. Instill in my heart a desire to know and love you more each day.

Consciousness
Knowing that God loves me unconditionally, I can afford to be honest about how I am. How has the past day been, and how do I feel now? I share my feelings openly with the Lord.

The Word
I read the Word of God slowly, a few times over, and I listen to what God is saying to me. (Please turn to the Scripture on the following pages. Inspiration points are provided should you need them. When you are ready, return here to continue.)

Conversation
What feelings are rising in me as I pray and reflect on God's Word? I imagine Jesus himself sitting or standing near me, and I open my heart to him.

Conclusion
I thank God for these few moments we have spent alone together and for any insights I may have been given concerning the text.

Sunday 14th August
Twentieth Sunday in Ordinary Time
Luke 12:49–53

Jesus said to the crowds, "I came to bring fire to the earth, and how I wish it were already kindled! I have a baptism with which to be baptized, and what stress I am under until it is completed! Do you think that I have come to bring peace to the earth? No, I tell you, but rather division! From now on five in one household will be divided, three against two and two against three; they will be divided: father against son and son against father, mother against daughter and daughter against mother, mother-in-law against her daughter-in-law and daughter-in-law against mother-in-law."

- Gentle Jesus, meek and mild? Conformity and harmony are never to be imposed or sought for themselves. They are not a mold into which life is to be forced. When life is properly arranged, they will be the result.

- Jesus is anxious to see the fire of God's love blaze across the globe. John the Baptist had promised that Jesus would baptize his disciples with the Holy Spirit and fire. The fire of God's love was in fact visibly cast upon the earth at Pentecost, and we thank God for it. Lord, that we might experience the fire of your love in our hearts today. Saint Ignatius of Loyola was "ablaze with God," and we wish that for ourselves, too. Only so will we be your true disciples.

Monday 15th August
The Assumption of the Blessed Virgin Mary (Day)
Luke 1:39–56

In those days Mary set out and went with haste to a Judean town in the hill country, where she entered the house of Zechariah and greeted Elizabeth. When Elizabeth heard Mary's greeting, the child leapt in her womb. And Elizabeth was filled with the Holy Spirit and exclaimed with a loud cry, "Blessed are you among women, and blessed is the fruit of your womb. And why has this happened to me, that the mother of my Lord comes to me? For as soon as I heard the sound of your greeting, the child in my womb leapt for joy. And blessed is she who believed that there would be a fulfilment of what was spoken to her by the Lord." And Mary said, "My soul magnifies the Lord, and my spirit rejoices in God my Savior, for he has looked with favor on the lowliness of his servant. Surely, from now on all generations will call me blessed; for the Mighty One has done great things for me, and holy is his name. His mercy is for those who fear him from generation to generation. He has shown strength with his arm; he has scattered the proud in the thoughts of their hearts. He has brought down the powerful from their thrones, and lifted up the lowly; he has filled the hungry with good things, and sent the rich away empty. He has helped his servant Israel, in remembrance of his mercy, according to the promise he made to our ancestors, to Abraham and to his descendants forever." And Mary remained with her for about three months and then returned to her home.

- Mary and Elizabeth are kindred spirits, sharing a bond and relationship that goes beyond words. Such friendship is a real gift from God and, as with every blessing, awaits the appreciation of prayer. I bring to mind my best experiences of friendship and let them speak to me about who God is to me and who God calls me to be.

- The Feast of the Assumption recognizes that Mary responded fully to God's invitation; it invites me to consider what holds me back and to ask for God's help.

Tuesday 16th August
Matthew 19:23–30

Then Jesus said to his disciples, "Truly I tell you, it will be hard for a rich person to enter the kingdom of heaven. Again I tell you, it is easier for a camel to go through the eye of a needle than for someone who is rich to enter the kingdom of God." When the disciples heard this, they were greatly astounded and said, "Then who can be saved?" But Jesus looked at them and said, "For mortals it is impossible, but for

God all things are possible." Then Peter said in reply, "Look, we have left everything and followed you. What then will we have?" Jesus said to them, "Truly I tell you, at the renewal of all things, when the Son of Man is seated on the throne of his glory, you who have followed me will also sit on twelve thrones, judging the twelve tribes of Israel. And everyone who has left houses or brothers or sisters or father or mother or children or fields, for my name's sake, will receive a hundredfold, and will inherit eternal life. But many who are first will be last, and the last will be first."

• Consider how much of our news coverage, conversation, and attention is directed to the rich and famous, yet we often see how their lives are lacking, how the peace that Jesus promises remains out of their reach. Without letting go, we can go nowhere; we are left where we are if we cannot trust.

• We must get our priorities right and put Jesus first in our lives. No sacrifice that we make to draw closer to God will go unrewarded. Our prayer today, Lord, is that we will not be afraid that you will ask anything of us that we cannot do. Help us to surrender totally to you, trusting that you, and you alone, are all we need.

Wednesday 17th August
Matthew 20:1–16

Jesus said to his disciples, "For the kingdom of heaven is like a landowner who went out early in the morning to hire laborers for his vineyard. After agreeing with the laborers for the usual daily wage, he sent them into his vineyard. When he went out about nine o'clock, he saw others standing idle in the marketplace; and he said to them, 'You also go into the vineyard, and I will pay you whatever is right.' So they went. When he went out again about noon and about three o'clock, he did the same. And about five o'clock he went out and found others standing around; and he said to them, 'Why are you standing here idle all day?' They said to him, 'Because no one has hired us.' He said to them, 'You also go into the vineyard.' When evening came, the owner of the vineyard said to his manager, 'Call the laborers and give them their pay, beginning with the last and then going to the first.' When those hired about five o'clock came, each of them received the usual daily wage. Now when the first came, they thought they would receive more; but each of them also received the usual daily wage. And when they received it, they grumbled against the landowner, saying, 'These last worked only one hour, and you have made them equal to us who have borne the burden of the day and the scorching heat.' But he replied to one of them, 'Friend, I am doing you no wrong; did you not agree with me for the usual daily wage? Take what belongs to you and go; I choose to give to this last the same as I give to you. Am I not allowed to do what I choose with what belongs to me? Or are you envious because I am generous?' So the last will be first, and the first will be last."

- When I look at my life and see what is good, I am drawn to give thanks. When I turn my attention to what others have, I may be distracted and notice what I lack. Lord, if I am to raise my eyes, let me direct them only to you and never to look with envy at others. They may be blessed in ways that I seem not to be, but help me not to think that I am without blessing or that you love me less.

- How different God's ways are to our ways! He uses dramatic images to turn upside-down our ideas of our self-importance. There is no place for competitiveness in the kingdom of God. Forgive us, Lord, for our jealous attitudes. Help us to be grateful for what we have and not to begrudge others any good fortune that comes their way. Help us to be generous in our treatment of others and never think of ourselves as more deserving.

Thursday 18th August
Matthew 22:1–14

Once more Jesus spoke to them in parables, saying: "The kingdom of heaven may be compared to a king who gave a wedding banquet for his son. He sent his slaves to call those who had been invited to the wedding banquet, but they would not come. Again he sent other slaves, saying, 'Tell those who have been invited: Look, I have prepared my dinner, my oxen and my fat calves have been slaughtered, and everything is ready; come to the wedding banquet.' But they made light of it and went away, one to his farm, another to his business, while the rest seized his slaves, maltreated them, and killed them. The king was enraged. He sent his troops, destroyed those murderers, and burned their city. Then he said to his slaves, 'The wedding is ready, but those invited were not worthy. Go therefore into the main streets, and invite everyone you find to the wedding banquet.' Those slaves went out into the streets and gathered all whom they found, both good and bad; so the wedding hall was filled with guests. But when the king came in to see the guests, he noticed a man there who was not wearing a wedding robe, and he said to him, 'Friend, how did you get in here without a wedding robe?' And he was speechless. Then the king said to the attendants, 'Bind him hand and foot, and throw him into the outer darkness, where there will be weeping and gnashing of teeth.' For many are called, but few are chosen."

- God invites us to draw close, not because of our worthiness or in thanks for our efforts but in a generous sharing of life. This time of prayer is part of my response: I give it wholeheartedly to God.

- The "wedding robe" I wear is my awareness of my hand before God. I pray that I may remain humble, be conscious of how I am blessed, and grow in trust as I respond to God's Spirit in my life.

Friday 19th August
Matthew 22:34–40

When the Pharisees heard that he had silenced the Sadducees, they gathered together, and one of them, a lawyer, asked him a question to test him. "Teacher, which commandment in the law is the greatest?" He said to him, "'You shall love the Lord your God with all your heart, and with all your soul, and with all your mind.' This is the greatest and first commandment. And a second is like it: 'You shall love your neighbor as yourself.' On these two commandments hang all the law and the prophets."

- Jesus calls us to more than mindfulness; paying attention is not enough. He wants us to be where he is, drawn fully into the life of God. Heart, soul, and mind show me just how fully Jesus thinks of love. Nothing is to be left out, nor is anyone to be excluded as the love of God draws me beyond myself into loving contact with those around me.

- Lord, if these two commandments could become my way of life, my religion would be simple, without arguments or complications. Let your words sink deeply into my heart and soul.

Saturday 20th August
Matthew 23:1–12

Then Jesus said, "The scribes and the Pharisees sit on Moses' seat; therefore, do whatever they teach you and follow it; but do not do as they do, for they do not practice what they teach. They tie up heavy burdens, hard to bear, and lay them on the shoulders of others; but they themselves are unwilling to lift a finger to move them. They do all their deeds to be seen by others; for they make their phylacteries broad and their fringes long. They love to have the place of honor at banquets and the best seats in the synagogues, and to be greeted with respect in the marketplaces, and to have people call them rabbi. But you are not to be called rabbi, for you have one teacher, and you are all students. And call no one your father on earth, for you have one Father—the one in heaven. Nor are you to be called instructors, for you have one instructor, the Messiah. The greatest among you will be your servant. All who exalt themselves will be humbled, and all who humble themselves will be exalted."

- Jesus does not take issue with how the Pharisees live, but he sees how they have become distracted from God by thinking using human measures and scales. Could it be that I am sometimes misled by wanting my way, by establishing my kingdom instead of seeking the reign of God?

- Religion can be heavy going! Jesus came to lighten our religious loads and focus on loving and serving others. We can put religious burdens and expectations on others, even in our judgments on them. Prayer is a time of growing in humility and joy before the God who calls us in the name of Jesus who came to serve.

August 21—August 27

Something to think and pray about each day this week:

Dare We Hope?

Pope Francis created a stir when he suggested that atheists might be saved. On the other hand, Pope Benedict alarmed many people when he insisted on the translation "for you and for many" rather than "for you and for all" in the Mass. Clearly the question put to Jesus, "Will only a few be saved?" (Luke 13:23), has not lost its urgency over the past two thousand years.

The Jews believed that on Judgment Day the wicked would receive the punishment they richly deserved. This notion appeals to us if we think that we ourselves will be among the "good." But the good news of Jesus upsets this. Paul puts it dramatically: "God gave up his Son for all of us. It is God who justifies. Who is to condemn?" (Romans 8:31–34). This hope that all may be saved appeals to us when we think of ourselves as "sinners," which we indeed are! We can hope that against all the odds God will win a total victory over evil, and that the Body of Christ will lack none of its members.

The church has long faltered regarding the salvation of all humankind. But Vatican II and the *Catechism of the Catholic Church* now tell us that we must indeed dare to hope that God, to whom nothing is impossible, will achieve his purposes. We work, pray, and endure all things for this.

The Presence of God

I pause for a moment and think of the love and the grace that God showers on me, creating me in his image and likeness, making me his temple.

Freedom

Lord, you granted me the great gift of freedom. In these times, O Lord, grant that I may be free from any form of racism or intolerance. Remind me, Lord, that we are all equal in your loving eyes.

Consciousness

To be conscious about something is to be aware of it. Dear Lord, help me to remember that you gave me life. Thank you for the gift of life. Teach me to slow down, to be still, and to enjoy the pleasures created for me. To be aware of the beauty that surrounds me. The marvel of mountains, the calmness of lakes, the fragility of a flower petal. I need to remember that all these things come from you.

The Word

God speaks to each one of us individually. I listen attentively to hear what he is saying to me. Read the text a few times, then listen. (Please turn to the Scripture on the following pages. Inspiration points are provided should you need them. When you are ready, return here to continue.)

Conversation

Begin to talk to Jesus about the piece of Scripture you have just read. What part of it strikes a chord in you? Perhaps the words of a friend— or some story you have heard recently—will slowly rise to the surface of your consciousness. If so, does the story throw light on what the Scripture passage may be trying to say to you?

Conclusion

Glory be to the Father, and to the Son, and to the Holy Spirit, as it was in the beginning, is now and ever shall be, world without end. Amen.

Sunday 21st August
Twenty-First Sunday in Ordinary Time
Luke 13:22–30

Jesus went through one town and village after another, teaching as he made his way to Jerusalem. Someone asked him, "Lord, will only a few be saved?" He said to them, "Strive to enter through the narrow door; for many, I tell you, will try to enter and will not be able. When once the owner of the house has got up and shut the door, and you begin to stand outside and to knock at the door, saying, 'Lord, open to us,' then in reply he will say to you, 'I do not know where you come from.' Then you will begin to say, 'We ate and drank with you, and you taught in our streets.' But he will say, 'I do not know where you come from; go away from me, all you evildoers!' There will be weeping and gnashing of teeth when you see Abraham and Isaac and Jacob and all the prophets in the kingdom of God, and you yourselves thrown out. Then people will come from east and west, from north and south, and will eat in the kingdom of God. Indeed, some are last who will be first, and some are first who will be last."

- Every artist, musician, and athlete whose performance I enjoy will speak of training, dedication, and commitment. Jesus calls us to think of what is important to us and to consider the efforts we make. Salvation remains God's gift, but I demonstrate my readiness and desire by my "striving." My time of prayer trains me to listen and prepares me to respond to the Word of God.

- Jesus cautions us against being presumptuous about salvation. Let us not be late arrivals at the gates of heaven! It can be a painful experience to realize that I am not as perfect as I might like to believe. What matters most is that I should have a loving and forgiving heart that embraces all my fellow sinners. Lord, you are not saying that many will be lost at the End. But you are warning us to deepen our relationship with you and to accept others. Let me play my small but essential part to ensure that all of us may be gathered safely into your kingdom.

Monday 22nd August

Matthew 23:13–22

Then Jesus said, "But woe to you, scribes and Pharisees, hypocrites! For you lock people out of the kingdom of heaven. For you do not go in yourselves, and when others are going in, you stop them. Woe to you, scribes and Pharisees, hypocrites! For you cross sea and land to make a single convert, and you make the new convert twice as much a child of hell as yourselves. Woe to you, blind guides, who say, 'Whoever swears by the sanctuary is bound by nothing, but whoever swears by the gold of the sanctuary is bound by the oath.' You blind fools! For which is greater, the gold or the sanctuary that has made the gold sacred? And you say, 'Whoever swears by the altar is bound by nothing, but whoever swears by the gift that is on the altar is bound by the oath.' How blind you are! For which is greater, the gift or the altar that makes the gift sacred? So whoever swears by the altar, swears by it and by everything on it; and whoever swears by the sanctuary, swears by it and by the one who dwells in it; and whoever swears by heaven, swears by the throne of God and by the one who is seated upon it."

- Jesus condemns the Pharisees for speaking about what is unknown to them; he was referring, of course, to what was in their hearts, not in their knowledgeable minds. There would be much silence if people spoke only about what they knew about! When it comes to faith, many people speak about what is in their heads. The silent work of God in my prayer defies explanation and suggests discretion—but can I give witness to the working of God in my heart? I don't want to be like the Pharisees when I speak of faith, letting my head do the talking. I consider how God works in the depth of my being.

- Jesus uses the strongest language to condemn those who confuse the externals of religion with what might be at its heart. I let God lead me in my time of prayer, prepared to let go even of habits, rituals, and externals—all so that I may better hear the voice of God. I pray for the community with which I worship; may we never confuse the beautiful things we have or do with their source, but may we grow together in humble service of God.

Tuesday 23rd August
Matthew 23:23–26

Jesus said, "Woe to you, scribes and Pharisees, hypocrites! For you tithe mint, dill, and cumin, and have neglected the weightier matters of the law: justice and mercy and faith. It is these you ought to have practiced without neglecting the others. You blind guides! You strain out a gnat but swallow a camel! Woe to you, scribes and Pharisees, hypocrites! For you clean the outside of the cup and of the plate, but inside they are full of greed and self-indulgence. You blind Pharisee! First clean the inside of the cup, so that the outside also may become clean."

• Attention to outward appearance is not a modern phenomenon: archaeologists find cosmetics and body art in almost every ancient culture. Jesus reminds us that the more attention we pay to the outside, the less likely we are to give care to where life really is. I consider how God sees me and how God wants me to resist any urge to present only my best side. God loves me as I am and invites me to see myself for who I am.

• Outsiders are often shocked at the hypocrisy of Christians who worship God on Sundays and then tear apart their neighbor's reputation during the rest of the week. Am I ever guilty? Cleaning "the inside of the cup" takes constant vigilance.

Wednesday 24th August
John 1:45–51

Philip found Nathanael and said to him, "We have found him about whom Moses in the law and also the prophets wrote, Jesus son of Joseph from Nazareth." Nathanael said to him, "Can anything good come out of Nazareth?" Philip said to him, "Come and see." When Jesus saw Nathanael coming toward him, he said of him, "Here is truly an Israelite in whom there is no deceit!" Nathanael asked him, "Where did you get to know me?" Jesus answered, "I saw you under the fig tree before Philip called you." Nathanael replied, "Rabbi, you are the Son of God! You are the King of Israel!" Jesus answered, "Do you believe because I told you that I saw you under the fig tree? You will see greater things than these." And he said to him, "Very truly, I tell you, you will see heaven opened and the angels of God ascending and descending upon the Son of Man."

- Jesus describes the heart and character of Nathanael as if he had looked into his soul. Would you want to think that anyone can see into your very soul? We can say to others, "You don't really know me!" But we cannot say that to Jesus. Jesus knows us and loves us just as we are. What a gift that is to us: we don't have to hide anything—and he loves us!

- The more we think about you, Jesus, the more we find it hard to believe that you love us just as we are. We do not have to change a thing for you. All we need is to learn how to spend time in your presence and let you do the work of transforming us.

Thursday 25th August
Matthew 24:42–51

Jesus said to his disciples, "Keep awake therefore, for you do not know on what day your Lord is coming. But understand this: if the owner of the house had known in what part of the night the thief was coming, he would have stayed awake and would not have let his house be broken into. Therefore you also must be ready, for the Son of Man is coming at an unexpected hour. Who then is the faithful and wise slave, whom his master has put in charge of his household, to give the other slaves their allowance of food at the proper time? Blessed is that slave whom his master will find at work when he arrives. Truly I tell you, he will put that one in charge of all his possessions. But if that wicked slave says to himself, 'My master is delayed,' and he begins to beat his fellow slaves, and eats and drinks with drunkards, the master of that slave will come on a day when he does not expect him and at an hour that he does not know. He will cut him in pieces and put him with the hypocrites, where there will be weeping and gnashing of teeth."

- Jesus speaks of being alert to the coming of the kingdom. We do not know the day the Lord is coming, so there is a need for constant watchfulness. We must waken from slumber and live out our lives before God, so that when the Lord does come we will be ready.

- Keep guard over us, Jesus, so that we may always be aware of your hand on the tiller of our lives, directing us and steering us on the right path through life. Help us to be awake to the whisperings and promptings of your Holy Spirit in our hearts.

Friday 26th August
Matthew 25:1–13

Jesus said to his disciples, "Then the kingdom of heaven will be like this. Ten bridesmaids took their lamps and went to meet the bridegroom. Five of them were foolish, and five were wise. When the foolish took their lamps, they took no oil with them; but the wise took flasks of oil with their lamps. As the bridegroom was delayed, all of them became drowsy and slept. But at midnight there was a shout, 'Look! Here is the bridegroom! Come out to meet him.' Then all those bridesmaids got up and trimmed their lamps. The foolish said to the wise, 'Give us some of your oil, for our lamps are going out.' But the wise replied, 'No! there will not be enough for you and for us; you had better go to the dealers and buy some for yourselves.' And while they went to buy it, the bridegroom came, and those who were ready went with him into the wedding banquet; and the door was shut. Later the other bridesmaids came also, saying, 'Lord, Lord, open to us.' But he replied, 'Truly I tell you, I do not know you.' Keep awake therefore, for you know neither the day nor the hour."

- Being always ready is not about activity, preparing, and doing more. We make ourselves ready by recognizing how God is at work. My time of prayer helps me to notice what God is doing so that I am poised to respond to God's invitation at any time. I give God this time of prayer now. I resist the urge to rush off to do something else—even something I think good—so that I might do something better.

• I grow in relationship with God in my prayer. God sees my desire to seek out these times of prayer and recognizes what is in my heart. In these quiet moments I come to know God and to know myself in relation to God. Help me, Lord, not to wait for some far-off day when things are quieter or better, but to respond now to your invitation to receive love, hope, and life.

Saturday 27th August
Matthew 25:14–30

Jesus said to his disciples, "For it is as if a man, going on a journey, summoned his slaves and entrusted his property to them; to one he gave five talents, to another two, to another one, to each according to his ability. Then he went away. The one who had received the five talents went off at once and traded with them, and made five more talents. In the same way, the one who had the two talents made two more talents. But the one who had received the one talent went off and dug a hole in the ground and hid his master's money. After a long time the master of those slaves came and settled accounts with them. Then the one who had received the five talents came forward, bringing five more talents, saying, 'Master, you handed over to me five talents; see, I have made five more talents.' His master said to him, 'Well done, good and trustworthy slave; you have been trustworthy in a few things, I will put you in charge of many things; enter into the joy of your master.' And the one with the two talents also came forward, saying, 'Master, you handed over to me two talents; see, I have made two more talents.' His master said to him, 'Well done, good and trustworthy slave; you have been trustworthy in a few things, I will put you in charge of many things; enter into the joy of your master.' Then the one who had received the one talent also came forward, saying, 'Master, I knew that you were a harsh man, reaping where you did not sow, and gathering where you did not scatter seed; so I was afraid, and I went and hid your talent in the ground. Here you have what is yours.' But his master replied, 'You wicked and lazy slave! You knew, did you, that I reap where I did not sow, and gather where I did not scatter? Then you ought to have invested my money with the bankers, and on my return I would have received what was my own with interest. So take the talent from him, and give it to the one with the ten talents. For to all those who have, more will be given, and they will have an abundance; but from those who have nothing, even what they have will be taken away. As for this worthless slave, throw him into the outer darkness, where there will be weeping and gnashing of teeth.'"

• This is a parable of wasted opportunities! We are each gifted uniquely by God, and we must use our giftedness as God wishes. What matters isn't what we are given but what we do with our gift. Do not be afraid to use your talents: stop comparing your gifts with others; share what you have received. To bury your giftedness leads only to sorrow and regret—the "gnashing of teeth."

• The parable can remind us of the beautiful hymn attributed to Saint Teresa of Ávila: "Christ has no body now but yours. No hands, no feet on earth but yours. Yours are the eyes through which he looks compassion on this world, yours are the feet with which he walks to do good."

The Twenty-Second Week of Ordinary Time
August 28—September 3

Something to think and pray about each day this week:

Giving without Getting

How often my giving is corrupted by self-interest and the hope of favors in return. Jesus gave to us without hope of return. I can do him no favors, but he taught me that love means giving without expectations, that there is more happiness in giving than in receiving. We do what we do out of love, out of care, and out of following him, not expecting thanks. We invite people to share in what we have who have nothing to give in return. The good we do will not be forgotten in his heart. The good we do is written in our "book of life." In prayer we offer what we do for God to God, knowing that this is reward enough. Although he promises reward, Jesus wants us to do good simply because it is good. I ask that I may recognize what is best and act with confidence. Giving without hope of reward means letting go of even my rational satisfaction. Sometimes I may not be sure about the best thing to do, but I ask God to strengthen my faith as I do what I can.

The Presence of God

I pause for a moment and think of the love and the grace that God showers on me: I am created in the image and likeness of God; I am God's dwelling place.

Freedom

Saint Ignatius of Loyola thought that a thick and shapeless tree trunk would never believe that it could become a statue, admired as a miracle of sculpture, and would never submit itself to the chisel of the sculptor, who sees by her genius what she can make of it. I ask for the grace to let myself be shaped by my loving Creator.

Consciousness

Where do I sense hope, encouragement, and growth areas in my life? By looking back over the last few months, I may be able to see which activities and occasions have produced rich fruit. If I do notice such areas, I will determine to give those areas both time and space in the future.

The Word

I take my time to read the Word of God slowly, a few times, allowing myself to dwell on anything that strikes me. (Please turn to the Scripture on the following pages. Inspiration points are provided should you need them. When you are ready, return here to continue.)

Conversation

What is stirring in me as I pray? Am I consoled, troubled, left cold? I imagine Jesus himself standing or sitting at my side, and I share my feelings with him.

Conclusion

I thank God for these few moments we have spent alone together and for any insights I may have been given concerning the text.

Sunday 28th August
Twenty-Second Sunday in Ordinary Time
Luke 14:1, 7–14

On one occasion when Jesus was going to the house of a leader of the Pharisees to eat a meal on the sabbath, they were watching him closely. When he noticed how the guests chose the places of honor, he told them a parable. "When you are invited by someone to a wedding banquet, do not sit down at the place of honor, in case someone more distinguished than you has been invited by your host; and the host who invited both of you may come and say to you, 'Give this person your place,' and then in disgrace you would start to take the lowest place. But when you are invited, go and sit down at the lowest place, so that when your host comes, he may say to you, 'Friend, move up higher'; then you will be honored in the presence of all who sit at the table with you. For all who exalt themselves will be humbled, and those who humble themselves will be exalted." He said also to the one who had invited him, "When you give a luncheon or a dinner, do not invite your friends or your brothers or your relatives or rich neighbours, in case they may invite you in return, and you would be repaid. But when you give a banquet, invite the poor, the crippled, the lame, and the blind. And you will be blessed, because they cannot repay you, for you will be repaid at the resurrection of the righteous."

• How difficult it is to practice the art of humility! How difficult it is not to take the best seat, grab the best bargain, and be first in line for the concert I must see! Jesus asks us to think of others, be more aware of others' needs, and step back a bit and allow others to be center stage for a change. Heavenly Father, teach us how to follow in Jesus' footsteps, how to be compassionate, more understanding, and more generous in our thinking and in our actions.

• As I read Jesus' parable, does it ring any bells with me? Do I remember either the elation of being considered more special than I thought I was, or the deflation of being thought more ordinary than seemed right to me? What do these memories tell me about my sense of the world and my place in it?

Monday 29th August
The Passion of Saint John the Baptist
Mark 6:17–29

Herod himself had sent men who arrested John, bound him, and put him in prison on account of Herodias, his brother Philip's wife, because Herod had married her. For John had been telling Herod, "It is not lawful for you to have your brother's wife." And Herodias had a grudge against him, and wanted to kill him. But she could not, for Herod feared John, knowing that he was a righteous and holy man, and he protected him. When he heard him, he was greatly perplexed; and yet he liked to listen to him. But an opportunity came when Herod on his birthday gave a banquet for his courtiers and officers and for the leaders of Galilee. When his daughter Herodias came in and danced, she pleased Herod and his guests; and the king said to the girl, "Ask me for whatever you wish, and I will give it." And he solemnly swore to her, "Whatever you ask me, I will give you, even half of my kingdom." She went out and said to her mother, "What should I ask for?" She replied, "The head of John the baptizer." Immediately she rushed back to the king and requested, "I want you to give me at once the head of John the Baptist on a platter." The king was deeply grieved; yet out of regard for his oaths and for the guests, he did not want to refuse her. Immediately the king sent a soldier of the guard with orders to bring John's head. He went and beheaded him in the prison, brought his head on a platter, and gave it to the girl. Then the girl gave it to her mother. When his disciples heard about it, they came and took his body, and laid it in a tomb.

• What a horrible story! The gospel does not mince its words or soften its picture of the martyrdom of John the Baptist. Maybe our prayer about this death will remind us of the people who suffer in the cause of justice and rightness, and we will pray for them.

- Discipleship is demanding. Like Jesus, each of us in our own way is called to serve and to give our lives for the sake of others (Mark 10:45). Lord, do not let me lose courage when things go wrong. Let me keep on trying to do good.

Tuesday 30th August
Luke 4:31–37

Jesus went down to Capernaum, a city in Galilee, and was teaching them on the sabbath. They were astounded at his teaching, because he spoke with authority. In the synagogue there was a man who had the spirit of an unclean demon, and he cried out with a loud voice, "Let us alone! What have you to do with us, Jesus of Nazareth? Have you come to destroy us? I know who you are, the Holy One of God." But Jesus rebuked him, saying, "Be silent, and come out of him!" When the demon had thrown him down before them, he came out of him without having done him any harm. They were all amazed and kept saying to one another, "What kind of utterance is this? For with authority and power he commands the unclean spirits, and out they come!" And a report about him began to reach every place in the region.

- They say you can get used to anything; could it be that I am so used to Jesus and his ways that I no longer remark on them or consider how they challenge me? The people of Jesus' time were astonished and surprised. His teachings stood in stark contrast not only to the unclean spirits, but also to the good and established teachers. Help me, Jesus, to hear your voice and to accept your authority as you seek to lead me to life.

- The spirit that was not of God cried out, "Let us alone." The message of Jesus may often disturb and unsettle. I pray that I may receive more fully now, in this time of prayer, strength from the Spirit of Jesus and not settle for other, meaner spirits that promise me comfort. The authority of Jesus is unlike any other; it is not coercive or forceful, but it calls to my heart. This time of prayer is the time for my heart to speak to his heart, and for me to acknowledge the authority I give him.

Wednesday 31st August
Luke 4:38–44

After leaving the synagogue he entered Simon's house. Now Simon's mother-in-law was suffering from a high fever, and they asked him about her. Then he stood over her and rebuked the fever, and it left her. Immediately she got up and began to serve them. As the sun was setting, all those who had any who were sick with various kinds of diseases brought them to him; and he laid his hands on each of them and cured them. Demons also came out of many, shouting, "You are the Son of God!" But he rebuked them and would not allow them to speak, because they knew that he was the Messiah. At daybreak he departed and went into a deserted place. And the crowds were looking for him; and when they reached him, they wanted to prevent him from leaving them. But he said to them, "I must proclaim the good news of the kingdom of God to the other cities also; for I was sent for this purpose." So he continued proclaiming the message in the synagogues of Judea.

- To whom can a family go in their troubles? How many will take their troubles to the Lord in prayer? Let me then be an ambassador of prayer for those who cannot pray.

- Jesus pledges to be with spouses as they give themselves unconditionally to each other, for richer, for poorer, in hard times, in good times. Lord, may we find you in a deserted place in our hearts leading us to a deeper trust in you and in your promises.

Thursday 1st September
Luke 5:1–11

Once while Jesus was standing beside the lake of Gennesaret, and the crowd was pressing in on him to hear the Word of God, he saw two boats there at the shore of the lake; the fishermen had gone out of them and were washing their nets. He got into one of the boats, the one belonging to Simon, and asked him to put out a little way from the shore. Then he sat down and taught the crowds from the boat. When he had finished speaking, he said to Simon, "Put out into the deep water and let down your nets for a catch." Simon answered, "Master, we have worked all night long but have caught nothing. Yet if you say so, I will let down the nets." When they had done this, they caught so many fish that their nets were beginning to break. So they signaled to their partners in the other boat to come and help them. And they came and filled both boats, so that they began to sink. But when Simon Peter saw it, he fell down at Jesus' knees, saying, "Go away from me, Lord, for I am a sinful man!" For he and all who were with him were amazed at the catch of fish that they had taken; and so also were James and John, sons of Zebedee, who were partners with Simon. Then Jesus said to Simon, "Do not be afraid; from now on you will be catching people." When they had brought their boats to shore, they left everything and followed him.

- Peter recognized who Jesus was and realized that being close to Jesus would make demands on him. Jesus recognized who Peter was and saw that Peter had the capacity to respond to what he might ask of him. Jesus invited Peter to use his practiced skill in a new way, for the good of the gospel. I lay my skills and talents before Jesus, asking him to show me how I might use them for good.

- "Put out into the deep water." I fear the unknown just as I fear the sea, for I can't swim. So I pray for Peter's faith when I'm asked to "let down my nets" into unknown territory. Don't go away from me, Lord, for I am a sinful person and I need you so much.

Friday 2nd September
Luke 5:33–39

Then the Pharisees and the scribes said to Jesus, "John's disciples, like the disciples of the Pharisees, frequently fast and pray, but your disciples eat and drink." Jesus said to them, "You cannot make wedding guests fast while the bridegroom is with them, can you? The days will come when the bridegroom will be taken away from them, and then they will fast in those days." He also told them a parable: "No one tears a piece from a new garment and sews it on an old garment; otherwise the new will be torn, and the piece from the new will not match the old. And no one puts new wine into old wineskins; otherwise the new wine will burst the skins and will be spilled, and the skins will be destroyed. But new wine must be put into fresh wineskins. And no one after drinking old wine desires new wine, but says, 'The old is good.'"

- The disciples did what people often do: they made comparisons. Jesus invites them not to look out but to look in and to notice their own attitudes. He does not want them—or us—to be a patchwork of mismatched patterns and practices. He invites us to be made anew, to let go of anything that might hold us back or impair our ability to receive the good news.

- The Pharisees saw different ways of living and made comparisons; Jesus simply sought life. Jesus saw the ordinary things of the world—torn clothes, spilled wine—and recognized how God is at work in us. How might I look more closely at the bits and pieces of my every day?

Saturday 3rd September

Luke 6:1–5

One sabbath while Jesus was going through the grainfields, his disciples plucked some heads of grain, rubbed them in their hands, and ate them. But some of the Pharisees said, "Why are you doing what is not lawful on the sabbath?" Jesus answered, "Have you not read what David did when he and his companions were hungry? He entered the house of God and took and ate the bread of the Presence, which it is not lawful for any but the priests to eat, and gave some to his companions?" Then he said to them, "The Son of Man is lord of the sabbath."

- Looking outward, the Pharisees noticed the shortcomings of others; looking inward, they congratulated themselves on their good performance. Jesus invites them to look to God and to seek not just the letter of the law but to search out what lies in the heart of God. God is the real key for our well-being: God does not give up when our performance disappoints.

- Is Sunday a day of rest for me? Sunday can be a gift, a privileged moment to find inner calm. It is a time to shed the stress of work and let cares fall away. It is a time to walk leisurely with my God in his world of nature. It is a time to recapture reverence for the holy world gifted to us. It is a time for speaking the names of each member of the family with love and gratitude. Is Sunday my day for meeting the Lord of the sabbath? Is it the day of resurrection, when I celebrate the joy that the Lord Jesus is with me forever?

September 4—September 10

Something to think and pray about each day this week:

Discipleship Costs

"Whoever comes to me and does not hate father and mother, wife and children, brothers and sisters, yes, and even life itself, cannot be my disciple," Jesus says (Luke 14:25). The strong contrast in Jesus' words ("hate" father and mother) is Hebrew idiom for what we would call establishing priorities. We may have to make choices between the call of the Lord and the pull of family. What do you ask of me, Lord? Let me know the cost. In prayer it is just me and God; for a while all else is given up. I need nothing to pray except myself. This can be an experience of great freedom.

Prayer is the moment of offering the self to God—the true and real self without the "possessions" that can sometimes block God's invitation and grace. How much am I able to let go? I ask God to help me to grow in freedom, to be ready to follow, and to serve in new ways. As I consider the freedom to which Jesus calls me, patterns and habits that limit me may come to mind. I bring them before God for the healing that I need. Jesus tells us that discipleship costs. I think of how I sometimes resist the difficulties that the gospel presents, and I ask for help.

The Presence of God

I remind myself that, as I sit here now, God is gazing on me with love and holding me in being. I pause for a moment and think of this.

Freedom

Lord, grant me the grace to have freedom of the spirit. Cleanse my heart and soul so I may live joyously in your love.

Consciousness

In the presence of my loving Creator, I look honestly at my feelings over the past day—the highs, the lows, and the level ground. Can I see where the Lord has been present?

The Word

I take my time to read the Word of God slowly, a few times, allowing myself to dwell on anything that strikes me. (Please turn to the Scripture on the following pages. Inspiration points are provided should you need them. When you are ready, return here to continue.)

Conversation

Jesus, you speak to me through the words of the gospels. May I respond to your call today. Teach me to recognize your hand at work in my daily living.

Conclusion

Glory be to the Father, and to the Son, and to the Holy Spirit, as it was in the beginning, is now and ever shall be, world without end. Amen.

Sunday 4th September
Twenty-Third Sunday in Ordinary Time
Luke 14:25–33

Now large crowds were traveling with him; and he turned and said to them, "Whoever comes to me and does not hate father and mother, wife and children, brothers and sisters, yes, and even life itself, cannot be my disciple. Whoever does not carry the cross and follow me cannot be my disciple. For which of you, intending to build a tower, does not first sit down and estimate the cost, to see whether he has enough to complete it? Otherwise, when he has laid a foundation and is not able to finish, all who see it will begin to ridicule him, saying, 'This fellow began to build and was not able to finish.' Or what king, going out to wage war against another king, will not sit down first and consider whether he is able with ten thousand to oppose the one who comes against him with twenty thousand? If he cannot, then, while the other is still far away, he sends a delegation and asks for the terms of peace. So therefore, none of you can become my disciple if you do not give up all your possessions."

- "Take up your cross daily." This sounds manageable until we come to the details! For example, there is no perfect marriage. A good marriage demands huge homework around compatibility and open communication. Marriage and children are nature's school in which self-giving is taught to us day after day.

- A celibate life can be considered to cost no less than everything. The celibate renounces wealth, sex, and power. But in practice there is the danger of sliding into comfort and selfishness. Lord, may we be guided by you and your demanding standards. Give us the grace to be faithful to the calling you have invited us to.

Monday 5th September
Luke 6:6–11

On another sabbath Jesus entered the synagogue and taught, and there was a man there whose right hand was withered. The scribes and the

Pharisees watched him to see whether he would cure on the sabbath, so that they might find an accusation against him. Even though he knew what they were thinking, he said to the man who had the withered hand, "Come and stand here." He got up and stood there. Then Jesus said to them, "I ask you, is it lawful to do good or to do harm on the sabbath, to save life or to destroy it?" After looking around at all of them, he said to him, "Stretch out your hand." He did so, and his hand was restored. But they were filled with fury and discussed with one another what they might do to Jesus.

- Isn't it intriguing that the authorities expected Jesus to perform the miracle, but they had no interest in the compassion that absorbed him, which outweighed all ritual? He was upset that their religious practice was so empty of heart. "If I am without love, I am nothing."

- Lord, put heart and forgiveness and mercy into every prayer I utter. Take every last vestige of self-pity out of my concerns. Draw me more and more toward compassionate action for the weak and the suffering.

Tuesday 6th September
Luke 6:12–19

Now during those days Jesus went out to the mountain to pray; and he spent the night in prayer to God. And when day came, he called his disciples and chose twelve of them, whom he also named apostles: Simon, whom he named Peter, and his brother Andrew, and James, and John, and Philip, and Bartholomew, and Matthew, and Thomas, and James son of Alphaeus, and Simon, who was called the Zealot, and Judas son of James, and Judas Iscariot, who became a traitor. He came down with them and stood on a level place, with a great crowd of his disciples and a great multitude of people from all Judea, Jerusalem, and the coast of Tyre and Sidon. They had come to hear him and to be healed of their diseases; and those who were troubled with unclean spirits were cured. And all in the crowd were trying to touch him, for power came out from him and healed all of them.

- We never cease to be amazed at just how ordinary those men were whom Jesus chose as his closest followers. They had no wealth, education, or position. They could be petty, cowardly, and ambitious. But they did have something to offer: they allowed themselves to be drawn to Jesus.

- Lord, remove whatever blocks me from accepting your personal invitation to me. Take me to you. I want to serve as your friend and witness. May I accept you gratefully as my brother.

Wednesday 7th September
Luke 6:20–26

Jesus looked up at his disciples and said: "Blessed are you who are poor, for yours is the kingdom of God. Blessed are you who are hungry now, for you will be filled. Blessed are you who weep now, for you will laugh. Blessed are you when people hate you, and when they exclude you, revile you, and defame you on account of the Son of Man. Rejoice on that day and leap for joy, for surely your reward is great in heaven; for that is what their ancestors did to the prophets. But woe to you who are rich, for you have received your consolation. Woe to you who are full now, for you will be hungry. Woe to you who are laughing now, for you will mourn and weep. Woe to you when all speak well of you, for that is what their ancestors did to the false prophets."

- There are no glossy images here! Who wants to be poorer, sad, in conflict, excluded, or demeaned? Jesus does not ask us to seek out discomfort, but he wants us to realize that God always holds a brighter promise for us. We seek and find God where we are but always realize that God calls us further—we have not arrived.

- God's mercy means doing justice for the poorest and the most humiliated. Jesus meets families on his travels who are barely surviving and are defenseless against powerful landowners. We, too, see poor and powerless people today. Are we, his followers, defenders of the poor? What meaningful action will I do today to bring a smile to the lips of someone who is poor or broken? Christian living is neither an armchair occupation nor a spectator sport.

Thursday 8th September
The Nativity of the Blessed Virgin Mary
Matthew 1:18–23

Now the birth of Jesus the Messiah took place in this way. When his mother Mary had been engaged to Joseph, but before they lived together, she was found to be with child from the Holy Spirit. Her husband Joseph, being a righteous man and unwilling to expose her to public disgrace, planned to dismiss her quietly. But just when he had resolved to do this, an angel of the Lord appeared to him in a dream and said, "Joseph, son of David, do not be afraid to take Mary as your wife, for the child conceived in her is from the Holy Spirit. She will bear a son, and you are to name him Jesus, for he will save his people from their sins." All this took place to fulfill what had been spoken by the Lord through the prophet: "Look, the virgin shall conceive and bear a son, and they shall name him Emmanuel," which means, "God is with us."

- Joseph was able to change his mind even when he had determined a conscientious and careful path. Like Mary he was alert to a greater plan and was able to put even his good decision aside when God directed his attention to a better one. There may be conclusions to which I have come that are logical and sensible but that will never fit properly within the framework of the gospel. Instead of trying to figure it out entirely on my own, I ask God for light.

- Jesus' name—"Emmanuel," or "God is with us"—can be like a mantra. We can look at everything he does and everything that happens to him with these words echoing like a chorus or featured like a backdrop behind him. Because of him we are all Emmanuel; God is with us still in a special way because he was in Jesus in a special way. We could look this day at everyone we meet and say, "Emmanuel."

Friday 9th September
Luke 6:39–42

Jesus also told them a parable: "Can a blind person guide a blind person? Will not both fall into a pit? A disciple is not above the teacher, but everyone who is fully qualified will be like the teacher. Why do you see the speck in your neighbor's eye, but do not notice the log in your own eye? Or how can you say to your neighbor, 'Friend, let me take out the speck in your eye,' when you yourself do not see the log in your own eye? You hypocrite, first take the log out of your own eye, and then you will see clearly to take the speck out of your neighbor's eye."

- Instead of seeking healing, the person with the plank in their eye can become adept at spotting the splinters of others. If I cannot look out at the world and find what is to be praised and blessed, I need to look in to see what is hampering me, to recognize how I may be blinded to the work of God in others. As I pray for my daily bread, I pray also that I may recognize and accept it.

- God sees each of us from the inside. God sees us with a generous and compassionate gaze. God does not despise or condemn us for our shortcomings and failings. Lord, today make me gaze at annoying people as kindly as you do.

Saturday 10th September
Luke 6:43–49

Jesus said, "No good tree bears bad fruit, nor again does a bad tree bear good fruit; for each tree is known by its own fruit. Figs are not gathered from thorns, nor are grapes picked from a bramble bush. The good person out of the good treasure of the heart produces good, and the evil person out of evil treasure produces evil; for it is out of the abundance of the heart that the mouth speaks. Why do you call me 'Lord, Lord,' and do not do what I tell you? I will show you what someone is like who comes to me, hears my words, and acts on them. That one is like a man building a house, who dug deeply and laid the foundation on rock; when a flood arose, the river burst against that house but could not shake it, because it had been well built. But the one who hears and does not act is like a man who built a house on the ground without a foundation. When the river burst against it, immediately it fell, and great was the ruin of that house."

- If I think of my life as a tree, I can ask how it is nourished and reflect on its vital quality. What "water" do I soak in from the ground around me, what "light" do I bask in, what "shade" or "fruit" do I have for the good of others? I take care of any negative conclusions of mine, remembering that judgment belongs to God alone. I ask only that the words of Jesus open me to God's wisdom and truth.

- Even the strongest building needs care and repair. I think of the image that Jesus presents and let it speak to me. I work with God to make a worthy dwelling, a refuge, a place from which to set forth. The foundations of a building are often its least recognized feature, usually hidden and seemingly insignificant. My "faith foundations" may not be known to many but are cherished by God, to whom I bring them now in prayer, that they may be blessed and strengthened.

The Twenty-Fourth Week of Ordinary Time
September 11—September 17

Something to think and pray about each day this week:

What Is Truly Important
Who are today's sinners, reviled by the media? Whenever I see a finger-pointing headline in a tabloid, denouncing someone who has been caught, I will think like you, Lord. Instead of letting my anger be harnessed against them, let me feel some compassion, realizing that, but for the grace of God, I could be in their shoes. A painting of the scene from this Sunday's gospel shows a woman bent over, looking intently for what she has lost. The coin was precious to her—a tenth of her wealth. Jesus compares his care for us to this—he really wants us near him, faults and all. Prayer time is that—the whole self is the self I bring to prayer, searching for the God who loves all of creation. The finding of the coin seems such a simple joy. I realize that possessions and property may blind me to simple blessings. As I think of what is really of value, I may realize that I have to seek it again, perhaps sweeping and searching. Those around me may know what is really important to me. Thinking of the woman in Jesus' story, I may need to remind them of what I really value.

The Presence of God
Lord, help me to be fully alive to your holy presence. Enfold me in your love. Let my heart become one with yours.

Freedom
Lord, may I never take the gift of freedom for granted. You gave me the great blessing of freedom of spirit. Fill my spirit with your peace and your joy.

Consciousness
Knowing that God loves me unconditionally, I can afford to be honest about how I am. How has the past day been, and how do I feel now? I share my feelings openly with the Lord.

The Word
The Word of God comes down to us through the Scriptures. May the Holy Spirit enlighten my mind and my heart to respond to the gospel teachings. (Please turn to the Scripture on the following pages. Inspiration points are provided should you need them. When you are ready, return here to continue.)

Conversation
Jesus, you always welcomed little children when you walked on this earth. Teach me to have a childlike trust in you, to live in the knowledge that you will never abandon me.

Conclusion
I thank God for these few moments we have spent alone together and for any insights I may have been given concerning the text.

Sunday 11th September
Twenty-Fourth Sunday in Ordinary Time
Luke 15:1–10

Now all the tax collectors and sinners were coming near to listen to him. And the Pharisees and the scribes were grumbling and saying, "This fellow welcomes sinners and eats with them." So he told them this parable: "Which one of you, having a hundred sheep and losing one of them, does not leave the ninety-nine in the wilderness and go after the one that is lost until he finds it? When he has found it, he lays it on his shoulders and rejoices. And when he comes home, he calls together his friends and neighbors, saying to them, 'Rejoice with me, for I have found my sheep that was lost.' Just so, I tell you, there will be more joy in heaven over one sinner who repents than over ninety-nine righteous people who need no repentance. Or what woman having ten silver coins, if she loses one of them, does not light a lamp, sweep the house, and search carefully until she finds it? When she has found it, she calls together her friends and neighbors, saying, 'Rejoice with me, for I have found the coin that I had lost.' Just so, I tell you, there is joy in the presence of the angels of God over one sinner who repents."

- Jealousy rears its ugly head as the Pharisees listen to the words of Jesus. They do not like the fact that Jesus welcomes everyone unconditionally. No judging, no condemnation. In him is found pure love and acceptance. Jesus, you welcome all into your warm embrace. When we are lost, you come to find us. When we are in despair, you come to lift us up. When we feel forsaken, you remind us of your great love for each one of us. Thank you for loving us just as we are.

- Would I join in with the present-day tax collectors and sinners as they flock to Jesus? Or would I want a private audience? I talk with Jesus about this. This passage reveals the heart of God, who searches for the lost. Can I admit that I often get lost and forget where my true home is? How does it feel to imagine Jesus going in search of me and finding me?

Monday 12th September
Luke 7:1–10

After Jesus had finished all his sayings in the hearing of the people, he entered Capernaum. A centurion there had a slave whom he valued highly, and who was ill and close to death. When he heard about Jesus, he sent some Jewish elders to him, asking him to come and heal his slave. When they came to Jesus, they appealed to him earnestly, saying, "He is worthy of having you do this for him, for he loves our people, and it is he who built our synagogue for us." And Jesus went with them, but when he was not far from the house, the centurion sent friends to say to him, "Lord, do not trouble yourself, for I am not worthy to have you come under my roof; therefore I did not presume to come to you. But only speak the word, and let my servant be healed. For I also am a man set under authority, with soldiers under me; and I say to one, 'Go,' and he goes, and to another, 'Come,' and he comes, and to my slave, 'Do this,' and the slave does it." When Jesus heard this he was amazed at him, and turning to the crowd that followed him, he said, "I tell you, not even in Israel have I found such faith." When those who had been sent returned to the house, they found the slave in good health.

- The mutual respect among the characters in this scene is very evident. The eucharistic prayer "Lord, I am not worthy . . ." has its origin in the compassion and love of a centurion for a slave. Let me be respectful not only to Jesus but to all I meet.

- The love and concern of this long-dead soldier for his slave dignifies and sanctifies not just his slave but all people. What can we do to promote justice for those in need of it today?

Tuesday 13th September
Luke 7:11–17

Soon afterwards Jesus went to a town called Nain, and his disciples and a large crowd went with him. As he approached the gate of the town, a man who had died was being carried out. He was his mother's only son, and she was a widow; and with her was a large crowd from the town.

When the Lord saw her, he had compassion for her and said to her, "Do not weep." Then he came forward and touched the bier, and the bearers stood still. And he said, "Young man, I say to you, rise!" The dead man sat up and began to speak, and Jesus gave him to his mother. Fear seized all of them; and they glorified God, saying, "A great prophet has risen among us!" and "God has looked favorably on his people!" This word about him spread throughout Judea and all the surrounding country.

- Funeral processions rely on custom and tradition, yet even here Jesus is prepared to act in a new way. He recognizes life in the hope and love of the distressed mother and sympathetic crowd. He shows them that their hopes are not dashed, that love is not over. Help me, Lord, to see how you are at work, bringing life even in seemingly impossible circumstances.

- Our life is a gradual learning of letting go and saying an unqualified "Yes." We can let God in a little more each day by becoming more free, more emptied. "For all that has been, thanks. For all that shall be, yes" (Dag Hammarskjöld).

Wednesday 14th September

John 3:13–17

Jesus said, "No one has ascended into heaven except the one who descended from heaven, the Son of Man. And just as Moses lifted up the serpent in the wilderness, so must the Son of Man be lifted up, that whoever believes in him may have eternal life. For God so loved the world that he gave his only Son, so that everyone who believes in him may not perish but may have eternal life. Indeed, God did not send the Son into the world to condemn the world, but in order that the world might be saved through him."

- God sent Jesus not to condemn us but to save us. I let the meaning of this truth sink in, recognizing that Jesus reaches out to me that I may be saved. I admit that, in ways I do not fully understand, Jesus' cross calls me to life by asking me to resist whatever reduces, diminishes, or seeks to kill.

- When I am lifted up from the earth, Jesus said, I shall draw all people to myself (John 12:32). In the cross of Christ is our freedom and birth to a new life. The Father generously gave us his own Son so that we might all truly live. Do I deeply desire this life for all the world?

Thursday 15th September
Luke 2:33–35

The child Jesus' father and mother were amazed at what was being said about him. Then Simeon blessed them and said to his mother Mary, "This child is destined for the falling and the rising of many in Israel, and to be a sign that will be opposed so that the inner thoughts of many will be revealed—and a sword will pierce your own soul too."

- Even before Jesus' birth, Mary and Joseph began hearing amazing things about their child. While not always fully understanding those messages at first, they had faith in God's intentions and pondered these things in their hearts. We don't always see God's will for us clearly, but we can trust that our best efforts to discern and follow it will bear good fruit.

- Simeon's prophecy bore a mixed message: falling as well as rising. Opposition. Pain. While God's salvation goes out to all, not everyone will welcome it. Following Jesus will not always be easy, and it will mean at times embracing his way of sacrifice and suffering. His disciples need to know this.

Friday 16th September
Luke 8:1–3

Soon afterwards Jesus went on through cities and villages, proclaiming and bringing the good news of the kingdom of God. The twelve were with him, as well as some women who had been cured of evil spirits and infirmities: Mary, called Magdalene, from whom seven demons had gone out, and Joanna, the wife of Herod's steward Chuza, and Susanna, and many others, who provided for them out of their resources.

- We know little about Susanna and Joanna other than that they were happy to follow Jesus and were recognized by Luke as disciples. I think of all those quiet disciples whose lives and prayer have contributed to the church but who have left little evident legacy. I pray for all who support others through their presence—especially women—that they may draw encouragement from knowing how Jesus sees, recognizes, and loves their humble service.

- The generous women who cared for Jesus are usually out of sight—like so many women who give of themselves for others. I pray for all who enrich my life by their discreet service. Jesus did not just proclaim the good news—he was the good news. Saint Francis of Assisi's advice about preaching the gospel—using words, if necessary—comes to mind. As I receive the Word of God, I pray that I may embody it and proclaim it.

Saturday 17th September

Luke 8:4–15

When a great crowd gathered and people from town after town came to him, he said in a parable: "A sower went out to sow his seed; and as he sowed, some fell on the path and was trampled on, and the birds of the air ate it up. Some fell on the rock; and as it grew up, it withered for lack of moisture. Some fell among thorns, and the thorns grew with it and choked it. Some fell into good soil, and when it grew, it produced a hundredfold." As he said this, he called out, "Let anyone with ears to hear listen!" Then his disciples asked him what this parable meant. He said, "To you it has been given to know the secrets of the kingdom of God; but to others I speak in parables, so that 'looking they may not perceive, and listening they may not understand.' Now the parable is this: The seed is the Word of God. The ones on the path are those who have heard; then the devil comes and takes away the word from their hearts, so that they may not believe and be saved. The ones on the rock are those who, when they hear the word, receive it with joy. But these have no root; they believe only for a while and in a time of testing fall away. As for what fell among the thorns, these are the ones who hear;

but as they go on their way, they are choked by the cares and riches and pleasures of life, and their fruit does not mature. But as for that in the good soil, these are the ones who, when they hear the word, hold it fast in an honest and good heart, and bear fruit with patient endurance."

• Jesus has scattered the seed of his word; what will happen to it? He does not imagine that everything he says will find a positive reception, and he allows for evident failure. I consider how it is that I sometimes look for success and feel disappointed when things don't turn out as I want. Critical and judgmental attitudes seem foreign to Jesus as he recognizes and cherishes where there is life.

• Jesus uses parables to change our way of seeing things. The fruitfulness of the seed is determined by the quality of the soil in which it falls. Similarly, the fruitfulness of the Word of God is determined by the openness of heart of the person who receives it. We grow at our own pace. God is patient with this growth. God, grant me a heart of flesh to receive your holy word. May I spend time each day listening to the song of the seed that you plant in my heart. May it transform me ever more fully into the likeness of your Son.

September 18—September 24

Something to think and pray about each day this week:

The Prayer of Love
The great mystic Saint Teresa of Ávila says that in the Song of Songs, the Lord is teaching the soul how to pray. We can, she tells us, make the bride's prayer our own. Your reaction to the experience of praying the Song of Songs might be a revelation, even completely alien—almost shocking in its loving, desiring, tactile imagery: "I am faint with love. O that his left hand were under my head and that his right hand embraced me!" But perhaps Teresa was right, and this is the kind of language in which God longs to hear the soul speak. This would mean that we might have to radically shift our perception of what it truly is to love and be loved by God. Ecstatic delight in God's presence is not the preserve of mystics, inaccessible to people living among the commonplace realities of everyday life. Prayer as passionate seeking, as desolation in the absence of the beloved and rapture in finding him—this kind of prayer is not only possible for all of us, it is the kind of prayer that God, himself passionately in love with us, wants to hear.

The Presence of God

My soul longs for your presence, Lord. When I turn my thoughts to you, I find peace and contentment.

Freedom

Lord, you created me to live in freedom. May your Holy Spirit guide me to follow you freely. Instill in my heart a desire to know and love you more each day.

Consciousness

To be conscious about something is to be aware of it. Dear Lord, help me to remember that you gave me life. Thank you for the gift of life. Teach me to slow down, to be still, and to enjoy the pleasures created for me. To be aware of the beauty that surrounds me. The marvel of mountains, the calmness of lakes, the fragility of a flower petal. I need to remember that all these things come from you.

The Word

I read the Word of God slowly, a few times over, and I listen to what God is saying to me. (Please turn to the Scripture on the following pages. Inspiration points are provided should you need them. When you are ready, return here to continue.)

Conversation

Remembering that I am still in God's presence, I imagine Jesus himself standing or sitting beside me, and I say whatever is on my mind, whatever is in my heart, speaking as one friend to another.

Conclusion

Glory be to the Father, and to the Son, and to the Holy Spirit, as it was in the beginning, is now and ever shall be, world without end. Amen.

Sunday 18th September
Twenty-Fifth Sunday in Ordinary Time
Luke 16:10–13

Jesus said, "Whoever is faithful in a very little is faithful also in much; and whoever is dishonest in a very little is dishonest also in much. If then you have not been faithful with the dishonest wealth, who will entrust to you the true riches? And if you have not been faithful with what belongs to another, who will give you what is your own? No slave can serve two masters; for a slave will either hate the one and love the other, or be devoted to the one and despise the other. You cannot serve God and wealth."

- True wealth consists not in what we keep but in what we give away. As soon as a person has more than they need, the extra they have belongs by right to the person who has not enough. We are God's stewards. All that we have belongs to him—our time, our talents, our money, our property.

- There is an African proverb that says: "When you pray, move your feet." It is good to be silent and attentive in prayer. But the love that grows in me through meeting the Lord in quiet prayer must translate into deeds of love. Saint Ignatius of Loyola says that "love is found in deeds rather than in words."

Monday 19th September
Luke 8:16–18

Jesus said to his disciples, "No one after lighting a lamp hides it under a jar, or puts it under a bed, but puts it on a lampstand, so that those who enter may see the light. For nothing is hidden that will not be disclosed, nor is anything secret that will not become known and come to light. Then pay attention to how you listen; for to those who have, more will be given; and from those who do not have, even what they seem to have will be taken away."

- Jesus asks me to pay attention to how I listen, to notice how I notice. If my prayer is full of distraction or if my mind is always racing, I need to do as Jesus asks and pay attention. If I see only deficiency I will lose everything; if I am able to recognize, appreciate, and receive blessing, I can trust in God's goodness and love.

- Does it fill me with joy to know that I am grace-filled in Jesus? Do I wake up to a fresh day knowing that a loving Father is holding me in the palm of his hand?

Tuesday 20th September
Luke 8:19–21

Then Jesus' mother and his brothers came to him, but they could not reach him because of the crowd. And he was told, "Your mother and your brothers are standing outside, wanting to see you." But he said to them, "My mother and my brothers are those who hear the Word of God and do it."

- Calling God our father or Mary our mother is not a pious notion; it springs from the heart of Jesus, who embraces everyone who follows him and invites us to find life where he has received it. Jesus invites us to be his next of kin, his close relations, his family. His story is our story; he gives us his word to be our own.

- The compass of God's family is not limited by blood or heritage, but is thrown open to include all who receive and enact the Word of God. I review any boundaries I tolerate and look beyond them in response to Jesus' words. Hear and "do"; this is my time for listening closely, for attending to where God is speaking in my life. Later I will move into the "doing" when I express my responses to what this time of prayer brings me to understand. I ask God now to help me later.

Wednesday 21st September
Matthew 9:9–13

As Jesus was walking along, he saw a man called Matthew sitting at the tax booth; and he said to him, "Follow me." And he got up and followed him. And as he sat at dinner in the house, many tax collectors and sinners came and were sitting with him and his disciples. When the Pharisees saw this, they said to his disciples, "Why does your teacher eat with tax collectors and sinners?" But when he heard this, he said, "Those who are well have no need of a physician, but those who are sick. Go and learn what this means, 'I desire mercy, not sacrifice.' For I have come to call not the righteous but sinners."

- Jesus is inclusive—even "tax collectors and sinners" are welcomed. They represent those whose professions and social status are "not respectable." But Jesus shows that he has come for all people, without exception, and especially the weak and the vulnerable, the "sick" and the "sinners."

- How inclusive and compassionate Jesus is in his ministry! I ask myself whether I am prejudiced against any individuals or groups. Lord, help me to become more like you in thought, word, and deed. Make me large-hearted.

Thursday 22nd September
Luke 9:7–9

Now Herod the ruler heard about all that had taken place, and he was perplexed, because it was said by some that John had been raised from the dead, by some that Elijah had appeared, and by others that one of the ancient prophets had arisen. Herod said, "John I beheaded; but who is this about whom I hear such things?" And he tried to see him.

- It seemed to Herod that his use of force would silence John the Baptist. Like every bullying person and nation, he learned that truth is not so easily kept at bay. When conscience brings past wrongdoings to mind, it may not be to torment, but so that God may lead me to truth and light.

- Jesus, you are the gracious gift of the Father, dwelling among us. You bring us into God's friendship. Thus you touch us at the deepest core of our being. "In him I have found the heart of a king, the heart of a friend, the heart of a brother" (Saint Richard).

Friday 23rd September

Luke 9:18–22

Once when Jesus was praying alone, with only the disciples near him, he asked them, "Who do the crowds say that I am?" They answered, "John the Baptist; but others, Elijah; and still others, that one of the ancient prophets has arisen." He said to them, "But who do you say that I am?" Peter answered, "The Messiah of God." He sternly ordered and commanded them not to tell anyone, saying, "The Son of Man must undergo great suffering, and be rejected by the elders, chief priests, and scribes, and be killed, and on the third day be raised."

- The crowds referred to their history, recognizing how God had worked in the past. The disciples realized how God was working among them in their present. I give thanks for my history, for my story. As I see where God has worked, I pray for confidence that God is working now, for hope in God's continuing goodness, and for the strength I need to follow God's Word.

- This is a crucial moment in Jesus' life. He asks the question that lies at the heart of Christian faith and theology: "Who do you say that I am?" Peter becomes the spokesperson for this little contingent of believers. Only later will they grasp how the term *Messiah* is understood by Jesus. Suffering, rejection, and death await him, but they are followed by glory. Lord, to follow you I, too, must embark on a personal discovery of who you are. Give me the grace to walk this faith journey. May I not keep you at arm's length by putting a protective shield around myself, but help me rather to daily embrace you on the path of discipleship, with its pains and joys.

Saturday 24th September

Luke 9:43b–45

And all were astounded at the greatness of God. While everyone was amazed at all that he was doing, Jesus said to his disciples, "Let these words sink into your ears: The Son of Man is going to be betrayed into human hands." But they did not understand this saying; its meaning was concealed from them, so that they could not perceive it. And they were afraid to ask him about this saying.

- See how Jesus emphasizes his words? He knows that the disciples will find them difficult to accept. It is still the case. Sometimes it is easier for me to accept that I might betray Jesus than it is for me to receive his assurance of continuing love and presence. I ask, now, that I might listen to Jesus' words and not be preoccupied by my own hesitation.

- The disciples were not prepared for the Passion of Jesus. Are we prepared for the Passion that so many people endure today and every day? We need a new way of seeing. When we are broken by trouble, Jesus is walking most closely by our side. He gives us the courage to take one more step.

September 25—October 1

Something to think and pray about each day this week:

The Needs Under Our Noses
The parable of the rich man and Lazarus (Luke 16:19–31) is one of startling contrasts, but its central message is simple: be alert to the needs under your nose. It is not concerned with patterns of good living on the part of Lazarus, nor of evildoing on the part of the rich man. But the latter closed his eyes to the needy at his gate. And without an eye for the needy around us, our life becomes self-centered and callous. Jesus is asking his listeners to open their eyes to what is around them, and to open their ears to the simple commands of the gospel: love your neighbor. This is a great story with no ambiguity about it. We have an obligation as Christians to feed the hungry. Every hungry man and woman in the world is on our conscience. While we did not create the problem, we can be part of the solution. Our hearts go out to the millions of old and young in the world just because they are hungry, like Lazarus was at the rich man's gate. Allow some prayer today to enlarge your compassion for the hungry and your desire to do what you can to feed them, for in feeding them, we feed Jesus.

The Presence of God

The more we call on God, the more we can feel God's presence. Day by day we are drawn closer to the loving heart of God.

Freedom

Lord, grant me the grace to be free from the excesses of this life. Let me not get caught up with the desire for wealth. Keep my heart and mind free to love and serve you.

Consciousness

Where do I sense hope, encouragement, and growth areas in my life? By looking back over the last few months, I may be able to see which activities and occasions have produced rich fruit. If I do notice such areas, I will determine to give those areas both time and space in the future.

The Word

God speaks to each one of us individually. I listen attentively to hear what he is saying to me. Read the text a few times, then listen. (Please turn to the Scripture on the following pages. Inspiration points are provided should you need them. When you are ready, return here to continue.)

Conversation

Sometimes I wonder what I might say if I were to meet you in person, Lord. I think I might say, "Thank you, Lord" for always being there for me.

Conclusion

Glory be to the Father, and to the Son, and to the Holy Spirit, as it was in the beginning, is now and ever shall be, world without end. Amen.

Sunday 25th September
Twenty-Sixth Sunday in Ordinary Time
Luke 16:19–31

Jesus said to the Pharisees, "There was a rich man who was dressed in purple and fine linen and who feasted sumptuously every day. And at his gate lay a poor man named Lazarus, covered with sores, who longed to satisfy his hunger with what fell from the rich man's table; even the dogs would come and lick his sores. The poor man died and was carried away by the angels to be with Abraham. The rich man also died and was buried. In Hades, where he was being tormented, he looked up and saw Abraham far away with Lazarus by his side. He called out, 'Father Abraham, have mercy on me, and send Lazarus to dip the tip of his finger in water and cool my tongue; for I am in agony in these flames.' But Abraham said, 'Child, remember that during your lifetime you received your good things, and Lazarus in like manner evil things; but now he is comforted here, and you are in agony. Besides all this, between you and us a great chasm has been fixed, so that those who might want to pass from here to you cannot do so, and no one can cross from there to us.' He said, 'Then, father, I beg you to send him to my father's house—for I have five brothers—that he may warn them, so that they will not also come into this place of torment.' Abraham replied, 'They have Moses and the prophets; they should listen to them.' He said, 'No, father Abraham; but if someone goes to them from the dead, they will repent.' He said to him, 'If they do not listen to Moses and the prophets, neither will they be convinced even if someone rises from the dead.'"

- The rich man in the story is totally self-centered. Jesus warns us that we must instead care for others and stand for justice. Consider the following poem: "Me and my wife; my son John and his wife; us four; no more." Can I, too, be absorbed in my small, self-sufficient life and fail to notice the needs of those around me, and the cry of pain in the wider world?

- "You just need to be a flea against injustice. Enough committed fleas biting strategically can make even the biggest dog uncomfortable and transform even the biggest nation" (Marian Wright Edelman).

Monday 26th September
Luke 9:46–50

An argument arose among them as to which one of them was the greatest. But Jesus, aware of their inner thoughts, took a little child and put it by his side, and said to them, "Whoever welcomes this child in my name welcomes me, and whoever welcomes me welcomes the one who sent me; for the least among all of you is the greatest." John answered, "Master, we saw someone casting out demons in your name, and we tried to stop him, because he does not follow with us." But Jesus said to him, "Do not stop him; for whoever is not against you is for you."

- Jesus turns everything on its head. For him the kingdom of God is the only absolute value. The creative power of the Holy Spirit is active in every person, even in those who belong to no Christian denomination. Can I rejoice in that? "In the evening of life we will be examined in love" (Saint John of the Cross).

- What makes a person great? Is it power, or wealth, or skills, or beauty, or giftedness of one kind or another? In the kingdom of God greatness is judged by one's capacity to serve others. So it is the little people of the earth, those who serve the rest of us, who turn out to be the greatest! Will I be considered great in God's Kingdom?

Tuesday 27th September
Luke 9:51–56

When the days drew near for him to be taken up, Jesus set his face to go to Jerusalem. And he sent messengers ahead of him. On their way they entered a village of the Samaritans to make ready for him; but they did not receive him, because his face was set toward Jerusalem. When his disciples James and John saw it, they said, "Lord, do you want us to command fire to come down from heaven and consume them?" But he turned and rebuked them. Then they went on to another village.

- The disciples thought, "If only everybody were like us" as they asked Jesus to teach a lesson to the obstinate Samaritans. Even as he had set his face to Jerusalem, Jesus recognized how his followers did not understand his heart. Help me, Jesus, to follow you in humility, to seek your way. Let the logic of my head be tempered by the compassion of your heart.

- The antagonism between Jews and Samaritans was strong in Jesus' time. It highlights the worst of religious intolerance and racism. Jesus seems to want to break through the barriers and walls separating these people. Sometimes it worked, as with the woman of Samaria and in the parable of the Good Samaritan. Other times he moves on, knowing that in that specific situation at least, nothing could be done.

Wednesday 28th September
Luke 9:57–62

As they were going along the road, someone said to him, "I will follow you wherever you go." And Jesus said to him, "Foxes have holes, and birds of the air have nests; but the Son of Man has nowhere to lay his head." To another he said, "Follow me." But he said, "Lord, first let me go and bury my father." But Jesus said to him, "Let the dead bury their own dead; but as for you, go and proclaim the kingdom of God." Another said, "I will follow you, Lord; but let me first say farewell to those at my home." Jesus said to him, "No one who puts a hand to the plow and looks back is fit for the kingdom of God."

- Jesus wants to help us to know ourselves, so he questions us, leading us to deeper self-knowledge. Even our excuses are opportunities to recognize what really attracts us and to bring those things to Jesus.

- We can remember that we have said "Yes" in baptism; we may need to take care not to undermine ourselves by focusing on our unworthiness. Instead, we can remember who calls us in love.

Thursday 29th September
John 1:47–51

When Jesus saw Nathanael coming toward him, he said of him, "Here is truly an Israelite in whom there is no deceit!" Nathanael asked him, "Where did you get to know me?" Jesus answered, "I saw you under the fig tree before Philip called you." Nathanael replied, "Rabbi, you are the Son of God! You are the King of Israel!" Jesus answered, "Do you believe because I told you that I saw you under the fig tree? You will see greater things than these." And he said to him, "Very truly, I tell you, you will see heaven opened and the angels of God ascending and descending upon the Son of Man."

• What a beautiful tribute Jesus gives to Nathanael! Here is a man without guile—sincere, faithful, and upright before God. Our deepest identity lies in our relationship with God. Lord, I come toward you this day. You know my heart. Is it without deceit? "In the presence of his glory, closely watch your heart, so your thoughts won't shame you, for he sees guilt, opinion, and desire as plainly as a dark hair in pure milk" (Rumi).

• Nathanael's answer seemed cynical, but he was prepared to go and see, as Philip invited him. I pray for the strength I need to put up with dismissive answers, and I ask God to work gently in skeptical hearts. What might it have been that Jesus saw under the fig tree? What actions or words of Nathanael's impressed him? I think of how Jesus sees me under the fig trees of my life, of how he values what may be hidden from others.

Friday 30th September
Luke 10:13–16

Jesus said to his disciples, "Woe to you, Chorazin! Woe to you, Bethsaida! For if the deeds of power done in you had been done in Tyre and Sidon, they would have repented long ago, sitting in sackcloth and ashes. But at the judgment it will be more tolerable for Tyre and Sidon than for you. And you, Capernaum, will you be exalted to heaven? No, you will be brought down to Hades. Whoever listens to you listens to me, and whoever rejects you rejects me, and whoever rejects me rejects the one who sent me."

- We take great pride in our cities; we score and rank our favorite destinations. Jesus tells us to take care not to be carried away by the admirable achievements of civilization. Abundance of noise does not always communicate meaning; mass communication does not always uncover truth. Regardless of where I live or what I admire, I pray that local pride might not distract me from what is really important.

- Jesus laments the fact that people reject the Good News despite all he does for them. The truth can be painful at times and challenging to hear. When we speak our truths and live our lives according to the teaching of Christ, then we have chosen the better part and it cannot be taken away from us. I come back to you, God, as your loving disciple, again and again, in all my sinfulness. But you do not "bring me down to Hades." Instead you revive my drooping spirit as you enfold me in your loving forgiveness.

Saturday 1st October
Luke 10:17–24

The seventy returned with joy, saying, "Lord, in your name even the demons submit to us!" He said to them, "I watched Satan fall from heaven like a flash of lightning. See, I have given you authority to tread on snakes and scorpions, and over all the power of the enemy; and nothing will hurt you. Nevertheless, do not rejoice at this, that the spirits submit to you, but rejoice that your names are written in heaven." At that same hour Jesus rejoiced in the Holy Spirit and said, "I thank you, Father, Lord of heaven and earth, because you have hidden these things from the wise and the intelligent and have revealed them to infants; yes, Father, for such was your gracious will. All things have been handed over to me by my Father; and no one knows who the Son is except the Father, or who the Father is except the Son and anyone to whom the Son chooses to reveal him." Then turning to the disciples, Jesus said to them privately, "Blessed are the eyes that see what you see! For I tell you that many prophets and kings desired to see what you see, but did not see it, and to hear what you hear, but did not hear it."

• Learning and knowledge are often confused with education and intelligence. The truth that Jesus proclaims is available to all. The important question is not what do I know but what education do I have? My prayer helps me to appreciate whom I know, who knows me, and who loves me.

• In Hebrew culture, snakes and scorpions were symbols of various kinds of evil. But triumph over evil is not to be the main cause of joy for the disciples. The deepest joy of these anonymous disciples is to come from knowing that they are loved by God and are the chosen sisters and brothers of Jesus. Jesus, I may not be particularly wise or smart! I am like a child before you. But I hand myself over to you. Remain with me always, especially in my times of doubt. Increase my insight to the needs of others and keep me tuned in to your word.

October 2—October 8

Something to think and pray about each day this week:

A Place in the Wilderness

If the Spirit is to take over in our prayer, we need to be somewhere like the wilderness, where nothing much is happening. In Hosea 2:14, God says of his people Israel,

> "I will now allure her,
> And bring her into the wilderness,
> And speak to her heart."

Your dedicated time for prayer can feel like the wilderness when you turn off your cell phone, iPad, radio, or TV. You have drawn back from the noise and chatter that imprisons you on the surface of yourself, and you may wonder if anything worthwhile can happen now. But God wants to draw you deep into your own heart and meet you there. So it is good to create those wilderness conditions that heighten your sensitivity to God's Word. You will be allured by God's attractiveness, and God will speak to your heart. God is active in your prayer, too. Your wilderness is a graced place. Be still and let the things of God touch your heart. Invite God to whisper your name, to light a little flame in your heart, and to tell you how he loves you.

The Presence of God

Dear Jesus, as I call on you today I realize that I often come asking for favors. Today I'd like just to be in your presence. Let my heart respond to your love.

Freedom

Lord, grant me the grace to have freedom of the spirit. Cleanse my heart and soul so I may live joyously in your love.

Consciousness

I ask how I am within myself today. Am I particularly tired, stressed, or off-form? If any of these characteristics apply, can I try to let go of the concerns that disturb me?

The Word

I take my time to read the Word of God slowly, a few times, allowing myself to dwell on anything that strikes me. (Please turn to the Scripture on the following pages. Inspiration points are provided should you need them. When you are ready, return here to continue.)

Conversation

I know with certainty there were times when you carried me, Lord. When it was through your strength I got through the dark times in my life.

Conclusion

I thank God for these few moments we have spent alone together and for any insights I may have been given concerning the text.

Sunday 2nd October
Twenty-Seventh Sunday in Ordinary Time
Luke 17:5–10

The apostles said to the Lord, "Increase our faith!" The Lord replied, "If you had faith the size of a mustard seed, you could say to this mulberry tree, 'Be uprooted and planted in the sea,' and it would obey you. Who among you would say to your slave who has just come in from ploughing or tending sheep in the field, 'Come here at once and take your place at the table'? Would you not rather say to him, 'Prepare supper for me, put on your apron and serve me while I eat and drink; later you may eat and drink'? Do you thank the slave for doing what was commanded? So you also, when you have done all that you were ordered to do, say, 'We are worthless slaves; we have done only what we ought to have done!'"

- Jesus draws attention to the greatness hidden in something tiny. We too are tiny, but God empowers those who truly follow him to do great things. God can work through us, beyond all our hopes and dreams, when we do not get in the way.

- Lord, you fill me with your unlimited love, and you invite me to share that love with a needy world. Let it be my joy to do that. That is my greatness, to serve in love. And the opportunities are endless.

Monday 3rd October
Luke 10:25–37

Just then a lawyer stood up to test Jesus. "Teacher," he said, "what must I do to inherit eternal life?" He said to him, "What is written in the law? What do you read there?" He answered, "You shall love the Lord your God with all your heart, and with all your soul, and with all your strength, and with all your mind; and your neighbor as yourself." And he said to him, "You have given the right answer; do this, and you will live." But wanting to justify himself, he asked Jesus, "And who is my neighbor?" Jesus replied, "A man was going down from Jerusalem to Jericho, and fell into the hands of robbers, who stripped him, beat him, and went away, leaving him half dead. Now by chance a priest was going down that road; and when he saw him, he passed by on the other side. So likewise a Levite, when he came to the place and saw him, passed by on the other side. But a Samaritan while traveling came near him; and when he saw him, he was moved with pity. He went to him and bandaged his wounds, having poured oil and wine on them. Then he put him on his own animal, brought him to an inn, and took care of him. The next day he took out two denarii, gave them to the innkeeper, and said, 'Take care of him; and when I come back, I will repay you whatever more you spend.' Which of these three, do you think, was a neighbor to the man who fell into the hands of the robbers?" He said, "The one who showed him mercy." Jesus said to him, "Go and do likewise."

- Modern urban life trains us to walk on by, to be like the priest or Levite in the parable. I ask God to help me to preserve the compassion to which Jesus calls us.

- To be a neighbor is to be one who shows mercy. I consider my attitude to those among whom I live and imagine how I might be merciful to them as God is to me.

Tuesday 4th October
Luke 10:38–42

Now as they went on their way, Jesus entered a certain village, where a woman named Martha welcomed him into her home. She had a sister named Mary, who sat at the Lord's feet and listened to what he was saying. But Martha was distracted by her many tasks; so she came to him and asked, "Lord, do you not care that my sister has left me to do all the work by myself? Tell her then to help me." But the Lord answered her, "Martha, Martha, you are worried and distracted by many things; there is need of only one thing. Mary has chosen the better part, which will not be taken away from her."

- It is easy to be distracted and fragmented when many things call for attention—even what is good can lose its luster if we forget what busyness is about. Martha seems to have been distracted by the many things she had to do; she forgot whom she was doing them for.

- I pray that I, like Mary, can be drawn to the presence of Jesus and, like Martha, can be honest with him about what distracts me.

Wednesday 5th October
Luke 11:1–4

Jesus was praying in a certain place, and after he had finished, one of his disciples said to him, "Lord, teach us to pray, as John taught his disciples." He said to them, "When you pray, say: Father, hallowed be your name. Your kingdom come. Give us each day our daily bread. And forgive us our sins, for we ourselves forgive everyone indebted to us. And do not bring us to the time of trial."

- The disciples were looking outward at John and his disciples, at Jesus in prayer. Jesus suggests to them that their prayer might begin by looking in, by starting with their most important relationships. To call God "Father" is to recognize where my life comes from and to establish me in relation to others. If I focus on my needs, it is so that I might grow in trust as I recognize who is ready to answer them.

- It is clear that prayer was essential for Jesus—for his identity and his mission. Prayer expressed Jesus' relationship with his Father. He taught his followers how to pray, and he made time for it himself, no matter what needs and demands pressed on him. Do I do likewise? The Lord's Prayer is the model for all prayer. It contains the essential petitions for truly Christian prayer and living. Do I allow this prayer to mold me as a person and to directly influence my relationship with God and with my neighbor?

Thursday 6th October
Luke 11:5–13

And he said to them, "Suppose one of you has a friend, and you go to him at midnight and say to him, 'Friend, lend me three loaves of bread; for a friend of mine has arrived, and I have nothing to set before him.'

And he answers from within, 'Do not bother me; the door has already been locked, and my children are with me in bed; I cannot get up and give you anything.' I tell you, even though he will not get up and give him anything because he is his friend, at least because of his persistence he will get up and give him whatever he needs. So I say to you, Ask, and it will be given to you; search, and you will find; knock, and the door will be opened for you. For everyone who asks receives, and everyone who searches finds, and for everyone who knocks, the door will be opened. Is there anyone among you who, if your child asks for a fish, will give a snake instead of a fish? Or if the child asks for an egg, will give a scorpion? If you then, who are evil, know how to give good gifts to your children, how much more will the heavenly Father give the Holy Spirit to those who ask him!"

• There are people to whom I would like to be generous; there may be some to whom I would give anything. Can I imagine that, in God's eyes, I am one of those people? God may not seem to give me everything I ask, but he arranges what is for my good and lasting benefit. I pray for the trust I need.

• I bring different intentions to my prayer as my priorities shift. I review what is really important to me and see what I might let go. I ask God for the faith I need. My prayer may be less in the waiting for the answer than in approaching God with a child's confident trust.

Friday 7th October
Luke 11:15–26

Some of them said, "He casts out demons by Beelzebul, the ruler of the demons." Others, to test him, kept demanding from him a sign from heaven. But he knew what they were thinking and said to them, "Every kingdom divided against itself becomes a desert, and house falls on house. If Satan also is divided against himself, how will his kingdom stand?—for you say that I cast out the demons by Beelzebul. Now if I cast out the demons by Beelzebul, by whom do your exorcists cast them out? Therefore they will be your judges. But if it is by the finger of

God that I cast out the demons, then the kingdom of God has come to you. When a strong man, fully armed, guards his castle, his property is safe. But when one stronger than he attacks him and overpowers him, he takes away his armor in which he trusted and divides his plunder. Whoever is not with me is against me, and whoever does not gather with me scatters. When the unclean spirit has gone out of a person, it wanders through waterless regions looking for a resting place, but not finding any, it says, 'I will return to my house from which I came.' When it comes, it finds it swept and put in order. Then it goes and brings seven other spirits more evil than itself, and they enter and live there; and the last state of that person is worse than the first."

• God's Spirit will always lead us to life and truth. Other spirits may distract us with false promises, but we need not fear them when we honestly seek God's way and follow Jesus' words. I pray that I may respect and love those who follow God in sincerity even if they differ from me. I ask that I be alert to any voice that distracts me from my path of discipleship.

• The opposition that Jesus faced was endless. Here he argues that demons can only be cast out by "the finger of God," which symbolizes divine power. With every victory over evil, the kingdom of God becomes more firmly established. It is said that if those in recovery from an addiction lapse into their former negative lifestyle, their new condition may be far worse than before. Am I resolved, with the help of God's power, to continue to progress on the path of health and growth?

Saturday 8th October

Luke 11:27–28

While Jesus was speaking this, a woman in the crowd raised her voice and said to him, "Blessed is the womb that bore you and the breasts that nursed you!" But he said, "Blessed rather are those who hear the Word of God and obey it!"

- The woman's comment drew attention to Jesus' mother, suggesting why she was blessed. His answer invites us all to be blessed as Mary was by receiving God's Word in our hearts and living in its light.

- What do I make of Jesus' reaction here? He risks being blunt with the woman in the crowd and dismissive of his mother. What is he getting at? What does he really want to say? What does it say to me? Here is an encounter with a woman who is adoring and envious of Jesus' mother. He responds unexpectedly, not downgrading Mary but pointing to the source of her blessedness, as her cousin Elizabeth did at the Visitation: Blessed is she who believed in the Lord's promise.

October 9—October 15

Something to think and pray about each day this week:

The One Who Came Back

Can I imagine this scene? Ten miserable individuals have to call on Jesus from a distance for fear of contaminating him. What is going on within them? What happens? I have done it myself, Lord. I go looking for something, advertising my need, seeking sympathy. And when somebody helps me, part of me is muttering, "He was only doing his job" or "That's what you'd expect of a neighbor." I take kindness for granted and do not bother to say, "Thank you." It was a stranger, a Samaritan, who took the trouble to go back to Jesus and then became an icon of gratitude. The other nine went away thinking, "Sure, that's only what the priests/doctors/healers are there for."

Thank you, Lord, that I am alive and able to speak to you. Our daily prayer at its best includes praise of God—for who God is and for what God does for us. Jesus often praised God himself and asked others to do the same. We all share our faith in the God who creates us and the world day by day. We share faith, too, in the God who helps us in life, regardless of creed or color. All prayer echoes the praise of Mary: "My soul glorifies the Lord and my spirit rejoices in God my Savior" (Luke 1:46).

The Presence of God

Dear Jesus, I come to you today longing for your presence. I desire to love you as you love me. May nothing ever separate me from you.

Freedom

God is not foreign to my freedom. Instead the Spirit breathes life into my most intimate desires, gently nudging me toward all that is good. I ask for the grace to let myself be enfolded by the Spirit.

Consciousness

How do I find myself today? Where am I with God? With others? Do I have something to be grateful for? Then I give thanks. Is there something I am sorry for? Then I ask forgiveness.

The Word

The Word of God comes down to us through the Scriptures. May the Holy Spirit enlighten my mind and my heart to respond to the gospel teachings. (Please turn to the Scripture on the following pages. Inspiration points are provided should you need them. When you are ready, return here to continue.)

Conversation

Remembering that I am still in God's presence, I imagine Jesus himself standing or sitting beside me, and I say whatever is on my mind, whatever is in my heart, speaking as one friend to another.

Conclusion

Glory be to the Father, and to the Son, and to the Holy Spirit, as it was in the beginning, is now and ever shall be, world without end. Amen.

Sunday 9th October
Twenty-Eighth Sunday in Ordinary Time
Luke 17:11–19

On the way to Jerusalem Jesus was going through the region between Samaria and Galilee. As he entered a village, ten lepers approached him. Keeping their distance, they called out, saying, "Jesus, Master, have mercy on us!" When he saw them, he said to them, "Go and show yourselves to the priests." And as they went, they were made clean. Then one of them, when he saw that he was healed, turned back, praising God with a loud voice. He prostrated himself at Jesus' feet and thanked him. And he was a Samaritan. Then Jesus asked, "Were not ten made clean? But the other nine, where are they? Was none of them found to return and give praise to God except this foreigner?" Then he said to him, "Get up and go on your way; your faith has made you well."

- How long does gratitude last? These lepers were respectful, even fawning, when they were still suffering: "Jesus, Master, have mercy on us!" In their misery they joined forces, waiving the old hostility between Jews and Samaritans. But when they saw their leprosy healed, and felt themselves whole, nine of them took their blessing for granted and forgot to say thank you.

- Lord, all throughout my life I have known kindnesses; there have been people whom I thanked after a big favor, using inflated language and saying that I would never forget them. But my gratitude grows cold. Let me count my blessings, not take them for granted.

Monday 10th October
Luke 11:29–32

When the crowds were increasing, Jesus began to say, "This generation is an evil generation; it asks for a sign, but no sign will be given to it except the sign of Jonah. For just as Jonah became a sign to the people of Nineveh, so the Son of Man will be to this generation. The queen of the South will rise at the judgment with the people of this generation and condemn them, because she came from the ends of the earth to listen to the wisdom of Solomon, and see, something greater than Solomon is here! The people of Nineveh will rise up at the judgment with this generation and condemn it, because they repented at the proclamation of Jonah, and see, something greater than Jonah is here!"

- Jesus uses the imagination to help his audience catch on to the mystery of who he is. So he reminds them of famous characters in stories they already know well. He then tries to open their minds further by saying twice that "something greater" is here in his person.

- This is a mysterious assertion. But God is mysterious, so coming closer to the truth about God means being led along the path of mystery. Do I cultivate my capacity for mystery, or do I live on the surface of life? Do I reduce the wonders of nature and the cosmos to mere facts, or do I let myself ponder what their author must be like? Everything is a divine mystery because all comes from God. Let me sit with Jesus and ask him to enliven the mystical dimension that may be dormant in me.

Tuesday 11th October
Luke 11:37–41

While Jesus was speaking, a Pharisee invited him to dine with him; so he went in and took his place at the table. The Pharisee was amazed to see that he did not first wash before dinner. Then the Lord said to him, "Now you Pharisees clean the outside of the cup and of the dish, but inside you are full of greed and wickedness. You fools! Did not the one who made the outside make the inside also? So give for alms those things that are within; and see, everything will be clean for you."

- Perhaps it was their fear of God that led the Pharisees to mask their greed and wickedness. As I come to know Jesus, I know that I have nothing to fear. I realize that God knows me thoroughly and loves me fully. All God asks of me is that I be honest, humbly recognize my need, and grow toward God's light.

- Have you ever been surprised when others do not ritually "toe the line"? Does this make me dismiss them? Jesus once again places love and inner goodness above the commands of law. What inner alms have I to share with others? Do I believe that even my little prayers for the world are blessed by God? Lord, you search me and you know me better than I know myself. Cleanse my heart of any traces of "greed and wickedness" and sow in me your generous spirit.

Wednesday 12th October
Luke 11:42–46

Jesus said, "But woe to you Pharisees! For you tithe mint and rue and herbs of all kinds, and neglect justice and the love of God; it is these you ought to have practiced, without neglecting the others. Woe to you Pharisees! For you love to have the seat of honor in the synagogues and to be greeted with respect in the marketplaces. Woe to you! For you are like unmarked graves, and people walk over them without realizing it." One of the lawyers answered him, "Teacher, when you say these things, you insult us too." And he said, "Woe also to you lawyers! For you load people with burdens hard to bear, and you yourselves do not lift a finger to ease them."

• Jesus saw that the Pharisees and lawyers were self-satisfied and realized they were starving themselves. They paid attention to what was outside while neglecting the life of the spirit. Life is not about cosmetics and advertising, nor is it measured by conformity and approval.

• In our time there are industries and advertising campaigns whose only purpose is to attract my attention, consume my resources, and give me a "better" identity. Can I hear Jesus call me back to life?

Thursday 13th October
Luke 11:47–54

Jesus said: "Woe to you! For you build the tombs of the prophets whom your ancestors killed. So you are witnesses and approve of the deeds of your ancestors; for they killed them, and you build their tombs. Therefore also the Wisdom of God said, 'I will send them prophets and apostles, some of whom they will kill and persecute,' so that this generation may be charged with the blood of all the prophets shed since the foundation of the world, from the blood of Abel to the blood of Zechariah, who perished between the altar and the sanctuary. Yes, I tell you, it will be charged against this generation. Woe to you lawyers! For you have taken away the key of knowledge; you did not enter yourselves, and you hindered those who were entering." When he went outside, the scribes and the Pharisees began to be very hostile toward him and to cross-examine him about many things, lying in wait for him, to catch him in something he might say.

- Jesus recognized that the Pharisees had a true inspiration, but he regretted how they arranged their lives. What can I learn from those who "oppose" me? What "key of knowledge" do they hold that I might use wisely to enrich my life?

- To be prophetic is a risky business! It means to speak and do as God would wish. I need to be attentive in prayer to hear what God is trying to say to me. Do I try to notice the promptings of the Holy Spirit so that I can be the Spirit's spokesperson?

Friday 14th October
Luke 12:1–7

Meanwhile, when the crowd gathered by the thousands, so that they trampled on one another, Jesus began to speak first to his disciples, "Beware of the yeast of the Pharisees, that is, their hypocrisy. Nothing is covered up that will not be uncovered, and nothing secret that will not become known. Therefore whatever you have said in the dark will be heard in the light, and what you have whispered behind closed doors will be proclaimed from the housetops. I tell you, my friends, do not fear those who kill the body, and after that can do nothing more. But I will warn you whom to fear: fear him who, after he has killed, has authority to cast into hell. Yes, I tell you, fear him! Are not five sparrows sold for two pennies? Yet not one of them is forgotten in God's sight. But even the hairs of your head are all counted. Do not be afraid; you are of more value than many sparrows."

- Even when there were thousands present, Jesus spoke first to his disciples. Among all those who pray now, Jesus chooses to speak to me. He invites me to honesty and integrity, helping me to realize that I need not pretend in his presence but can be fully who I am. If I can relax in the company of Jesus, of what need I be afraid?

- The actions of hypocrites do not conform to their words. Jesus calls us to personal integrity: coherence between what we believe, say, and do. Jesus speaks encouraging words to his followers in the face of opposition—the reassurance of God's faithful love, care, and support. God cares for the smallest and most vulnerable of his creatures. How much more is God present for all who believe and trust in him?

Saturday 15th October
Luke 12:8–12

Jesus said to the disciples, "And I tell you, everyone who acknowledges me before others, the Son of Man also will acknowledge before the angels of God; but whoever denies me before others will be denied before the angels of God. And everyone who speaks a word against the Son of Man will be forgiven; but whoever blasphemes against the Holy Spirit will not be forgiven. When they bring you before the synagogues, the rulers, and the authorities, do not worry about how you are to defend yourselves or what you are to say; for the Holy Spirit will teach you at that very hour what you ought to say."

- Fear alienates and disables people. It can be employed as an instrument of manipulation, and it can lead to disintegration. Jesus is saying that the follower of Christ has nothing to fear. Disciples will be enabled by the Holy Spirit to speak out in the right way.

- As I pray with you, Lord, I thank you for your forgiveness when I have been disabled by fear. Your love can eliminate my fear. Over and over you tell me not to be afraid. Plant in me your spirit of courage so that I may speak clearly and confidently to others about your word.

October 16—October 22

Something to think and pray about each day this week:

Patience in Prayer

We can be so impatient sometimes and feel that God has not heard our prayers when they are not answered immediately. We live in a world of instant gratification, instant coffee, instant contact—a touch of a button on our computer and we can be anywhere in the world! But Jesus in today's gospel is asking us to be patient, to "pray always and do not lose heart." Our prayers will be answered—maybe not in the way we are expecting, but in the way that is beneficial to us.

Saint Luke shows that Jesus prayed consistently during his public life and his Passion. I am Jesus' disciple, and he needs me to be a person of prayer also. Prayer is like a magnet that keeps us close to God. If I let the magnet go, I drift away from God. Jesus, teach us to trust you and not lose heart when we call on you in prayer. The prayer of intercession will never go unanswered, but our ways are not your ways and our thoughts not your thoughts. Keep us faithful in prayer, Lord, for you will never be outdone in generosity. I pray: "Jesus, when you search my heart, do you find any faith inside it? Stretch my small heart so that I may take the risk of entrusting myself more to you."

The Presence of God
At any time of the day or night we can call on Jesus. He is always waiting, listening for our call. What a wonderful blessing. No phone needed, no e-mails, just a whisper.

Freedom
Everything has the potential to draw forth from me a fuller love and life. Yet my desires are often fixed, caught on illusions of fulfillment. I ask that God through my freedom may orchestrate my desires in a vibrant, loving melody rich in harmony.

Consciousness
Help me, Lord, to be more conscious of your presence. Teach me to recognize your presence in others. Fill my heart with gratitude for the times your love has been shown to me through the care of others.

The Word
I read the Word of God slowly, a few times over, and I listen to what God is saying to me. (Please turn to the Scripture on the following pages. Inspiration points are provided should you need them. When you are ready, return here to continue.)

Conversation
Jesus, you speak to me through the words of the gospels. May I respond to your call today. Teach me to recognize your hand at work in my daily living.

Conclusion
I thank God for these few moments we have spent alone together and for any insights I may have been given concerning the text.

Sunday 16th October
Twenty-Ninth Sunday in Ordinary Time
Luke 18:1–8

Then Jesus told them a parable about their need to pray always and not to lose heart. He said, "In a certain city there was a judge who neither feared God nor had respect for people. In that city there was a widow who kept coming to him and saying, 'Grant me justice against my opponent.' For a while he refused; but later he said to himself, 'Though I have no fear of God and no respect for anyone, yet because this widow keeps bothering me, I will grant her justice, so that she may not wear me out by continually coming.'" And the Lord said, "Listen to what the unjust judge says. And will not God grant justice to his chosen ones who cry to him day and night? Will he delay long in helping them? I tell you, he will quickly grant justice to them. And yet, when the Son of Man comes, will he find faith on earth?"

• Lord, you puzzle me. I hear you telling me to persist in prayer, to entreat God until he is weary of me. You say he will quickly grant justice. But then I think of good people suffering famine, AIDS, loss of children, sickness, and death though they pray to God. I think of the Jews in Auschwitz, still singing the psalms as they walked into the gas chambers. Surely there are times when you delay in helping us? At times like this I turn to the memory of your Passion and your agonized prayer in the Garden. You have faced a dark and apparently empty heaven yet stayed faithful. Keep me with you.

• Our persistence in prayer does not change God's mind. Instead it prepares our own heart by strengthening our desire for God! Jesus wishes us to pray always and not lose heart. Help me to be constant, Lord. Renew my failing confidence when your answer is, "Wait . . . wait . . . wait a little longer."

Monday 17th October

Luke 12:13–21

Someone in the crowd said to Jesus, "Teacher, tell my brother to divide the family inheritance with me." But he said to him, "Friend, who set me to be a judge or arbitrator over you?" And he said to them, "Take care! Be on your guard against all kinds of greed; for one's life does not consist in the abundance of possessions." Then he told them a parable: "The land of a rich man produced abundantly. And he thought to himself, 'What should I do, for I have no place to store my crops?' Then he said, 'I will do this: I will pull down my barns and build larger ones, and there I will store all my grain and my goods. And I will say to my soul, "Soul, you have ample goods laid up for many years; relax, eat, drink, be merry."' But God said to him, 'You fool! This very night your life is being demanded of you. And the things you have prepared, whose will they be?' So it is with those who store up treasures for themselves but are not rich toward God."

- Whenever Jesus meets the crowds, he meets many different needs. People present their sicknesses, tell him of the illnesses of others, seek out God's ways, and, here, speak of their ordinary concerns. It is often so as I come to pray: needs of different kinds come into my head, petitions surface, and arguments come to mind. As Jesus replied to the person in the crowd, he speaks to me to help me see what is of lasting importance. Help me, Jesus, not to be distracted by the waves on the surface but to be sensitive to the deeper current that draws me to you.

- Jesus is asked to settle an inheritance case. He cautions his listeners against any kind of greed. He tells them that their lives are not made secure by what they own. They must grow into a true sense of values and recognize that their real life cannot be measured in terms of material possessions. Jesus, how patient you are with us as we struggle with our earthly desires. We want more and yet more. We look with envy on what others seem to have—better homes, better jobs, better ways of living. Help us instead to be grateful for what we have, for your goodness to us, and for who we are as children of God.

Tuesday 18th October

Luke 10:1–9

After this the Lord appointed seventy others and sent them on ahead of him in pairs to every town and place where he himself intended to go. He said to them, "The harvest is plentiful, but the laborers are few; therefore ask the Lord of the harvest to send out laborers into his harvest. Go on your way. See, I am sending you out like lambs into the midst of wolves. Carry no purse, no bag, no sandals; and greet no one on the road. Whatever house you enter, first say, 'Peace to this house!' And if anyone is there who shares in peace, your peace will rest on that person; but if not, it will return to you. Remain in the same house, eating and drinking whatever they provide, for the laborer deserves to be paid. Do not move about from house to house. Whenever you enter a town and its people welcome you, eat what is set before you; cure the sick who are there, and say to them, 'The kingdom of God has come near to you.'"

- Jesus' advice to travel light applies to all of us. How many unneeded and unused purses, bags, sandals, and other stuff clutter my drawers? My friend John, flying to his mission in Zimbabwe, can fit all he carries into his cabin luggage. Confiscation and theft are not a worry to him. I admire and envy him.

- Lord, make me content with you as my baggage.

Wednesday 19th October

Luke 12:39–48

Jesus said to the disciples, "But know this: if the owner of the house had known at what hour the thief was coming, he would not have let his house be broken into. You also must be ready, for the Son of Man is coming at an unexpected hour." Peter said, "Lord, are you telling this parable for us or for everyone?" And the Lord said, "Who then is the faithful and prudent manager whom his master will put in charge of his slaves, to give them their allowance of food at the proper time? Blessed is that slave whom his master will find at work when he arrives.

Truly I tell you, he will put that one in charge of all his possessions. But if that slave says to himself, 'My master is delayed in coming,' and if he begins to beat the other slaves, men and women, and to eat and drink and get drunk, the master of that slave will come on a day when he does not expect him and at an hour that he does not know, and will cut him in pieces, and put him with the unfaithful. That slave who knew what his master wanted, but did not prepare himself or do what was wanted, will receive a severe beating. But one who did not know and did what deserved a beating will receive a light beating. From everyone to whom much has been given, much will be required; and from one to whom much has been entrusted, even more will be demanded."

- Remaining alert doesn't mean living in a state of nervous anxiety. Perhaps it's like a tuned-in radio or a properly configured e-mail account that is ready to receive any message that arrives. Could there be settings in my life I need to adjust or tune more finely? Are there filters I need to help me not to be distracted by less-important signals?

- The parable shows Jesus' awareness that authority and power can be abused. God hears the cry of the poor who are being dominated. He will not "cut to pieces" such people, but their hearts will have to be torn open until they ask forgiveness of their victims and become reconciled. Bless my work, Lord. May I be just in all my dealings and never disrespectful.

Thursday 20th October
Luke 12:49–53

Jesus said to the crowds, "I came to bring fire to the earth, and how I wish it were already kindled! I have a baptism with which to be baptized, and what stress I am under until it is completed! Do you think that I have come to bring peace to the earth? No, I tell you, but rather division! From now on five in one household will be divided, three against two and two against three; they will be divided: father against son and son against father, mother against daughter and daughter against mother, mother-in-law against her daughter-in-law and daughter-in-law against mother-in-law."

- Gentle Jesus, meek and mild? Conformity and harmony are never to be imposed or sought for themselves. They are not a mold into which life is to be forced. When life is properly arranged, they will be the result.

- *Shalom,* the Hebrew word for "peace," has a rich spectrum of meaning to it. It focuses on integrity, well-being, harmony, and unity. When we wish people shalom, we ask for them a whole way of living at peace with God and with themselves. How am I living my faith today? Does it challenge others? For Jesus, here it means being "under stress." But there is also unhelpful stress that comes from anxiety. Let me then pray with Saint Teresa of Ávila:

"Let nothing disturb you,
Let nothing frighten you,
All things are passing away:
God never changes.
Patience obtains all things.
Whoever has God lacks nothing;
God alone suffices."

Friday 21st October
Luke 12:54–59

Jesus also said to the crowds, "When you see a cloud rising in the west, you immediately say, 'It is going to rain'; and so it happens. And when you see the south wind blowing, you say, 'There will be scorching heat'; and it happens. You hypocrites! You know how to interpret the appearance of earth and sky, but why do you not know how to interpret the present time? And why do you not judge for yourselves what is right? Thus, when you go with your accuser before a magistrate, on the way make an effort to settle the case, or you may be dragged before the judge, and the judge hand you over to the officer, and the officer throw you in prison. I tell you, you will never get out until you have paid the very last penny."

- We have elevated weather forecasting far beyond conversation: the weather has become an industry, a science, an art about which we are constantly informed. Jesus invites us to look at the microclimates of our own lives, to recognize the light that calls us to life, to be alert to the damaging storm, and to avoid the conditions that might lead to our overheating. Direct me, Lord, to recognize how your Spirit moves and to become responsive to your prompting.

- We are asked to interpret our present times rightly. This will involve standing out against injustice and domination. I cannot do this alone, so daily I beg for God's strength, just as Jesus did in his prayer. Jesus tells me to judge for myself what is right. Do I allow the Spirit to speak to me in my conscience, so that I no longer go with the trends of the day but follow instead the inspiration of God?

Saturday 22nd October

Luke 13:1–9

At that very time there were some present who told him about the Galileans whose blood Pilate had mingled with their sacrifices. He asked them, "Do you think that because these Galileans suffered in this way they were worse sinners than all other Galileans? No, I tell you; but unless you repent, you will all perish as they did. Or those eighteen who were killed when the tower of Siloam fell on them—do you think that they were worse offenders than all the others living in Jerusalem? No, I tell you; but unless you repent, you will all perish just as they did." Then he told this parable: "A man had a fig tree planted in his vineyard; and he came looking for fruit on it and found none. So he said to the gardener, 'See here! For three years I have come looking for fruit on this fig tree, and still I find none. Cut it down! Why should it be wasting the soil?' He replied, 'Sir, let it alone for one more year, until I dig round it and put manure on it. If it bears fruit next year, well and good; but if not, you can cut it down.'"

- Jesus comments on the news stories of his time. Just as in our time, narratives of destruction and distress capture the attention. As always, Jesus is telling us not only to look out but also to look in; he is concerned not only with what is going on in our heads but also what is happening in our hearts. He wants us to ask ourselves how God is opening us to compassion, prompting us to repentance, and leading us to life.

- Jewish belief was that whatever evil befell people was a punishment for sin. The more a person had to suffer, the greater their sin must have been! Jesus rejects this simplistic notion. Instead he emphasizes repentance, which means a turning around toward God and one's neighbor. Cultivating and fertilizing the fig tree is a symbol of God's mercy in action. Lord, you know my strengths and my frailties better than I do. You are a patient and loving God, and you have planted the seeds of change in my heart. Now is the time for these seeds to bear fruit.

October 23—October 29

Something to think and pray about each day this week:

Have Mercy on Me

The parable of the Pharisee and the tax collector Jesus tells in the gospel reading this Sunday was meant to sting. Can I get in touch with the power of Jesus' rebuke? Do I hear the call to a different way of living? What does it say to me? The Pharisee and the tax collector spoke about themselves to God. Their attitudes toward others were in stark contrast. As I come to pray, I may speak to God humbly about me and about my neighbors so that I make sure to take time to listen for the voice of the Lord. I allow my prayer to be, "God, be merciful to me, a sinner." I identify myself without excuses, and I address myself to God, confident of being met with love and mercy. Jesus cautions me against anything that elevates me or sets me apart from others. I ask God to help me to be aware of any attitudes or words that demean other people. I place myself with the humble tax collector, asking God for mercy as I realize that I am a sinner. I ask God to help me to know my needs without becoming disheartened. The Pharisee did not just think well of himself but did so at the expense of other people, looking down on them from the height to which he had exalted himself. Are there ways in which I promote myself?

The Presence of God

The more we call on God, the more we can feel God's presence. Day by day we are drawn closer to the loving heart of God.

Freedom

By God's grace I was born to live in freedom. Free to enjoy the pleasures he created for me. Dear Lord, grant that I may live as you intended, with complete confidence in your loving care.

Consciousness

How do I find myself today? Where am I with God? With others? Do I have something to be grateful for? Then I give thanks. Is there something I am sorry for? Then I ask forgiveness.

The Word

The Word of God comes down to us through the Scriptures. May the Holy Spirit enlighten my mind and my heart to respond to the gospel teachings. (Please turn to the Scripture on the following pages. Inspiration points are provided should you need them. When you are ready, return here to continue.)

Conversation

How has God's Word moved me? Has it left me cold? Has it consoled me or moved me to act in a new way? I imagine Jesus standing or sitting beside me. I turn and share my feelings with him.

Conclusion

Glory be to the Father, and to the Son, and to the Holy Spirit, as it was in the beginning, is now and ever shall be, world without end. Amen.

Sunday 23rd October
Thirtieth Sunday in Ordinary Time
Luke 18:9–14

Jesus also told this parable to some who trusted in themselves that they were righteous and regarded others with contempt: "Two men went up to the temple to pray, one a Pharisee and the other a tax collector. The Pharisee, standing by himself, was praying thus, 'God, I thank you that I am not like other people: thieves, rogues, adulterers, or even like this tax collector. I fast twice a week; I give a tenth of all my income.' But the tax collector, standing far off, would not even look up to heaven, but was beating his breast and saying, 'God, be merciful to me, a sinner!' I tell you, this man went down to his home justified rather than the other; for all who exalt themselves will be humbled, but all who humble themselves will be exalted."

• The contrast between the Pharisee and tax collector has entered so deeply into our culture that it is sometimes reversed, and people are more anxious to hide at the back of the church than to be in the front pews.

• How does the story hit me? I would hate to be the object of people's contempt. But Lord, if they knew me as you do, they might be right to feel contempt. And I have no right to look down on those whose sins are paraded in the media. Be merciful to me.

Monday 24th October
Luke 13:10–17

Now Jesus was teaching in one of the synagogues on the sabbath. And just then there appeared a woman with a spirit that had crippled her for eighteen years. She was bent over and was quite unable to stand up straight. When Jesus saw her, he called her over and said, "Woman, you are set free from your ailment." When he laid his hands on her, immediately she stood up straight and began praising God. But the leader of the synagogue, indignant because Jesus had cured on the sabbath, kept saying to the crowd, "There are six days on which work ought to be done; come on those days and be cured, and not on the sabbath day." But the Lord answered him and said, "You hypocrites! Does not each of you on the sabbath untie his ox or his donkey from the manger, and lead it away to give it water? And ought not this woman, a daughter of Abraham whom Satan bound for eighteen long years, be set free from this bondage on the sabbath day?" When he said this, all his opponents were put to shame; and the entire crowd was rejoicing at all the wonderful things that he was doing.

- Think of the perspective this woman had: never able to look anyone in the eye, unable to take her place among any ordinary crowd. She was likely to have been looked down on or overlooked, denied her dignity as a person. Jesus wants to free me of any improper impediments or restrictions. He does not ask me what I can bear, what I am used to, or what I can settle for. He wants to restore me to my proper stature and to let me see as he sees.

- Two things move me in this story: the joy of the woman who for the first time in eighteen years could stand up straight, and the confrontation with the leader of the synagogue, who loved systems more than people (the law said that healing was work and thus was forbidden on the sabbath). Straighten me up, Lord. Unshackle my heart from crippling attachments.

Tuesday 25th October
Luke 13:18–21

Jesus said, "What is the kingdom of God like? And to what should I compare it? It is like a mustard seed that someone took and sowed in the garden; it grew and became a tree, and the birds of the air made nests in its branches." And again he said, "To what should I compare the kingdom of God? It is like yeast that a woman took and mixed in with three measures of flour until all of it was leavened."

- Let me review today the daily chores of my life. Do they rise up to challenge me? Do I become discouraged when I do not see results?

- Lord, teach me to recognize the seeds of transformation that you have placed within me. Help me to understand that the kingdom is growing now in me and that you are making your presence known to me in small as well as big ways.

Wednesday 26th October
Luke 13:22–30

Jesus went through one town and village after another, teaching as he made his way to Jerusalem. Someone asked him, "Lord, will only a few be saved?" He said to them, "Strive to enter through the narrow door; for many, I tell you, will try to enter and will not be able. Indeed, some are last who will be first, and some are first who will be last."

- Jesus cautions us against being presumptuous about salvation. Let us not be late arrivals at the gates of heaven! It can be a painful experience to realize that I am not as perfect as I might like to believe. What matters most is that I should have a loving and forgiving heart that embraces all my fellow sinners.

- Lord, you are not saying that many will be lost at the End. But you are warning us to deepen our relationship with you and to accept others. Let me play my small but essential part to ensure that all of us may be gathered safely into your kingdom.

Thursday 27th October
Luke 13:31–35

At that very hour some Pharisees came and said to Jesus, "Get away from here, for Herod wants to kill you." He said to them, "Go and tell that fox for me, 'Listen, I am casting out demons and performing cures today and tomorrow, and on the third day I finish my work. Yet today, tomorrow, and the next day I must be on my way, because it is impossible for a prophet to be killed outside of Jerusalem.' Jerusalem, Jerusalem, the city that kills the prophets and stones those who are sent to it! How often have I desired to gather your children together as a hen gathers her brood under her wings, and you were not willing! See, your house is left to you. And I tell you, you will not see me until the time comes when you say, 'Blessed is the one who comes in the name of the Lord.'"

- Jesus sees things as they are: he has no illusions about Herod; it is clear to him that Jerusalem has missed its opportunity. I ask God to help me to be able to see clearly, to recognize where there are influences in my life that draw me away from God. I pray that I may be able to recognize and resist temptation and keep my heart set on what God wants for me.

- When Saint Ignatius of Loyola suggests that we look on the world as God does, we might have this image of Jesus in mind as he looked on Jerusalem. I think of the cities and towns around me, of all the people's occupations and businesses, and I consider how God's heart yearns for them all. Jesus accepted the cross not only in his crucifixion but also in the many small choices that led him to Jerusalem. I pray that I may be ready to embrace God's will not only in the dramatic moments but also in the smaller, painful ones.

Friday 28th October
Luke 6:12–16

Now during those days Jesus went out to the mountain to pray; and he spent the night in prayer to God. And when day came, he called his disciples and chose twelve of them, whom he also named apostles: Simon, whom he named Peter, and his brother Andrew, and James, and John, and Philip, and Bartholomew, and Matthew, and Thomas, and James son of Alphaeus, and Simon, who was called the Zealot, and Judas son of James, and Judas Iscariot, who became a traitor.

- Jesus called people to follow him, but not all in the same way. The disciples lived their calling by following Jesus on his journeys, by accompanying him in his mission. There are not grades of discipleship; each of us strives to live the call of Jesus as fully as we can in a way that is appropriate to our situation.

- Jesus chose and called his disciples after some time of prayer. Consider what was in Jesus' heart—the hope, trust, and love that he had for his disciples as he chose them to be close to him. Allow Jesus to look on you with the same hope, trust, and love. Hear yourself called; ask for the grace to be able to respond fully from your heart.

Saturday 29th October
Luke 14:1, 7–11

On one occasion when Jesus was going to the house of a leader of the Pharisees to eat a meal on the sabbath, they were watching him closely. When he noticed how the guests chose the places of honor, he told them a parable. "When you are invited by someone to a wedding banquet, do not sit down at the place of honor, in case someone more distinguished than you has been invited by your host; and the host who invited both of you may come and say to you, 'Give this person your place,' and then in disgrace you would start to take the lowest place. But when you are invited, go and sit down at the lowest place, so that when your host comes, he may say to you, 'Friend, move up higher'; then you will be honored in the presence of all who sit at the table with you. For all who exalt themselves will be humbled, and those who humble themselves will be exalted."

- When Jesus recommends genuine humility—and his parable is not about banquet etiquette!—what is he calling me to do? Jesus picks out that uneasy moment when I walk to the table and wonder if there is a place for me. Do I remember either the elation of being considered more special than I thought I was, or the deflation of being thought more ordinary than seemed right to me? Lord, if I am happy in my own skin, I'll be good company for whoever is beside me.

- As I come to pray, I take care to seat myself properly. I choose a lowly place because I am aware of my status; God invites me closer because of love. I realize that I sometimes want to earn God's love or feel that I deserve it, and I ask forgiveness. I think of how appreciation or recognition has encouraged me and consider how I might raise someone up with my words.

October 30—November 5

Something to think and pray about each day this week:

Climb a Tree to See

Wasn't Zacchaeus (Luke 19:1–10) very quick off the mark when he raced to a tree and climbed it in order to see Jesus? He was a man of the world, wealthy, and well positioned but not very popular in the community; tax collectors were not the most popular people. Yet something stirred in him that caused him to find some way to get above the crowds. Zacchaeus had a conversion experience when he looked into the eyes of Jesus, and his whole world turned around. I wonder what happened to him after Jesus left the village. Lord, you met Zacchaeus where he was and changed him completely, bringing, as you say, salvation to his house. *Repent* means "turn around"; help me to turn my life around and repent of its many faults and failings. I am small, so I ask Jesus to lift me up onto his shoulders, so that I may see the world as he sees it. This is what prayer is like. I pray: "Jesus, you became the guest of a sinner that day. Please be my guest every day, though I am a sinner, too." The practice of prayer is like climbing a tree. It gives me a daily glimpse of the Lord as he passes.

The Presence of God
My soul longs for your presence, Lord. When I turn my thoughts to you, I find peace and contentment.

Freedom
"In these days, God taught me as a schoolteacher teaches a pupil" (Saint Ignatius of Loyola). I remind myself that there are things God has to teach me yet, and ask for the grace to hear them and let them change me.

Consciousness
How am I really feeling? Lighthearted? Heavyhearted? I may be very much at peace, happy to be here. Equally, I may be frustrated, worried, or angry. I acknowledge how I really am. It is the real me that the Lord loves.

The Word
God speaks to each one of us individually. I listen attentively to hear what he is saying to me. Read the text a few times, then listen. (Please turn to the Scripture on the following pages. Inspiration points are provided should you need them. When you are ready, return here to continue.)

Conversation
Do I notice myself reacting as I pray with the Word of God? Do I feel challenged, comforted, angry? Imagining Jesus sitting or standing by me, I speak out my feelings, as one trusted friend to another.

Conclusion
Glory be to the Father, and to the Son, and to the Holy Spirit, as it was in the beginning, is now and ever shall be, world without end. Amen.

Sunday 30th October
Thirty-First Sunday in Ordinary Time
Luke 19:1–10

Jesus entered Jericho and was passing through it. A man was there named Zacchaeus; he was a chief tax collector and was rich. He was trying to see who Jesus was, but on account of the crowd he could not, because he was short in stature. So he ran ahead and climbed a sycamore tree to see him, because he was going to pass that way. When Jesus came to the place, he looked up and said to him, "Zacchaeus, hurry and come down; for I must stay at your house today." So he hurried down and was happy to welcome him. All who saw it began to grumble and said, "He has gone to be the guest of one who is a sinner." Zacchaeus stood there and said to the Lord, "Look, half of my possessions, Lord, I will give to the poor; and if I have defrauded anyone of anything, I will pay back four times as much." Then Jesus said to him, "Today salvation has come to this house, because he too is a son of Abraham. For the Son of Man came to seek out and to save the lost."

- In my prayer, Lord, I am often like Zacchaeus, making huge efforts to catch a glimpse of you, only to find that you are waiting for me, calling me by name, inviting yourself into my heart. Once I am with you, I find happiness in putting things right, ordering my life, and finding the springs of generosity and justice that have been stifled by old habits. Jesus, you look at me as you looked at Zacchaeus. You call me by name and invite me to join you. You do not make demands, but in your company I want to change something in myself and to offer it to you.

- Zacchaeus used his imagination to see above the heads of those who came between him and Jesus. Do I allow someone or something to stop me from seeing Jesus? Jesus saw what was holding Zacchaeus back from living fully and freely. I ask Jesus to speak to me about my life, to help and to heal me.

Monday 31st October
Luke 14:12–14

Jesus said also to the one who had invited him, "When you give a luncheon or a dinner, do not invite your friends or your brothers or your relatives or rich neighbors, in case they may invite you in return, and you would be repaid. But when you give a banquet, invite the poor, the crippled, the lame, and the blind. And you will be blessed, because they cannot repay you, for you will be repaid at the resurrection of the righteous."

- Jesus, how often my giving is corrupted by self-interest and the hope of favors in return. You gave to me without hope of return. I can do you no favors, but you taught me that love means giving without expectations, that there is more happiness in giving than in receiving.

- Jesus' words reveal his generous heart. I try again to accept that I am here in prayer not because I am worthy but so that I might become more open to accept the gifts that God offers to me. I call to mind those who are without the advantages I enjoy: Jesus wishes such blessings for them, too. How can I wish anything less for them? What might I do to express my gratitude to God for being so good to me?

Tuesday 1st November
The Solemnity of All Saints
Matthew 5:1–12a

When Jesus saw the crowds, he went up the mountain; and after he sat down, his disciples came to him. Then he began to speak, and taught them, saying: "Blessed are the poor in spirit, for theirs is the kingdom of heaven. Blessed are those who mourn, for they will be comforted. Blessed are the meek, for they will inherit the earth. Blessed are those who hunger and thirst for righteousness, for they will be filled. Blessed are the merciful, for they will receive mercy. Blessed are the pure in heart, for they will see God. Blessed are the peacemakers, for they will be called children of God. Blessed are those who are persecuted for righteousness sake, for theirs is the kingdom of heaven. Blessed are you when people revile you and persecute you and utter all kinds of evil against you falsely on my account. Rejoice and be glad, for your reward is great in heaven, for in the same way they persecuted the prophets who were before you."

- Today's feast includes all the saints who were never canonized, the mothers and fathers who stayed faithful to one another and their families, the single women and men who did good unseen, those who found God through the pain they endured, and all those we loved and thought much of, who would never have thought of themselves as holy but whose goodness was clear to those close to them. Do I belong with them?

- Today, and always, Jesus is "sitting down" in the sacred space of my heart. I listen to him and his words of life. Which beatitude do I find most affirming? Which gives me the most encouragement for my life's journey right now? Which beatitude challenges me the most? Whichever one I feel drawn to indicates the next step forward in my life's journey.

Wednesday 2nd November
The Commemoration of All the Faithful Departed
John 6:37–40

Jesus said to them, "Everything that the Father gives me will come to me, and anyone who comes to me I will never drive away; for I have come down from heaven, not to do my own will, but the will of him who sent me. And this is the will of him who sent me, that I should lose nothing of all that he has given me, but raise it up on the last day. This is indeed the will of my Father, that all who see the Son and believe in him may have eternal life; and I will raise them up on the last day."

- It is hard for me to understand what it means "to be raised up on the last day." I pray for the trust I need, for the faith to believe that God is working only for my good and lasting happiness.

- Jesus seeks to draw those who listen to him into a profound relationship. He asks them to believe in his wonderful promises about eternal life. Jesus, you invite me to partake in a life that is indestructible. I am to share in the very life of God. This sharing has already begun. May my life and prayer witness that I belong where you are. Bring me—and all others—home to you.

Thursday 3rd November

Luke 15:1–10

Now all the tax collectors and sinners were coming near to listen to him. And the Pharisees and the scribes were grumbling and saying, "This fellow welcomes sinners and eats with them." So he told them this parable: "Which one of you, having a hundred sheep and losing one of them, does not leave the ninety-nine in the wilderness and go after the one that is lost until he finds it? When he has found it, he lays it on his shoulders and rejoices. And when he comes home, he calls together his friends and neighbors, saying to them, 'Rejoice with me, for I have found my sheep that was lost.' Just so, I tell you, there will be more joy in heaven over one sinner who repents than over ninety-nine righteous people who need no repentance. Or what woman having ten silver coins, if she loses one of them, does not light a lamp, sweep the house, and search carefully until she finds it? When she has found it, she calls together her friends and neighbors, saying, 'Rejoice with me, for I have found the coin that I had lost.' Just so, I tell you, there is joy in the presence of the angels of God over one sinner who repents."

- This is not the sort of doctrine you learn in business school. It sounds outlandish, to abandon the well behaved and spend your energies on the outside chance of rescuing the delinquent 1 percent. Yet over the centuries these words have inspired good Christians to plug the gaps in social systems and reach out to those who have drifted into isolation and despair. Common sense urges us to spend ourselves on those who reward our efforts. Jesus worked in another direction: the healthy have no need of a doctor.

- The Pharisees "were grumbling." Am I a grumbler, dissatisfied with the way God goes about things? My greatest difficulty may be that I cannot allow myself to be real and vulnerable with Jesus. Can I let him put me on his shoulders in my weakness? Can I pray, "Carry me, Lord"?

Friday 4th November

Luke 16:1–8

Jesus said to the disciples, "There was a rich man who had a manager, and charges were brought to him that this man was squandering his property. So he summoned him and said to him, 'What is this that I hear about you? Give me an accounting of your management, because you cannot be my manager any longer.' Then the manager said to himself, 'What will I do, now that my master is taking the position away from me? I am not strong enough to dig, and I am ashamed to beg. I have decided what to do so that, when I am dismissed as manager, people may welcome me into their homes.' So, summoning his master's debtors one by one, he asked the first, 'How much do you owe my master?' He answered, 'A hundred jugs of olive oil.' He said to him, 'Take your bill, sit down quickly, and make it fifty.' Then he asked another, 'And how much do you owe?' He replied, 'A hundred containers of wheat.' He said to him, 'Take your bill and make it eighty.' And his master commended the dishonest manager because he had acted shrewdly; for the children of this age are more shrewd in dealing with their own generation than are the children of light."

- Jesus says that we can learn even from dishonest people who are smart! The manager adapts quickly to a crisis. When a crisis hits me, do I turn to God and work out what to do, or do I let the crisis ruin my life? Saint Luke highlights the importance of care for the poor. Those who listened to this story would have smiled at how the poor benefit from the dishonesty of the manager. I hear Jesus ask me: "Are the poor important to you?"

- Having money is a responsibility. I can use it selfishly or with a sensitivity to others' needs. God gave us temporal things to use. My wealth consists not in what I keep but in what I give away. You will judge me by how I use the things of which I am only a steward. The only riches we take from this world are those we have given away.

Saturday 5th November

Luke 16:9–15

Jesus said to the disciples, "And I tell you, make friends for yourselves by means of dishonest wealth so that when it is gone, they may welcome you into the eternal homes. Whoever is faithful in a very little is faithful also in much; and whoever is dishonest in a very little is dishonest also in much. If then you have not been faithful with the dishonest wealth, who will entrust to you the true riches? And if you have not been faithful with what belongs to another, who will give you what is your own? No slave can serve two masters; for a slave will either hate the one and love the other, or be devoted to the one and despise the other. You cannot serve God and wealth." The Pharisees, who were lovers of money, heard all this, and they ridiculed him. So he said to them, "You are those who justify yourselves in the sight of others; but God knows your hearts; for what is prized by human beings is an abomination in the sight of God."

- "Whoever is faithful in a very little is faithful also in much." Lord, you invite me to aim at zero tolerance in my heart for dishonesty, half-truths, and sly self-indulgence. Saint Thérèse of Lisieux based her Little Way on this: fidelity is the flower of love, to which nothing is little. When I prepare a gift for the one I love, every detail counts, and I do it with joy.

- To walk the narrow path of faithfulness and justice is not easy—to be true to oneself and honest with one another is a task we must work at. Jesus tells us that we cannot serve two masters; we cannot sit on the fence. We must come down on the side of righteousness or be bereft of all that is good. You ask us to believe in you, Lord, to trust in your goodness and care for each other. Look into our hearts and remove everything that causes us to stumble or fall, and as we walk through life help us keep our eyes on you.

November 6—November 12

Something to think and pray about each day this week:

Live in the Now of God

In this Sunday's gospel reading, Jesus is being hassled by a trick question from someone who denies the resurrection of the dead. How would I deal with this situation? Do I hear Jesus' strong affirmation of eternal life? How am I moved by it? The Sadducees scorned the idea of rising from the dead. Jesus lifts them from the human tangles in which their theology has trapped them to a cosmic vision. "He is God not of the dead but of the living, for to him all are alive." We are part of that cosmos that transcends space and time and embraces not merely Abraham, Isaac, and Jacob but my parents and all my ancestors to the beginning of creation. In the resurrection we will share the eternal Now of God. It may be that the conundrum of the Sadducees was offered more to confound Jesus than to seek illumination. I think of how the discussion that engages me is for my good or how much is less than helpful to my journey in faith. I pray with compassion for all those whose reason and intelligence is missing the humility to accept the truths that faith uncovers, and I give thanks for the intuitions and insights that have been given to me.

The Presence of God

Lord, help me to be fully alive to your holy presence. Enfold me in your love. Let my heart become one with yours.

Freedom

I am free. When I look at these words in writing they seem to create in me a feeling of awe. Yes, a wonderful feeling of freedom. Thank you, God.

Consciousness

Help me, Lord, to be more conscious of your presence. Teach me to recognize your presence in others. Fill my heart with gratitude for the times your love has been shown to me through the care of others.

The Word

I take my time to read the Word of God slowly, a few times, allowing myself to dwell on anything that strikes me. (Please turn to the Scripture on the following pages. Inspiration points are provided should you need them. When you are ready, return here to continue.)

Conversation

Conversation requires talking and listening. As I talk to Jesus, may I also learn to be still and listen. I picture the gentleness in his eyes and the smile full of love as he gazes on me. I can be totally honest with Jesus as I tell him of my worries and my cares. I will open up my heart to him as I tell him of my fears and my doubts. I will ask him to help me to place myself fully in his care, to abandon myself to him, knowing that he always wants what is best for me.

Conclusion

I thank God for these few moments we have spent alone together and for any insights I may have been given concerning the text.

Sunday 6th November
Thirty-Second Sunday in Ordinary Time
Luke 20:27–38

Some Sadducees, those who say there is no resurrection, came to Jesus and asked him a question, "Teacher, Moses wrote for us that if a man's brother dies, leaving a wife but no children, the man shall marry the widow and raise up children for his brother. Now there were seven brothers; the first married, and died childless; then the second and the third married her, and so in the same way all seven died childless. Finally the woman also died. In the resurrection, therefore, whose wife will the woman be? For the seven had married her." Jesus said to them, "Those who belong to this age marry and are given in marriage; but those who are considered worthy of a place in that age and in the resurrection from the dead neither marry nor are given in marriage. Indeed they cannot die anymore, because they are like angels and are children of God, being children of the resurrection. And the fact that the dead are raised Moses himself showed, in the story about the bush, where he speaks of the Lord as the God of Abraham, the God of Isaac, and the God of Jacob. Now he is God not of the dead, but of the living; for to him all of them are alive."

- At the doorway of death, life is changed, not ended. Jesus himself uses the image of the great banquet where all our yearnings are finally fulfilled and we become fully alive.

- When we fear that we have "lost" loved ones, we must believe that they are not lost. The relationship continues. Spend some time communing with someone you love who has gone before you.

Monday 7th November
Luke 17:1–6

Jesus said to his disciples, "Occasions for stumbling are bound to come, but woe to anyone by whom they come! It would be better for you if a millstone were hung around your neck and you were thrown into the sea than for you to cause one of these little ones to stumble. Be on your guard! If another disciple sins, you must rebuke the offender, and if there is repentance, you must forgive. And if the same person sins against you seven times a day, and turns back to you seven times and says, 'I repent,' you must forgive." The apostles said to the Lord, "Increase our faith!" The Lord replied, "If you had faith the size of a mustard seed, you could say to this mulberry tree, 'Be uprooted and planted in the sea,' and it would obey you."

- "Forgive us our trespasses," we repeatedly say to God—and we need to repeat it, as we trespass again and again. You tell me, Lord, to be as patient with others' repentance as you are with mine. Thank you, Lord. I needed this reminder. Forgiveness is not a cover-all blanket, but a reaching out toward the one who repents. You bid me to be discerning, not foolish; but when I forgive, it must be a burying of the hatchet without marking the spot.

- "Little ones" means vulnerable people who cannot defend themselves. Have I ever hurt or diminished someone weaker than myself? Am I a bully? If so, I beg forgiveness of God and pray for those whose happiness I have taken away. Do people think of me as someone who forgives easily? Jesus never holds grudges against anyone, and I must become like him to be a true disciple.

Tuesday 8th November
Luke 17:7–10

Jesus said to his disciples, "Who among you would say to your slave who has just come in from plowing or tending sheep in the field, 'Come here at once and take your place at the table'? Would you not rather say to him, 'Prepare supper for me, put on your apron and serve me while I eat and drink; later you may eat and drink'? Do you thank the slave for doing what was commanded? So you also, when you have done all that you were ordered to do, say, 'We are worthless slaves; we have done only what we ought to have done!'"

- This is a tough saying of Jesus'. We know that a little gratitude and recognition of work well done can raise the spirits! So let me find an opportunity today to recognize and affirm someone whose life is filled with work.

- We can never boast or rest on our laurels in our search for God. There will always be new challenges opening up before us. But perhaps I take on too much myself? Then let me learn from a saint who said: "I will do these things in love and freedom, or leave them alone."

Wednesday 9th November

John 2:13–22

The Passover of the Jews was near, and Jesus went up to Jerusalem. In the temple he found people selling cattle, sheep, and doves, and the money changers seated at their tables. Making a whip of cords, he drove all of them out of the temple, both the sheep and the cattle. He also poured out the coins of the money changers and overturned their tables. He told those who were selling the doves, "Take these things out of here! Stop making my Father's house a marketplace!" His disciples remembered that it was written, "Zeal for your house will consume me." The Jews then said to him, "What sign can you show us for doing this?" Jesus answered them, "Destroy this temple, and in three days I will raise it up." The Jews then said, "This temple has been under construction for forty-six years, and will you raise it up in three days?" But he was speaking of the temple of his body. After he was raised from the dead, his disciples remembered that he had said this; and they believed the Scripture and the word that Jesus had spoken.

- In my imagination I stand in the temple courtyard, as the young rabbi from Galilee enters. I notice the courtyard, the sounds, the smells, the rattle of coins on the tables, and the reek and cries of the animals. I watch Jesus, see the blood rush to his face. He has come to reverence the temple and to pray. Instead he finds all the focus is on business. Suddenly I sense a whirlwind of anger as he whips the hucksters and scatters their money. This is a new side of Jesus and it shakes me. I stay with it.

- There may be junk and clutter in the temple of my heart, too. How can I clear it to provide some sacred space for God today?

Thursday 10th November
Luke 17:20–25

Once Jesus was asked by the Pharisees when the kingdom of God was coming, and he answered, "The kingdom of God is not coming with things that can be observed; nor will they say, 'Look, here it is!' or 'There it is!' For, in fact, the kingdom of God is among you." Then he said to the disciples, "The days are coming when you will long to see one of the days of the Son of Man, and you will not see it. They will say to you, 'Look there!' or 'Look here!' Do not go, do not set off in pursuit. For as the lightning flashes and lights up the sky from one side to the other, so will the Son of Man be in his day. But first he must endure much suffering and be rejected by this generation."

- This is the tension of every Christian: to hope that God will intervene and bring about a better world, and at the same time to work and act knowing that it all depends on us. Lord, you are warning me not to be distracted by scaremongers and prophets who claim private revelations about the end of the world. It is our world; we have to shape it and care for it with patience and courage.

- We often look to the extraordinary for reassurance that God is in our present situation. Yet God is more often found in the quiet— in quiet endurance, quiet joy, quiet kindness, and quiet goodness. Lord, let me be quiet and still so that I may find you.

Friday 11th November
Luke 17:26–37

Jesus said to the Pharisees, "Just as it was in the days of Noah, so too it will be in the days of the Son of Man. They were eating and drinking, and marrying and being given in marriage, until the day Noah entered the ark, and the flood came and destroyed all of them. Likewise, just as it was in the days of Lot: they were eating and drinking, buying and selling, planting and building, but on the day that Lot left Sodom, it rained fire and sulphur from heaven and destroyed all of them—it will be like that on the day that the Son of Man is revealed. On that day, anyone on the housetop who has belongings in the house must not come down to take them away; and likewise anyone in the field must not turn back. Remember Lot's wife. Those who try to make their life secure will lose it, but those who lose their life will keep it. I tell you, on that night there will be two in one bed; one will be taken and the other left. There will be two women grinding meal together; one will be taken and the other left." Then they asked him, "Where, Lord?" He said to them, "Where the corpse is, there the vultures will gather."

- Three apocalyptic visions weave in and out of one another in these chapters of Luke: Jesus' sense of his own forthcoming Passion and death; his warning of the destruction of Jerusalem by the Romans; and the second coming of Jesus at the end of time. Jesus is on his way to Jerusalem to die. He does not have much time left. He knows that he faces the ultimate choice soon. Is that why he speaks so vehemently about the need to choose now, and about the insecurity of this life?

- Today's reading is meant to shatter my complacency. Lord, keep my spirit keen in its search for you. Keep my faith strong in times of crisis. When doubt or fear weigh down my spirit, Lord, give me the grace to surrender to you in hope. May I trust in "the plans of your heart which endure from age to age" (Psalm 33:11).

Saturday 12th November

Luke 18:1–8

Jesus told the people a parable about their need to pray always and not to lose heart. He said, "In a certain city there was a judge who neither feared God nor had respect for people. In that city there was a widow who kept coming to him and saying, 'Grant me justice against my opponent.' For a while he refused; but later he said to himself, 'Though I have no fear of God and no respect for anyone, yet because this widow keeps bothering me, I will grant her justice, so that she may not wear me out by continually coming.'" And the Lord said, "Listen to what the unjust judge says. And will not God grant justice to his chosen ones who cry to him day and night? Will he delay long in helping them? I tell you, he will quickly grant justice to them. And yet, when the Son of Man comes, will he find faith on earth?"

• Lord, you puzzle me. I hear you telling me to persist in prayer, to entreat God until he is weary of me. You say he will quickly grant justice. But then I think of good people suffering famine, AIDS, loss of children, sickness, and death though they pray to God. I think of the Jews in Auschwitz, still singing the psalms as they walked into the gas chambers. Surely there are times when you delay in helping us? At times like this I turn to the memory of your Passion, and your agonized prayer in the garden. You have faced a dark and apparently empty heaven, yet stayed faithful. Keep me with you.

• The model for our prayer has to be the widow in Jesus' parable. Her persistence does not falter. In prayer I can present my true self to God. God knows the real me anyway, and he is a God of justice. Do I really believe this? Do I pray and work for justice in the situations around me?

November 13—November 19

Something to think and pray about each day this week:

The Lover Gives All

Prior to the Second Vatican Council, Saint Ignatius of Loyola was often caricatured as a hard military man who insisted on rules and demanded blind obedience of his followers. But contemporary research reveals him as a deeply loving man. Before his conversion at the ripe age of thirty, he loved his feudal lord, and also a mysterious but important lady, about whom he would daydream endlessly. When the Christ of the New Testament was opened up to him, he fell in love again, and this love transformed his remaining thirty-five years. He fell in love, too, with all God's people, and his life's goal was simply expressed: "to help others." Even to help one person brought him joy, and he devoted much of his time to one-to-one spiritual conversation. His was a ministry of consolation. It was said that "no one went away from him sad."

"What ought I do for Christ?" was his abiding question. As one of the great mystics of the church, he saw God as the great Lover who gives everything to us. Filled with love and gratitude, he made himself over to God's service. He believed that God deals directly with us, and that we can thus "find God in all things."

The Presence of God
I remind myself that, as I sit here now, God is gazing on me with love and holding me in being. I pause for a moment and think of this.

Freedom
Your death on the cross has set me free. I can live joyously and freely without fear of death. Your mercy knows no bounds.

Consciousness
At this moment, Lord, I turn my thoughts to you. I will leave aside my chores and preoccupations. I will take rest and refreshment in your presence, Lord.

The Word
The Word of God comes down to us through the Scriptures. May the Holy Spirit enlighten my mind and my heart to respond to the gospel teachings. (Please turn to the Scripture on the following pages. Inspiration points are provided should you need them. When you are ready, return here to continue.)

Conversation
Begin to talk to Jesus about the piece of Scripture you have just read. What part of it strikes a chord in you? Perhaps the words of a friend— or some story you have heard recently—will slowly rise to the surface of your consciousness. If so, does the story throw light on what the Scripture passage may be trying to say to you?

Conclusion
Glory be to the Father, and to the Son, and to the Holy Spirit, as it was in the beginning, is now and ever shall be, world without end. Amen.

Sunday 13th November
Thirty-Third Sunday in Ordinary Time
Luke 21:5–19

When some were speaking about the temple, how it was adorned with beautiful stones and gifts dedicated to God, he said, "As for these things that you see, the days will come when not one stone will be left upon another; all will be thrown down." They asked him, "Teacher, when will this be, and what will be the sign that this is about to take place?" And he said, "Beware that you are not led astray; for many will come in my name and say, 'I am he!' and, 'The time is near!' Do not go after them. When you hear of wars and insurrections, do not be terrified; for these things must take place first, but the end will not follow immediately." Then he said to them, "Nation will rise against nation, and kingdom against kingdom; there will be great earthquakes, and in various places famines and plagues; and there will be dreadful portents and great signs from heaven. But before all this occurs, they will arrest you and persecute you; they will hand you over to synagogues and prisons, and you will be brought before kings and governors because of my name. This will give you an opportunity to testify. So make up your minds not to prepare your defense in advance; for I will give you words and a wisdom that none of your opponents will be able to withstand or contradict. You will be betrayed even by parents and brothers, by relatives and friends; and they will put some of you to death. You will be hated by all because of my name. But not a hair of your head will perish. By your endurance you will gain your souls."

- There are many temples in our world—the green cathedrals of nature and the temples of our own hearts. May my life be adorned with beauty of character, forged by a generous response to God.

- Words and wisdom will be given to us when we are put to the test. Have you ever experienced that what you need to say in regard to God's affairs is given to you?

Monday 14th November
Luke 18:35–43

As Jesus approached Jericho, a blind man was sitting by the roadside begging. When he heard a crowd going by, he asked what was happening. They told him, "Jesus of Nazareth is passing by." Then he shouted, "Jesus, Son of David, have mercy on me!" Those who were in front sternly ordered him to be quiet; but he shouted even more loudly, "Son of David, have mercy on me!" Jesus stood still and ordered the man to be brought to him; and when he came near, he asked him, "What do you want me to do for you?" He said, "Lord, let me see again." Jesus said to him, "Receive your sight; your faith has saved you." Immediately he regained his sight and followed him, glorifying God; and all the people, when they saw it, praised God.

• Jesus does not cure unbidden. He waits to be asked. What may seem from the outside a desperate need (for sight) could for the sightless be such a habitual state that they could not imagine themselves otherwise. So Jesus asks: What do you want me to do for you? Lord, there is a sort of sight I ask from you: to use my eyes fully, to relish every nuance of color that surrounds me, to pick up the life and feeling in others' faces and bodies, to appreciate and be open to the glorious world of vision that I would miss if I were like this blind man.

• If the Lord asked me: "What do you want me to do for you?" what would I answer? The blind, the starving, and the troubled know what they need and want. Some of the better-off seem to live without desires, not keen to change themselves, complacent. Lord, you interrupted what you were saying to meet the blind man's cry. For you, acting mattered more than talking. I know I can trust your kindness.

Tuesday 15th November
Luke 19:1–10

Jesus entered Jericho and was passing through it. A man was there named Zacchaeus; he was a chief tax collector and was rich. He was trying to see who Jesus was, but on account of the crowd he could not, because he was short in stature. So he ran ahead and climbed a sycamore tree to see him, because he was going to pass that way. When Jesus came to the place, he looked up and said to him, "Zacchaeus, hurry and come down; for I must stay at your house today." So he hurried down and was happy to welcome him. All who saw it began to grumble and said, "He has gone to be the guest of one who is a sinner." Zacchaeus stood there and said to the Lord, "Look, half of my possessions, Lord, I will give to the poor; and if I have defrauded anyone of anything, I will pay back four times as much." Then Jesus said to him, "Today salvation has come to this house, because he too is a son of Abraham. For the Son of Man came to seek out and to save the lost."

- In my prayer, Lord, I am often like Zacchaeus, making huge efforts to catch a glimpse of you only to find that you are waiting for me, calling me by name, inviting yourself into my heart. Once I am with you, I find happiness in putting things right, ordering my life, and finding the springs of generosity and justice that have been stifled by old habits. Jesus, you look at me as you looked at Zacchaeus. You call me by name and invite me to join you. You do not make demands, but in your company I want to change something in myself and offer it to you.

- Jesus "was passing through" Jericho. It seems that he did not intend to stay. Yet he changed his plans to be a guest of Zacchaeus. Lord, teach me not to be wooden but to be responsive to unexpected moments of grace. Lord, may I hear you say, "I must stay at your house today." Every day, please! Otherwise I am lost.

Wednesday 16th November
Luke 19:11–28

Jesus went on to tell a parable, because he was near Jerusalem, and because they supposed that the kingdom of God was to appear immediately. So he said, "A nobleman went to a distant country to get royal power for himself and then return. He summoned ten of his slaves, and gave them ten pounds, and said to them, 'Do business with these until I come back.' But the citizens of his country hated him and sent a delegation after him, saying, 'We do not want this man to rule over us.' When he returned, having received royal power, he ordered these slaves, to whom he had given the money, to be summoned so that he might find out what they had gained by trading. The first came forward and said, 'Lord, your pound has made ten more pounds.' He said to him, 'Well done, good slave! Because you have been trustworthy in a very small thing, take charge of ten cities.' Then the second came, saying, 'Lord, your pound has made five pounds.' He said to him, 'And you, rule over five cities.' Then the other came, saying, 'Lord, here is your pound. I wrapped it up in a piece of cloth, for I was afraid of you, because you are a harsh man; you take what you did not deposit, and reap what you did not sow.' He said to him, 'I will judge you by your own words, you wicked slave! You knew, did you, that I was a harsh man, taking what I did not deposit and reaping what I did not sow? Why then did you not put my money into the bank? Then when I returned, I could have collected it with interest.' He said to the bystanders, 'Take the pound from him and give it to the one who has ten pounds.' (And they said to him, 'Lord, he has ten pounds!') 'I tell you, to all those who have, more will be given; but from those who have nothing, even what they have will be taken away. But as for these enemies of mine who did not want me to be king over them—bring them here and slaughter them in my presence.'" After he had said this, he went on ahead, going up to Jerusalem.

- God takes risks for us, so let us take risks for God. By taking risks we gain confidence, experience, and productivity. Grant me initiative and courage, Lord, on all levels of living. Let it be said of me that I tried to do great things for you.

- The Kingdom does not appear in us immediately. Growth in relationship with God needs long, slow cultivation. In this instant age of ours, help me to be patient. May my commitment to prayer transform me over the years, so that I become more and more like you.

Thursday 17th November
Luke 19:41–44

As Jesus came near and saw the city, he wept over it, saying, "If you, even you, had only recognized on this day the things that make for peace! But now they are hidden from your eyes. Indeed, the days will come upon you, when your enemies will set up ramparts around you and surround you, and hem you in on every side. They will crush you to the ground, you and your children within you, and they will not leave within you one stone upon another; because you did not recognize the time of your visitation from God."

• Jesus wept over his city. The Semites who live there, some Arab, some Jew, still weep over it. We who live far away cannot forget Jesus' city. As the psalmist says, "If I forget you, O Jerusalem, let my right hand wither! Let my tongue cling to the roof of my mouth, if I do not remember you, if I do not set Jerusalem above my highest joy." Lord God of Jews, Muslims, and Christians, look with pity on Jerusalem so that she may cease to be a sign of contradiction and become a mother to all the children of Abraham.

• You did not force the hand of your people, Lord. You gave them their opportunity and wept when they were too blind to take it. So in my life you do not press me into goodness. I have the freedom to seize opportunities or to let them slip. Saint Augustine warned us: "Fear the Lord Jesus when he passes by, for he will not pass this way again." Don't we regret more the fullness of life we could have had, than the faults and failings that led us astray for a short while? Let prayer be a moment of fullness—the heart open to the fullness of God.

Friday 18th November
Luke 19:45–48

Jesus entered the temple and began to drive out those who were selling things there; and he said, "It is written, 'My house shall be a house of prayer'; but you have made it a den of robbers." Every day he was teaching in the temple. The chief priests, the scribes, and the leaders of the people kept looking for a way to kill him; but they did not find anything they could do, for all the people were spellbound by what they heard.

- The temple-goers seem not to have noticed what the hucksters had done to the holy place, as they changed money and sold animals for sacrifice. Commerce tends to grow and grow when it finds a market, so the temple, the place of prayer, degenerated into a sort of marketplace. Jesus needed to challenge that drift and reassert the place's holiness. Does it happen in my life, Lord? You desire to dwell in this temple that is my body, but first the pressure to survive and then the appetite for more money can so possess me that I find little space for you. Please make my soul a place of prayer.

- The house I live in can be a house of prayer, a place where God feels welcome and at home. I say to God: "Make yourself at home: you're always welcome!"

Saturday 19th November
Luke 20:27–40

Some Sadducees, those who say there is no resurrection, came to him and asked him a question, "Teacher, Moses wrote for us that if a man's brother dies, leaving a wife but no children, the man shall marry the widow and raise up children for his brother. Now there were seven brothers; the first married, and died childless; then the second and the third married her, and so in the same way all seven died childless. Finally the woman also died. In the resurrection, therefore, whose wife will the woman be? For the seven had married her." Jesus said to them, "Those who belong to this age marry and are given in marriage; but those who are considered worthy of a place in that age and in the resurrection from the dead neither marry nor are given in marriage. Indeed they cannot die any more, because they are like angels and are children of God, being children of the resurrection. And the fact that the dead are raised Moses himself showed, in the story about the bush, where he speaks of the Lord as the God of Abraham, the God of Isaac, and the God of Jacob. Now he is God not of the dead, but of the living; for to him all of them are alive." Then some of the scribes answered, "Teacher, you have spoken well." For they no longer dared to ask him another question.

- Lord, like the Sadducees sometimes I ask you the wrong questions. Grant me the gift of openness, wisdom, and discernment. May I come to see reality with your eyes.

- You are "God not of the dead but of the living." Those who have gone before me "are alive." I can communicate with them and ask their help, and surely they will answer.

November 20—November 26

Something to think and pray about each day this week:

Are We Freed?

When did you last hear a homily on "freedom"? The conviction that we have been radically freed by Jesus is central to Christianity. Saint Luke celebrates God's visitation of his people, which frees us from fear and saves us from the hands of our foes (Luke 1:71). Saint Paul asserts: "Brothers and sisters, you have been called to freedom. For freedom Christ has set us free" (Galatians 5:13; 5:1).

Could it be that we can't take in that Jesus has in fact set us free? Twice in the Acts of the Apostles prison doors are miraculously opened so the apostles can come out to preach the good news. Is this perhaps an image of Jesus' work of salvation? Has he not already opened the prison gates? But are we sitting inside waiting for something else to happen? And does this imagined imprisonment trap the divine energy latent within us, which is meant to be at the service of the world?

A teacher of highly gifted music students found that anxiety about their final grades inhibited the creative self-expression hidden in them. To liberate them he announced that every one of them would get good grades. Suddenly they began to play at their best! Are we like them, gifted with freedom and talent but needing reassurance that God loves to see us at our creative best, doing great works (John 14:12)?

The Presence of God

I pause for a moment and think of the love and the grace that God showers on me, creating me in his image and likeness, making me his temple.

Freedom

"There are very few people who realize what God would make of them if they abandoned themselves into his hands, and let themselves be formed by his grace" (Saint Ignatius of Loyola). I ask for the grace to trust myself totally to God's love.

Consciousness

Where do I sense hope, encouragement, and growth areas in my life? By looking back over the last few months, I may be able to see which activities and occasions have produced rich fruit. If I do notice such areas, I will determine to give those areas both time and space in the future.

The Word

I read the Word of God slowly, a few times over, and I listen to what God is saying to me. (Please turn to the Scripture on the following pages. Inspiration points are provided should you need them. When you are ready, return here to continue.)

Conversation

What is stirring in me as I pray? Am I consoled, troubled, left cold? I imagine Jesus himself standing or sitting at my side, and I share my feelings with him.

Conclusion

I thank God for these few moments we have spent alone together and for any insights I may have been given concerning the text.

Sunday 20th November
Our Lord Jesus Christ, King of the Universe
Luke 23:35–43

The people stood by, watching; but the leaders scoffed at Jesus, saying, "He saved others; let him save himself if he is the Messiah of God, his chosen one!" The soldiers also mocked him, coming up and offering him sour wine, and saying, "If you are the King of the Jews, save yourself!" There was also an inscription over him, "This is the King of the Jews." One of the criminals who were hanged there kept deriding him and saying, "Are you not the Messiah? Save yourself and us!" But the other rebuked him, saying, "Do you not fear God, since you are under the same sentence of condemnation? And we indeed have been condemned justly, for we are getting what we deserve for our deeds, but this man has done nothing wrong." Then he said, "Jesus, remember me when you come into your kingdom." He replied, "Truly I tell you, today you will be with me in Paradise."

- We find it hard to watch Jesus in such pain. He is innocent; he "has done nothing wrong." Yet by his cross he has redeemed the world. Can I believe that God somehow brings good out of the suffering of the innocent today?

- Salvation begins its work here and now: the second criminal recognizes Jesus as a just man and humbly asks his help. He hears the promise of eternal joy from Jesus' lips. When I am suffering I can turn to Jesus and hear the same words. "Today" means "in God's good time."

Monday 21st November
Luke 21:1–4

Jesus looked up and saw rich people putting their gifts into the treasury; he also saw a poor widow put in two small copper coins. He said, "Truly I tell you, this poor widow has put in more than all of them; for all of them have contributed out of their abundance, but she out of her poverty has put in all she had to live on."

- Generosity is all relative, of course. Solomon prayed: "Keep me from sacrifices that cost me nothing." Lord, teach me true large-heartedness like that of the poor widow—a generosity that gives in secret, my left hand not knowing what my right hand is doing, and that gives until it hurts. It does not matter what others see of my actions or neglect. You see into my heart and know my generosity or self-ishness. Save me, Lord, from sacrifices that cost me nothing. True generosity is not so much giving what I can easily spare as giving what I can't easily do without.

- Jesus tells us to be prepared, to remain firm in faith. He calls us to be rooted and stable while also being ready to shed everything. He reminds us that, without him as the center of our lives, we will be lost. The telling of the daily news makes it easy to believe that our times are worse than others. While technology is used to spread gloomy and disheartening news, I give thanks that it also leads me to Jesus' truth.

Tuesday 22nd November

Luke 21:5–11

When some were speaking about the temple, how it was adorned with beautiful stones and gifts dedicated to God, Jesus said, "As for these things that you see, the days will come when not one stone will be left upon another; all will be thrown down." They asked him, "Teacher, when will this be, and what will be the sign that this is about to take place?" And he said, "Beware that you are not led astray; for many will come in my name and say, 'I am he!' and, 'The time is near!' Do not go after them. When you hear of wars and insurrections, do not be terri-fied; for these things must take place first, but the end will not follow immediately." Then he said to them, "Nation will rise against nation, and kingdom against kingdom; there will be great earthquakes, and in various places famines and plagues; and there will be dreadful portents and great signs from heaven."

- The temple was not only the center of the Jews' civilization, it was also the place where God lived among them. Jesus told them that it was all going to fall apart! Is there any way in which my "secure center"—either personal or political—threatens to collapse? The key words from Jesus in all of this are: "Do not be terrified." Can I allow Jesus, the Consoler, to speak to me wherever I am?

- While our compassion and concern go out to victims of the disasters, violence, and unrest that we hear about on a daily basis, it's good for Christians to remember that they are citizens not only of this world but also of God's kingdom. Nothing on this earth can ultimately prevail against the relationship we have with God, both in the world to come but here and now as well.

Wednesday 23rd November
Luke 21:12–19

Jesus said to his disciples, "But before all this occurs, they will arrest you and persecute you; they will hand you over to synagogues and prisons, and you will be brought before kings and governors because of my name. This will give you an opportunity to testify. So make up your minds not to prepare your defense in advance; for I will give you words and a wisdom that none of your opponents will be able to withstand or contradict. You will be betrayed even by parents and brothers, by relatives and friends; and they will put some of you to death. You will be hated by all because of my name. But not a hair of your head will perish. By your endurance you will gain your souls."

- This picture of arrest and persecution seems remote from our experience—something hard to imagine happening to us. Most of us, however, have known betrayal and unjust treatment at some point in our lives. Whether at school, or in the family, or at work, or with acquaintances, we have tasted hatred at some stage. If Jesus could face it, so can we. He tells us to be unsurprisable. It is not the end. You will survive. Do not let the experience quench your love or your faith.

- "You will be betrayed" even by those close to you: when relation-ships fail, I know the truth of this warning. But do I believe that God is very close to me then, watching over "the hair of my head"? Does this help me to retain my equilibrium and integrity? "By your endurance you will gain your souls." I reflect on how I have dealt with adversity over the years. Have I grown through it? Perhaps I am more resilient now, knowing from experience that God is always working to bring good out of my troubles.

Thursday 24th November
Luke 21:20–28

Jesus said to his disciples, "When you see Jerusalem surrounded by armies, then know that its desolation has come near. Woe to those who are pregnant and to those who are nursing infants in those days! For there will be great distress on the earth and wrath against this people; they will fall by the edge of the sword and be taken away as captives among all nations; and Jerusalem will be trampled on by the Gentiles, until the times of the Gentiles are fulfilled. There will be signs in the sun, the moon, and the stars, and on the earth distress among nations confused by the roaring of the sea and the waves. People will faint from fear and foreboding of what is coming upon the world, for the powers of the heavens will be shaken. Then they will see 'the Son of Man coming in a cloud' with power and great glory. Now when these things begin to take place, stand up and raise your heads, because your redemption is drawing near."

- Millions of refugees—they number some 20 million—know the truth of this gospel passage today. We can do something to help them.

- How does the Son of Man "draw near" to his people in times of disaster? Saint Paul says that if one part of Christ's body suffers, "all the other parts suffer together with it" (1 Corinthians 12:26). We are asked to show solidarity with the afflicted, just as we would want them to show solidarity with us in our need.

Friday 25th November
Luke 21:29–33

Then Jesus told his disciples a parable: "Look at the fig tree and all the trees; as soon as they sprout leaves you can see for yourselves and know that summer is already near. So also, when you see these things taking place, you know that the kingdom of God is near. Truly I tell you, this generation will not pass away until all things have taken place. Heaven and earth will pass away, but my words will not pass away."

• That is a hard lesson to learn: that when our lives are disturbed and uncertain, the kingdom of God is near. Jesus is present in our sorrowful mysteries as well as in our joyful ones. Saint John of the Cross used to say: "Love is the fruit of faith, that is to say, of darkness." We cling to you, Lord, in our uncertainty. Lord, you are always telling us to be ready. Something is going to happen. Nature astonishes us with new life every spring, and in the same way, God will astonish us with a fresh spring in ourselves. Keep that sense of hope awake in me. I remember Hilaire Belloc's lines: "Kings live in palaces and pigs in sties but youth in expectation. Youth is wise."

• Jesus, you seem to have learned so much from nature! Grant me the same awareness so that I may learn the presence, action, and care of God in my life. Mention of this fig tree reminds me of the other fig tree that was given a second chance to bear fruit. Do I have the courage to start again when things don't work out the first time?

Saturday 26th November
Luke 21:34–36

Jesus said to the disciples, "Be on guard so that your hearts are not weighed down with dissipation and drunkenness and the worries of this life, and that day does not catch you unexpectedly, like a trap. For it will come upon all who live on the face of the whole earth. Be alert at all times, praying that you may have the strength to escape all these things that will take place, and to stand before the Son of Man."

- It's a curious phrase but it fits: "weighed down with dissipation and drunkenness." Drink is a narcotic; it does in fact dull the heart and blunt the appetites. As for dissipation, while it may be sold as fun and providing a laugh, on the morning after, most would agree with the philosopher Friedrich Nietzsche that the mother of dissipation is not joy but joylessness. Joy and moderation go hand in hand. When our hearts are happy, our own skins are a good place to be; we do not need to be blown out of our minds by alcohol or other drugs.

- The fourteenth-century mystic Meister Eckhart tells us that the Word of God is spoken continually in our soul. But where are we? He says bluntly: "God is with us in our inmost soul, provided he finds us within and not gone out on business." We so often use our five senses to anesthetize our souls, to blunt reality. But when we run away from ourselves, we are running away from the wonder at the heart of our being.

Continue the Conversation

If you enjoyed this book, then connect with Loyola Press to continue the conversation, engage with other readers, and find out about new and upcoming books from your favorite spiritual writers.

Visit us at **LoyolaPress.com** to create an account and register for our newsletters.

Or scan the code on the left with your smartphone.

Connect with us through:

 Facebook
facebook.com
/loyolapress

 Twitter
twitter.com
/loyolapress

 YouTube
youtube.com
/loyolapress